T0330363

The Valuation of Financial Companies

Tools and Techniques to Value Banks, Insurance Companies, and Other Financial Institutions

Mario Massari
Gianfranco Gianfrate
Laura Zanetti

Contents

Preface

If there is a lesson learnt from the on-going economic crisis, it is that financial companies play a key role in the economic life of nations. The understanding of how banks, insurance companies, and other financial institutions actually work is therefore of paramount importance, not just for scholars but also for managers, investors, regulators, and policy makers. A sound understanding of how financial companies work should be reflected in reliable methodologies in order to value them. However, how to value banks and other financial institutions is a topic that has not received due attention so far.

The most popular valuation manuals devote relatively little attention[1] (or no attention at all) to the valuation frameworks that should be applied to financial companies. Academia started to look in-depth into this issue only recently. In fact, for both practitioners and academics, the problem with the valuation of financial companies is that these are inherently complex organizations. The raw materials they process are often very complex risks embedded in highly sophisticated financial contracts. In some cases, to fully understand the structure of certain assets in the bank Balance Sheet – not to mention the estimation of the technical reserves of life insurance companies – a PhD in physics or mathematics is necessary. No wonder that, as vividly emerged from some official parliamentary hearings about the financial crisis and subsequent scandals, even top managers and board directors of global leading financial companies are often not aware about and proficient in what the organizations they lead are actually doing and about how much risk they carry.

If a proper comprehension of a financial company's actual situation is difficult for insiders in the top posts, the analysis and valuation from the outside is even more challenging. This is also because, unfortunately, the accounting standards leave the opacity and ambiguity that obfuscate the financial statements of banks and insurers mostly untouched – even the largest and "systemically important" ones.

---

[1] For example, Damodaran (2012) and Koller *et al.* (2010).

In this book we have not found the Holy Grail for the valuation of banks or of other financial institutions. But on the basis of our professional experience, academic research, and discussion with bankers and equity research analysts, we have encapsulated what appears to be the best practice for valuations in the financial sector. Our aim is to provide the reader, already familiar with the main corporate valuation models, with the coordinates to apply them specifically to financial companies. Therefore, the focus is eminently practical and we have tried to address the very problems that usually arise when dealing with the valuation of banks or insurance companies. Along the same lines, we have excluded the most complex econometric models, which are of intellectual fascination for academics but of little utility for real life application.

The book is structured as follows. Before presenting the bank valuation techniques (Chapter 5), we briefly introduce the various business models banks run (Chapter 1), the main accounting frameworks and issues that are relevant for banks (Chapter 2), and the regulations that define the capital to be held by banks (Chapter 3). Financial statements analysis and the comprehension of the regulatory frameworks are indeed the ingredients necessary to prepare and assess the business plan of a bank (Chapter 4).

We adopt a similar approach for the insurance companies. We first introduce insurers' business models and accounting practices (Chapter 6). A sketch of the main capital regulations follows (Chapter 7) along with the guidelines to assess and prepare the business plan (Chapter 8). The valuation issues that are peculiar to these companies are eventually presented (Chapter 9). We finally offer (Chapter 10) a few stylized elements about the valuation of other financial institutions such as funds and leasing, factoring, and asset management companies.

In terms of depth of discussion about business models, accounting features, and capital requirements, we have decided to present the bare minimum knowledge necessary to perform a proper valuation. This is because our objective is to offer the reader an agile reference book rather than a comprehensive encyclopedia on the topic. But the choice of being concise has also been made because the debate among policy makers – especially on accounting rules and capitalization requirements – is still (fiercely) going on and more details about current and proposed regulatory frameworks would become outdated quickly. The reader willing to know more about those aspects is strongly encouraged to refer to other sources and specialized handbooks (we shall provide some references in the footnotes where appropriate).

We have particularly focused our attention on the US and European financial industries because they are the ones we know best, but most of the considerations we make, especially in terms of valuation frameworks, apply to financial institutions located outside those geographies as well.

We expect financial companies' valuations to become a topic of growing interest in forthcoming years for both practitioners and scholars. We hope that this book will spark more curiosity and intriguing questions on the matter.

Acknowledgments

Of course, we owe a very great debt of thanks to friends, colleagues, and students who have contributed to this work. First, we thank greatly two extremely experienced professionals who read and commented on chapters: Paola Sabbione of Deutsche Bank and Giuseppe Sica of Morgan Stanley. A number of former students ran empirical analyses to test various propositions presented in the book: Isabella Baruzzi of Morgan Stanley, Paolo Bergamelli of UBS, Paolo De Bona of Citi, Davide Natale of Goldman Sachs, Kim Salvadori of Goldman Sachs, Matteo Santecchia of Credit Suisse, and Roberto Vincenzi of Bocconi University. We are grateful to the Wiley team who assisted us in the book preparation, and especially to: Werner Coetzee, Jennie Kitchin, Grace O'Byrne, and Vivienne Wickham. Finally, Lynette Woodward provided excellent professional support for the editing of the manuscript.

1

Bank Business Models

From an economic point of view, banks carry out the crucial role of intermediating between individuals and/or organizations (corporations, financial institutions, national and local governments, and non-profit entities) with financial surpluses and those suffering from (temporary) money deficits. Such a definition is quite general and falls short of fully representing the complexity and articulation of an industry that is essential for economic development and national growth. When the banking system does not work properly the costs for the economy may be severe as the last financial crisis has made painfully clear. To sketch the main features of the banking business, we will segment the industry into a few categories in order to identify the different business models' economics, profitability drivers, and, eventually, valuation metrics. Nevertheless, it's worth underlining that, as Paul Volcker,[1] former Federal Reserve Chairman used to say, fiduciary responsibility is at the very core of every banking organization, regardless of the specific activities carried out.

1.1   ECONOMICS OF BANKING

Bank valuation can build only on a sound understanding of what banking business involves, what the different business models are over time, and now coexist in most countries. For valuation purposes, we will identify the main revenue-generating activities that a bank may carry and outline the business models behind such activities. While some banks are "mono-business" in the sense that they offer solely one type of service, most actually are "multi-business" with a wide array of financial products and services. When the portfolio of financial products is wide and encompasses both commercial and investment banking services the bank is usually referred to as "universal". Table 1.1 introduces the relationship between business models and types of revenues that we will analyze in detail in the next paragraphs. The nature and mechanics of the insurance business will be presented in Chapter 6.

Historically the core source of revenues for commercial banks has been the issue of loans to customers (individuals and/or corporate) and the gathering of money in the form of deposits. Net interest income is typically the difference between the interest earned from loans and interest paid to depositors, in this sense commercial

---

[1] From the "Statement before US Senate, Committee on Banking, Housing, and Urban Affairs, January 21, 1987," *Federal Reserve Bulletin*.

Table 1.1   Types of banking revenues and business models

Types of revenues	Business model
Net interest income	Commercial banking
Fee and commission income	Commercial banking. Investment banking. Asset management
Trading income	Investment banking
Premium underwriting	Bank assurance

banking is a "spread business". Net interest income also includes earned and paid interest on other financial instruments. Collecting deposits and lending money are not value creating activities *per se*, but they are so if two more aspects are taken into account:

- Commercial banks usually perform a *maturity-transformation* activity: in fact, they receive short-term financing (deposits are usually regarded as short-term debt although money invested in most of them can be generally withdrawn upon request so they are "on demand debt") and issue long-term loans. Therefore, if the yield curve is upward sloping, part of the spread is due to the difference in the maturity of the instruments.
- There is a certain amount of risk embedded in the loans issued. Deposits, on the contrary, tend to have a very low risk (risk premium is generally assumed close to 0).

The second major source of revenue in the industry is fee and commission income. Services such as underwriting and placement of securities (mostly associated with investment banking), trust services and securities brokerage are commonly charged a fee or commission. The main difference between commercial and investment banks consists of the targeted segments of clients that commercial and investment banks strive to serve: while investment bank clients are usually large corporations to be served with tailored (costly) advisory services (especially related to extraordinary financial events such as IPO, seasoned equity offerings or M&A), commercial bank customers are individuals and small/medium enterprises for which less customized (expensive) services are provided. Typical fee-based services offered by banks are:

- *Asset Management.* Banks typically earn a management fee, as a fixed percentage of the Assets Under Management. Risk of financial investments carried out by the funds is held by clients.
- *Private Banking.* Banks provide advice to wealthy individual customers (including specialized advice on taxation) managing their financial assets.
- *Corporate Advisory.* Such services cover the entire spectrum of the events in the life of a company. So, they vary from risk management services (e.g.,

hedging foreign currency risk) and decisions on the optimal financial structure to the choice of issuing new securities, both debt and equity capital, and M&A transactions. In this sub-category, we consider the fees banks earn both for the piece of advice they provide to their clients and the fees earned to compensate for the risk involved in underwriting a security issue. Debt origination and specific advisory (e.g., project finance) is offered to sovereign, local governments and municipalities.

- *Brokerage and Dealership*. Commissions on trades are earned by banks in the secondary market. It's important to underline that the recent trend originated by an increasing competition and Internet-based trading has both augmented the volume of trades and reduced the per unit commission.

It's worth noting that banks' activities earning fees and commissions have different economics and value drivers from those that generate interest income, as the former are typically based on limited asset positions and minimal risk capital.

The third possible source of revenues is trading, which is mostly an investment banking activity even though commercial banks tend to have some exposure to that business. Proprietary trading involves trading of a wide variety of securities (in the name of the bank) on exchanges and OTC. For investment banks (an example is presented in Section 1.3) trading has always represented a large portion of total revenues, although trading results are quite volatile and predictable only under certain assumptions.

As a fourth source of income, we refer to non-banking activities, which range from real estate development to insurance activities and minority investment in non-banking companies. Universal banks, generally, cover most of this non-typical business.

1.2 COMMERCIAL BANKS

Commercial banks constitute the kind of banks people usually have in mind every time they speak of banks. They are basically engaged in the business of receiving money from their customers in the form of deposits and providing them with money in the form of loans. Even though these two activities are certainly the main part of the commercial banking business (in terms of the weight they have on the Balance Sheets of these organizations), both commercial banks' liabilities and assets are broader in range and don't fit such a narrow definition. Furthermore, commercial banks are also involved in providing their clients with trust services, namely managing their assets, and investment or financial advice.

1.2.1 Structure of the Industry in the US

In 2012, the number of institutions registered as commercial banks in the US was 6168, sub-divided by the value of their assets in commercial banks with assets

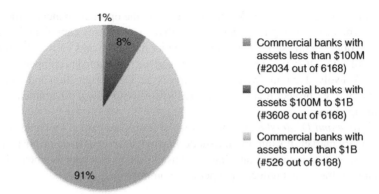

Figure 1.1   Structure of the US commercial banking business by assets
Source: Federal Deposit Insurance Corporation (2012), www.fdic.gov.

lower than $100M, commercial banks with assets ranging between $100M and $1B and those ones with assets more than $1B according to Figure 1.1. Even though in terms of their number, large banks (with assets over $1B) represent 8.53% of the total, they manage 91% of the total assets in the industry, as shown in Figure 1.1. Specifically, we have *community banks*, which are small banks (under $1B) specializing in retail and consumer banking. Therefore, what they do is simply receive money from their local customer base and lend this money out to consumers. *Savings banks*, although commonly regarded as different entities to commercial banks, can technically be considered as just banks offering a higher interest rate in order to attract money. However, they can choose not to lend any money as long as they invest the collected deposits and earn, with a certain degree of safety, a return high enough to repay their depositors. The bulk of assets are held by regional or superregional banks. Big banks carry out activities that are generally more complex and variegated than community banks and also have access to markets for purchased funds, for example, interbank or federal funds market.

Currently, five big players are also referred to as *money center banks*. In alphabetical order, they are: Bank of New York Mellon, Citigroup, Deutsche Bank, HSBC, and JPMorgan. It's worth noting that this title is not awarded because of the asset size of those banks (in fact, Bank of America or Wells Fargo are not included in the list and they are both larger in terms of assets than Bank of New York Mellon). Being considered a money center bank is the result of both reliance on non-deposit sources of funding and of geographic location (Chicago or New York).

Although the number of banks is currently shrinking and the assets are concentrated in the hands of the few largest players, it's unlikely that community banks will disappear. Even in a mature industry like US banking, there are several ways of competing successfully and niche business models (from a geographical and product offering point of view) may coexist.

1.2.2 Overview of the US Regulation

The current number of US banks is a direct reflection of intense merger and bankruptcy waves recorded in the industry in the past two decades. The US financial regulation, which, until some years ago, restricted the geographic expansion of players in the market, is commonly regarded as the main source for the consolidation trend. We will first analyze the rules about the gulf between commercial and investment banking, and then the regulations concerning the constraints on geographic extension.

In the early 1930s, after about 10 000 commercial banks went bankrupt in US, the Glass–Steagall Act was eventually promulgated (1933). Its goal was to rigidly separate commercial banks and investment banks. The distinction between investment and commercial banks is a peculiarity of the US banking history shared only with the Japanese one and some smaller contexts: in fact, in the rest of the world the universal banking model has been predominant for most of the twentieth century. The letter and spirit of Glass–Steagall Act were maintained intact for some decades. However, in the 1960s, after commercial banks somehow got involved in underwriting securities such as commercial papers and municipal bonds and in managing mutual funds, the rigid separation, hoped for by the original legislator, started losing *de facto* relevance. In 1987, commercial bank holdings were allowed by the Federal Reserve Board to establish investment bank affiliates (*Section 20 affiliates*) and all those "gray area" activities mentioned previously were transferred to these subsidiaries.

Finally, a revolutionary change occurred in 1997. In that year, first the Federal Reserve and then US Congress, through the Financial Service Modernization Act, eliminated the barrier between commercial and investment banks for good. As a consequence, looking from a commercial bank strategic standpoint, many commercial banking players (such as the Bank of America) entered the investment banking business in force. Nevertheless, investment banks, which were generally not subject to Federal Reserve rules and capital requirements, maintained their leading position in that business segment.

However, some new changes occurred after the recent crisis in 2008. Among the five big independent players (Merrill Lynch, Morgan Stanley, Goldman Sachs, Bear Sterns, and Lehman Brothers), just two companies survived and they all eventually applied to change their status into one of a Bank Holding Company (BHC).[2] Today, they all actually look very similar to commercial banks from a regulatory requirements point of view, as they have to comply with stricter rules and capital regulation, and higher levels of disclosure.

---

[2] A BHC, as provided by the Bank Holding Company Act of 1956 can be broadly defined as "any company that has control over a bank". The bank holding company status makes it easier for the firm to raise capital than as a traditional bank, allowing better and quicker access to liquidity and funding. The downside includes responding to additional regulatory authorities: e.g., all BHCs in the US are required to register with the Board of Governors of the Federal Reserve System.

As far as restrictions on interstate banking are concerned, the major piece of legislation shaping the industry until 1997 was the McFadden Act, which dated from the early 1930s. While state chartered banks were already generally constrained to state borders nationally chartered banks were also prohibited to expand. However, the potential loophole arising from this Act was that while a bank could not create a branch in a different state, subsidiaries could be established. The following period in fact, saw the growth of multi-bank holding companies (MBHCs) possessing subsidiaries in more than one state. Aware of that loophole, the Congress passed a law in 1956 constraining MBHCs from acquiring subsidiaries to only the extent allowed by the law of the *target* bank's state of. This is why we observe a huge growth in interstate banking pacts – namely agreements between states to outline the conditions for entrance for out-of-state banks – in that period. In 1997, the enactment of the Riegle–Neal Act, which allowed interstate banking in US, immediately triggered the consolidation wave that featured hundreds of mergers in the industry.

It's also worth underlining that the US banking system can be defined as dual. In fact, it is a system in which nationally chartered and state-chartered banks do coexist. Banks, instead of being nationally chartered by the *Office of the Comptroller of the Currency (OCC)*, a sub-agency of the US Treasury, can be chartered by one of the 50 state bank regulators. Finally, while all the nationally chartered banks are automatically members of the *Federal Reserve System*, just about 20% of all state chartered banks have decided to get membership.

1.2.3   Commercial Banks' Balance Sheets

The Balance Sheets of a commercial bank, unlike that of other financial institutions (e.g., insurance companies), can be considered as both asset- and liability-driven. Commercial banks, in order to become a major player in the industry, have to compete and succeed in both attracting money (for instance, in the form of deposits) and lending money (generally, issuance of loans). As shown in Figure 1.2, the ability to attract deposits at a cost sustainably lower than the return from the assets is the core of bank profitability.

Table 1.2 shows the consolidated balance sheet items for all the US commercial banks as of December 2012. On the asset side, as expected, loans and leases net of loan loss provisions (a balance sheet item generally related to the estimates of loan losses) account for the majority of the assets (51.5%). The other two main asset categories, with weights of almost 21% and 10% respectively, are securities (which don't include securities held in trading accounts) and cash (including due from depository institution).

As to the liability side, deposits represent about 83% of the total liabilities, while federal funds purchased and securities sold under the agreement to repurchase are close to 4%. Equity capital is not higher than 11.5% of total

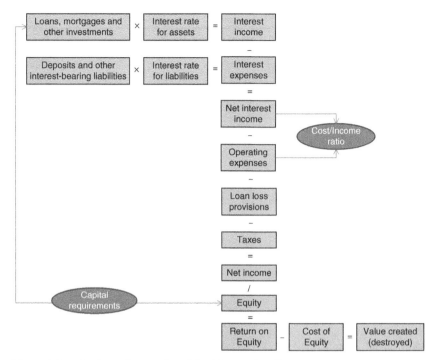

Figure 1.2   The determinants of retail banking profitability

funding. We will discuss the structure of bank financial statements in detail in the next chapter.

1.3 INVESTMENT BANKS

> We are investment bankers, not commercial bankers, which means that we underwrite
> to distribute, not to put a loan on our balance sheet.
>   *Matt Harris, Managing Director, Chase Securities*

At the bare minimum, investment banking involves helping corporations and governments to raise debt and equity securities in the market. Despite recent criticism, from an historical perspective, the financial intermediation role of investment banks has been crucial to the development of most developed countries' financial systems and economies. All large corporations have always relied on those organizations in order to find investors and, therefore, continue their "expansion". Investment banking activities range from the origination to the underwriting and placement of the issued securities. With the term *underwriting*, we refer to the practice of *purchasing securities from the issuer and then selling them in the market* (underwrite to distribute). When issuing securities, investment banks usually

Table 1.2   Balance Sheet for all FDIC-Insured Commercial Banks (in $000s)

Total assets	$13 390 970
Net loans and leases of which:	51.50%
Loans secured by real estate	*26.99%*
Commercial & industrial loans	*10.84%*
Loans to individuals	*9.22%*
Farm loans	*0.48%*
Other loans & leases	*5.11%*
Less: Unearned income	*0.01%*
Less: Reserve for losses	*1.14%*
Securities	20.54%
Other real estate owned	0.26%
Goodwill and other intangibles	2.62%
All other assets	25.08%
Total liabilities and capital	$13 390 970
Non-interest-bearing deposits	19.23%
Interest-bearing deposits	55.55%
Other borrowed funds	9.04%
Subordinated debt	0.88%
All other liabilities	4.08%
Equity capital	11.22%
Off-balance-sheet derivatives	*16.73x*

Source: Federal Deposit Insurance Corporation (www.fdic.gov), as of Dec. 2012.

distinguish between best effort practice and firm commitment. With firm commitment, investment banks underwrite the issuance, thus guaranteeing the full proceeds to the issuer regardless of the actual demand (the service so conceived tends to be very expensive for issuers). In case of best efforts, banks simply put these into selling the securities, not underwriting the issuance, so with no money commitment, which implies less risk for the bank and a lesser fee for issuing clients.

Investment banks are also involved in the stages following placement, which supports these securities in the secondary market through brokerage or dealing services and/or market making. Finally, the other two main activities of investment banks consist of advising their customers during M&A (mergers and acquisitions) transactions and corporate restructurings (not just liquidation) in exchange for a fee. Such services clearly do not involve any Balance Sheet commitment for the bank, unless some form of direct financing is attached to the transaction. Investment banks also usually engage in proprietary trading (also known as "prop trading"), which consists of systematic trading activities in stocks, bonds, currencies,

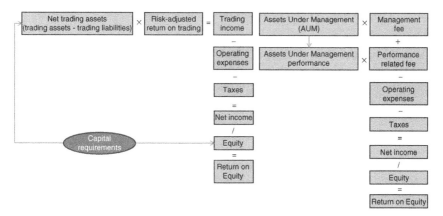

Figure 1.3   The determinants of profitability in asset management and trading

commodities, their derivatives, or other financial instruments. With proprietary trading, the firm's own money, as opposed to its customers' money, is invested and exposed to market related risks. The profitability of such activities depends therefore, not just on their return, but also on the level of risk associated with the trades (see Figure 1.3) as well as asset management of various securities (shares, bonds, and other financial instruments) and assets (e.g., real estate) in order to meet specified investment goals for the benefit of the investors. Usually the fees for asset management mandates are partly related to the volumes of managed assets and partly to the actual performance of the assets themselves (Figure 1.3).

1.3.1   Structure of the US Banking Industry

By segmenting the industry in few categories of investment banks, which differ from each other in size and shape, we can neatly distinguish between boutiques, regional, sub-majors, major, and bulge bracket firms. The distinguishing characteristic does not depend simply on the geographical scope or number of employees. Bulge bracket firms are the largest global and most profitable investment banks. They are referred to as the *bulge bracket* because of the tendency for these companies to be reported in large and bold characters in "tombstones" (written announcements placed during a security offering). Major and sub-major bracket banks are second and third tier banks, respectively, while regional banks are usually smaller institutions with operations limited to specific regions. Boutique firms, as opposed to one-stop shops (that offer the entire spectrum of investment banking services), are very specialized in terms of services provided (so, as they affirm, "avoiding the conflicts of interests naturally arising in larger firms") and/or geographic area.

1.3.2 Typical Balance Sheet for an Investment Bank

As an example of the main structure of an investment bank's economics, Table 1.3 shows the balance sheet of Morgan Stanley (as of December 2011). Unlike commercial banks – for which there is a significant investment in assets, typically loans, funded through deposits – investment banks do not require any significant investment in assets to run most operations. Even for securities trading, an activity usually run by investment banks and for corporate finance services, a huge medium-/long-term investment in assets is not necessary. As a consequence, the asset volume is often not an indication of the value of the bank.

Deposits represent a very low portion of total funding (8.76%) compared to standard commercial banks. The bank applied for the BHC status with the FED in the aftermath of Lehman's collapse (2008), but along with Goldman Sachs who made the same move, it essentially remains an investment bank.

For Morgan Stanley, the major categories of funding are represented by long-term borrowings, financial instruments sold and not yet purchased, securities sold under agreements to repurchase, and payables representing respectively 24.5, 15.5, 14 and 16.5% of the total funding. Financial instruments sold and not yet purchased are, generally speaking, securities involved in transactions where the bank borrowed those securities in order to sell them and the position has not been covered yet: they represent obligations for the seller. This category, together with the "securities sold under repurchase agreement", has always connoted the privileged source of funding in the investment banking business model. With the term payables (receivables), we are generally referring to payables to (receivables from) brokers, dealers, and clearing organizations. They include amounts payable (receivable) for securities not received (delivered) by Morgan Stanley by the settlement date ("fails to deliver"), payables to clearing organizations (margin deposits), commissions, and net receivables/payables arising from unsettled trades.

On the asset side, securities purchased under agreement to resell represent a relevant asset for Morgan Stanley and is a feature shared with other investment banking players. The last point we would like to stress, as far as an investment bank Balance Sheet is concerned, is that securities borrowed or loaned require the two parties (lender and borrower) to exchange securities with an amount of cash collateral. The amount of cash advanced or received is recorded as securities borrowed and securities loaned, respectively. Finally, "other assets" for an investment bank generally means a portion of prepaid expense.

Interest Income and *Interest Expense* in the Income Statement (Table 1.4) are constituted by interest earnings and expenses deriving from financial instruments owned and financial instruments sold, not yet purchased, securities available for sale, securities borrowed or purchased under agreements to resell, securities loaned or sold under agreements to repurchase, loans, deposits, commercial paper, and other short-term and long-term borrowings. The major expenses in an investment

Table 1.3 Morgan Stanley's 2011 Balance Sheet (in $ M)

Assets		Liabilities and Equity	
Cash and due from banks (including interest bearing deposits and cash deposited with clearing organization)	76 766	Deposits	65 662
		Commercial paper and other short-term borrowings	2843
Financial instruments owned, at fair value:			
US Government and agency securities	63 449	Total Financial instruments sold, not yet purchased, at fair value	116 147
Other sovereign government obligations	29 059		
Corporate and other debt	68 923	Obligation to return securities received as collateral, at fair value	15 394
Corporate equities	47 966		
Derivative and other contracts	48 064	Securities sold under agreements to repurchase	104 800
Investments	8195		
Physical commodities	9697	Securities loaned	30 462
Total Financial instruments owned, at fair value	275 353		
		Other secured financings	20 719
Securities available for sale, at fair value	30 495		
Securities received as collateral, at fair value	11 651	Payables (to customers, brokers, interest and dividends)	123 615
Federal funds sold and securities purchased under agreements to resell	130 155		
Securities borrowed	127 074	Other liabilities and accrued expenses	15 944
Receivables (from customers, brokers, fees, others)	48 669	Long-term borrowings	184 234
Loans	15 369	Total liabilities	679 820
Other investments	4832		
Premises, equipment and software costs	6457	Total equity	70 078
Goodwill	6686		
Intangible assets	4285		
Other assets	12 106		
TOTAL	749 898	TOTAL LIABILITIES AND EQUITY	749 898

Source: Morgan Stanley, December 2011.

Table 1.4   Morgan Stanley's Consolidated Statement of Income (in $ M)

Consolidated Statements of Income	
Investment banking	4991
Trading	12 392
Investments	573
Commissions and fees	5379
Asset management, distribution and administration fees	8502
Other	209
Total non-interest revenues	32 046
Interest income	7264
Interest expense	6907
Net interest	357
Non-interest expenses:	
Compensation and benefits	16 403
Occupancy and equipment	1564
Brokerage, clearing and exchange fees	1652
Information processing and communications	1815
Marketing and business development	602
Professional services	1803
Other	2450
Total non-interest expenses	26 289
Income from continuing operations before income taxes	6614

Source: Morgan Stanley, December 2011

bank are due to compensation and benefits to employees: human capital, in fact, is assumed to be the key success factor in the industry.

1.3.3   The Banking Industry outside the US

The strong development of the US economy and financial system has, over time, conferred global primacy to the US banking industry, and especially the US investment banking sector. To date, Europe is second to the US in terms of banking industry development. Similar to the US, most of the financial assets in Europe are concentrated in the hands of the few largest players. The segmentation provided by the European Central Bank (ECB) is similar from the point of view of the items recorded but differs regarding size ranges for categorizing banks (Figure 1.4).

Banks with more than 0.5% of the total European consolidated banking assets are considered large, those ones with assets ranging between 0.5 and 0.005% are defined medium, and those with assets lower than 0.005% of total consolidated assets are considered small. In terms of concentration, 14.33% of the banks hold 97.1% of total assets held by European domestic banks, and just the top 1% of banks control 74.28% of total assets.

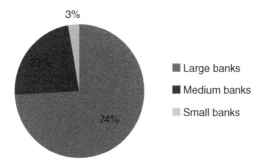

3%

- Large banks
- Medium banks
- Small banks

74%

Figure 1.4 Structure of European banking business by assets
Source: European Central Bank, June 2012, www.ecb.int/stats

Consolidated Balance Sheet data for European commercial banks is not available, because six countries (including Germany and the UK), still apply local Generally Accepted Accounting Principles (GAAP) instead of International Financial Reporting Standards (IFRS). Since IFRS and local GAAP differ substantially, the aggregation of IFRS and non-IFRS data would prove meaningless in some cases. This element already signals some difficulties faced by analysts who have to deal with relative valuation of banks that use different accounting principles.

Just as a rough indication of the values at play in the European financial system, loans represent about 56% of the total assets, debt instruments (which for the most part are governmental debt securities) about 15%, while equity is circa 5% of total assets (Table 1.5). In Chapter 4 we will further elaborate on the regulatory capital requirements in the US and Europe, and on why European banks apparently look relatively undercapitalized.

As it happens, in other industries globalization is opening up the financial services markets and new players are emerging challenging the secular leadership

Table 1.5 The European Banking assets

Assets IFRS and Non-IFRS reporting banks	In € B	Liabilities IFRS and Non-IFRS reporting banks	In € B
Total loans and advances	20 053	Total deposits from credit institutions	3 348
Total debt instruments	522	Total deposits (other than from credit institutions)	14 154
Total equity instruments	558	Total debt certificates (including bonds)	6050
		Total liabilities	34 107
Total assets	35 901	Total equity	1793

Table 1.6   The largest Chinese and Japanese banks

Institution name	Total assets ($ M)
Industrial & Commercial Bank of China (ICBC)	2 822 334
Mitsubishi UFJ Financial Group	2 382 911
China Construction Bank Corporation	2 248 062
Agricultural Bank of China	2 130 857
Japan Post Bank	2 104 219
Bank of China	2 040 160
Mizuho Financial Group	1 820 416
Sumitomo Mitsui Financial Group	1 518 478

Source: data from original financial statements. Exchange rates as of March 29, 2013.

of US and European banks. In Asia, for example, along with the leading Japanese financial institutions, four Chinese banks have assets worth more than $2 trillion (Table 1.6). However, the new emerging banking groups have so far adopted the same business models as Western banks. Therefore, the valuation frameworks presented in the next chapters easily apply to banks outside the US and Europe.

2

Financial Statements Analysis for Banks

Marco Grotteria

Accounting rules are supposed to help investors understand the companies whose shares they buy. Yet current disclosure requirements don't illuminate banks' financial statements; instead, they let the banks turn out the lights. And in that darkness, all sorts of unsavory practices can breed.

The Atlantic, January 2, 2013

The analysis of a company's financial statements is the first step of the valuation process. Considering the inherent complexity of financial business, such analysis is even more critical for banks. Financial statements of banks are not dissimilar to those of non-financial companies. They include the following documents: Balance Sheet, Income Statement, Statement of Shareholders' Equity, Statement of Cash Flows, Notes to the Accounts, and Management Analysis.

While all the documents convey useful information and insights for the valuation, analysis of the first two is paramount for assessment/preparation of the business plan, which in turn, is necessary to apply most valuation models.

2.1   BALANCE SHEET

Balance Sheets provide readers with information regarding the current financial situation of a bank and support the various bank stakeholders in making decisions. In the last two decades, the latter role of the Balance Sheet has gained in importance as it has transformed from a mere reporting document into a relationship management tool for a larger and wider audience of stakeholders – made of customers, investors, regulators, rating agencies – whose objectives are not overlapping. Well-written Balance Sheets have to satisfy all those needs. In this chapter we will first describe the relevant banks' Balance Sheet items according to the IAS/IFRS framework. We will then provide some real-life examples of financial statement issues for banks. We will assume that the reader is already familiar with the basic accounting concepts and terminology.[1]

---

[1] For a practical reference book, see e.g., Fridson and Alvarez (2011) *Financial Statement Analysis: A Practitioner's Guide*, John Wiley & Sons, Ltd.

2.1.1   Assets

IAS 1 defines assets as resources "*controlled* by the entity as a result of *past events* and from which *future economic benefits* are expected to flow to the entity". The definition implies that such benefits have to come in more than one year. Also, the indication that control must be the result of past events technically forbids the capitalization of potential assets not backed by any contractual right. Next, we briefly present the asset items that commonly show up in banks' Balance Sheets.

2.1.1.1   Fixed Tangible Assets (Operating)

Even though banks make a large portion of their profits from financial activities, a "tangible" infrastructure in order to distribute their services is almost always necessary. Security systems, real estate, furniture, and computers are just a few examples of tangible assets on which a bank relies to offer its services and compete in the market. The relevant IAS for the treatment of those assets is no. 16, which touches upon tangible assets held for "production" purposes or that are sold in the ordinary course of business, and n. 40, on investment properties (land or buildings held for the purpose of gaining a return via rents from third parties or via capital appreciation).

IAS 16 affirms that acquired assets must be recorded at costs and that all the complementary expenses necessary to bring the asset to its intended use must be added. The estimate of the expenses for dismantling and removing the asset shall also be added to the initial cost. As for banks, it's extremely unlikely – although not impossible – that long-lived assets are constructed internally, instead of being purchased, so we will skip the specific rules concerning internally constructed assets.

IAS 16 is of interest for the measurement methodologies related to tangible assets after their initial recognition. Banks can adopt either the cost method or the revaluation approach. The former implies that assets are carried at their initial cost – plus all the complementary expenses, if any – less any accumulated depreciation and impairment losses. The latter, on the contrary, requires the company to revalue their IAS 16 assets at fair value, at the revaluation date, and to subtract any accumulated depreciation and impairment losses. Revaluations must be performed with a defined periodicity but no indication on the specific frequency of that practice is provided by the framework. Moreover, the same model has to be applied to an entire class of asset (e.g., buildings) and not just to a single asset in a certain class although some exceptions are allowed.

Fair value generally refers to market value or value as assessed by experts. However, IFRS 13 defines fair value as "*the price that would be received to sell an asset or paid to transfer a liability in an orderly transaction between market participants at the measurement date*". It is not explicitly required that valuators should be external professionals, as long as the professionalism criterion is met. Any revaluation must increase *other items of comprehensive income* in the income statement (as in IAS 1) and a revaluation reserve (Equity side) on which further devaluations will have an impact afterwards, instead of impacting the Income Statement. Any exceeding devaluation will be expensed in Income Statement. If further revaluations need to be recorded, they will first increase income statements for the portion of devaluations mentioned previously and then the revaluation reserve. It's worth noting that the comparison must be carried out between the revaluated depreciated cost at the end of the year and the fair value of the same asset.

According to IAS 16, ordinary repair and maintenance must be expensed and cannot be capitalized. On the contrary, there are some (generally extraordinary) repair and maintenance costs, which satisfy capitalization requirements (as they generate future economic benefits and the costs can be estimated reliably) and that can be capitalized according to the IAS framework.

To complement the picture of IAS 16's scope, it is worth underlining that according to IAS 36, an entity is asked to evaluate at each reporting date whether or not there is evidence that an asset may be impaired and in case such an assessment suggests a positive answer, the entity is required to estimate the *recoverable amount* of the asset (for intangible assets with indefinite life and goodwill impairment test must be carried out each year regardless of the presence of any signal). An impairment loss has to be recorded whenever the carrying amount of an asset exceeds its recoverable amount (recoverable through its use or disposal). The recoverable amount is the greater of: (1) an asset's fair value less costs to sell; and (2) its value in use. Therefore, if it's impossible to compute the fair value of an asset, the company is required to estimate its value in use. The value in use is calculated (1) by measuring the future cash-flows expected to arise from the exploitation of the asset and its final removal; and (2) by determining the adequate discount rate for the estimated cash-flows.

No matter what valuation method is adopted (historical cost model or revaluation model) any asset may be subject to an impairment test at each reporting date. The difference, however, between cost and revaluation models is that while under the cost model any revaluation can never exceed the value the asset should have carried at, if no devaluation had occurred, in the revaluation model the possible revaluation is allowed to exceed the depreciated historical cost (and recorded against the revaluation reserve).

2.1.2 Investment Property

As for IAS 40, investment property is defined as land, building, or part of a building, utilized to earn rentals or gain from capital appreciation. The distinction proposed by IAS is not between operating and non-operating assets: real estate companies have to report real estate assets under IAS 40 even though their business consists of trading in those assets. What makes a certain real estate's assets an investment rather than a bank's operating facility is, in the IAS framework, the management objective for the use of that asset.

Initially, an investment property shall be recognized at its cost (transaction costs, as usual, should be added). Investment properties can be measured after their initial recognition at either fair value or depreciated cost – FASB prefer management to adopt the fair value model even though both methods are allowed. The bank should stick to the chosen methodology for the entire category of covered assets, with the only possible exception of investment properties posted as collateral for some specific bank debt (for which the return is linked to the assets value). Different to the assets encompassed by IAS 16, the IAS 40 assets (under the fair value model) should not depreciate because of the different purpose of investment properties. In case bank managers decide to adopt the cost method for some assets, they have to explicitly report the fair value of those assets in the notes to the accounts. Moreover, any revaluation of investment properties goes to the "standard" Income Statement instead of the section, *other items of comprehensive income*.

Fair value under IAS 40 is generally the market value. In fact, §53 in IAS 40 clearly states that *"there is a rebuttable presumption that an entity can reliably determine the fair value of an investment property on a continuing basis"*. The idea is that, unlike assets under IAS 16, the value of an investment property is related to the *external* value it has on the market and not to the value it could have if used *internally* for operating purposes.

Finally, changes in the assets' classification – from IAS 40 status to IAS 16, and *vice versa* – are allowed as long as an actual change in their use is occurred.

2.1.3   Intangibles

An intangible asset is defined in IAS 38 as "an identifiable non-monetary asset without physical substance" from which the company will benefit for more than a single year. For an asset to be recorded as an intangible in the Balance Sheet, some requirements must be met (§§ 11–17 and §§ 21–23 of IAS 38):

The asset must be separately identifiable;
The asset must be controlled by the company (thanks to a contract or law);
The asset must produce probable future benefits for the company;
The cost of the asset can be reliably measured.

Typical examples of intangible assets are provided by computer software, brand, or capitalized R&D. It's interesting for the reader to observe that in some cases, for example computer software, intangible assets may be embedded in tangible ones such as a CD. It's up to bank managers to assess which component is predominant and to record the asset accordingly. As for the requirement of control, employee know-how for example cannot be recognized as an intangible asset according to IAS, even if a contract "tying" the employee to the company is in place. The reason is that this resource is not controlled by the bank as it might vanish as soon as the employee leaves the organization.

The initial recognition of intangibles consists of recording the asset at its initial historical cost regardless of whether it was purchased or built internally. The cost of a separately acquired intangible asset beyond its price must include tariffs and any directly attributable cost of preparing the asset for its intended use. In case the asset is obtained within the acquisition of another company, different rules about business combinations (IFRS 3) apply. In such a case, intangible assets are recognized at the fair value they had on the acquisition date whether or not they had been previously recognized by the bought company. Fair value is usually the market value, however, if there is no active market where similar assets are traded, the value of the asset can be estimated, for example by discounting future cash flows expected from it or by assessing the royalty stream obtainable from licensing the asset to a third party in an arm's length transaction (same rule as before *ex.* IAS 36).

For any measurement after the initial recognition of intangibles, with the exception of goodwill, IAS 38 allows companies to choose between the cost method and revaluation method just as in IAS 16 for PPE (property, plant, and equipment). The very same method must be applied to all the assets in the same class and coherency over time is required: it may not be changed unless the used approach doesn't reveal the true representation of the situation anymore. However, unlike IAS 16, IAS 38 restricts the application of the revaluation model only to those assets for which a certain established active market exists. It's true that for most bank intangibles (e.g., brands) such a market doesn't generally exist, therefore banks are usually constrained to apply the cost model.

As far as depreciation is concerned, accountants need to estimate the useful life and the residual value of the asset. IAS 38 §§ 88–96 affirms that "An entity shall assess whether the useful life of an intangible asset is finite or indefinite and, if finite, the length of, or number of production or similar units constituting, that useful life". It's useful to highlight that *indefinite* is not the same as *infinite* and that an indefinite life simply refers to the fact that no specific boundary to the time period over which the asset may be reasonably foreseen to produce net cash inflows for the entity can be correctly estimated. While an intangible asset with definite useful life gets amortized over time, an intangible asset with an indefinite useful life is simply subject to impairment tests at each reporting date. Moreover, it's allowed to move some intangibles from one category (finite or indefinite life) to another if some major changes in technology, market, or competitive framework occur. In case of an intangible asset accounted for at fair value, any revaluation must follow the rules described in IAS 16: they accrue to a revaluation reserve and have an impact on *other items of comprehensive income*.

2.1.4   Research and Development

In the context of the banking business, research, and development costs, although typically of limited magnitude, are present and they mostly consist of new software for managing funds and innovative trading platforms. Research costs (IAS 38 §§ 54–56) are related to "an original and planned investigation" aimed at gaining from new scientific or technical knowledge. With the term *research*, IAS refer to the first stage of the research process, in which it's hard to measure economic benefits and, as a matter of fact, even to predict the existence of any benefit. Therefore, research costs will be expensed in the Income Statement. As to the development stage (§§ 57–64), IAS refer to "the application of research findings or other knowledge to a plan of new or substantially improved materials, devices, products, processes, systems or services before the start of commercial production or use". Development costs can be capitalized if and only if all of the following requirements are satisfied:

The intangible asset is technically feasible and can be potentially sold;
The company has both the intention and the ability to complete the intangible, use it and sell it;
There is clear and consistent way for the intangible to generate likely future benefits;
The bank owns appropriate technical, financial, and other necessary resources to complete the development activity, and to use the intangible internally or to sell it;
The expenditures allocated to the asset during its development activity are measured reliably.

2.1.5   Goodwill

According to IFRS 3, the so-called acquisition method shall be applied to account for a business combination. Under this method, all the assets and liabilities of the controlled entity must be recognized at fair value (including those items that were not previously recognized). Moreover, according to IFRS 3, even though the holding company owns less than 100%, assets and liabilities must be recognized at 100% of their fair value. The 100% recognition doesn't automatically apply to goodwill, for which bank management can opt either for the recognition of goodwill directly related to their portion or for the *full goodwill* method. Instead, the full goodwill method is the only accepted approach applicable to US companies under US GAAP from 2009. The idea to measure the items of the acquired entity at their fair value is based on the logic that, if the parent company had purchased the assets and the liabilities separately from the entity, their fair value would have been exactly equal to the amount to pay in a series of separate item-by-item transactions.

So we provide the reader with two simple formulas to compute goodwill, assuming no tax is involved:

- *Partial recognition of goodwill*: goodwill is equal to the cost of investment less the value of the share in subsidiary's Equity (computed at fair value) belonging to the parent company;
- *Full goodwill method*: goodwill to be recognized in the parent company's Balance Sheet also comprehends the portion belonging to minority share-holders and is computed as the sum of cost of investment and the fair value of non-controlling interests minus the subsidiary's Equity (measured at fair value).

From IAS 36 and 38, we know that goodwill cannot depreciate. However, an impairment test must be carried out at each reporting date. Goodwill shall, from the acquisition date, be allocated to each of the acquirer's *Cash-Generating Units* (CGU), or groups of cash-generating units, that will reasonably benefit from the synergies of the combination.

Each unit or group of units must:

- Correspond to the lowest level at which the goodwill is audited for purposes of internal management;
- Not exceed the size of an operating segment, measured according to what is established in IFRS 8 Operating Segments.

An impairment loss shall be recognized for a cash-generating unit if its recoverable amount is lower than its carrying amount. The impairment loss shall first reduce goodwill and only afterwards all the other assets belonging to the CGU *pro rata*. Finally, it's worth underlining that, once impaired, goodwill cannot be written back up in a subsequent period.

2.1.6 Securities

With the term securities in this paragraph we refer to fixed income securities, shares, and interests in funds held in the bank portfolio either in the *trading* book (which includes the securities that are actively traded by the bank in its daily operations and whose aim is short term gain) or the *banking* book (which includes the securities that are not actively traded by the bank, and which are generally held to maturity). All the previously mentioned terms – fixed income securities, shares, and investments in funds – do not have to be narrowly interpreted: fixed income securities, for instance, may be either fixed or variable bonds, or any bond with attached interest rate-structured products. For the accounting treatment of securities, the most relevant principle is the IAS 39, along with the definitions presented by IAS 32. The latter affirms that a *financial instrument* is any contract that gives rise to a *financial asset* of one entity and a *financial liability or equity* instrument of another entity and defines a financial asset as:

I. cash;
II. an equity instrument of another entity;
III. a contractual right:
    a. to receive cash or another financial asset from another entity; or
    b. to exchange financial assets or financial liabilities with another entity under conditions that are potentially favourable to the entity; or
IV. a contract that will or may be settled in the entity's own equity instruments and is:
    a. a non-derivative for which the entity is or may be obliged to receive a variable number of the entity's own equity instruments; or
    b. a derivative that will or may be settled other than by the exchange of a fixed amount of cash or another financial asset for a fixed number of the entity's own equity instruments.

For most financial assets, the proper measurement and classification is far from being a trivial task.

In general, according to IAS 39, there are two valuation criteria for securities: (1) the amortized cost with impairment test (ACIT); and (2) the fair value approach. When using the ACIT approach, banks have to record an impairment loss whenever the recoverable amount of an asset (i.e., recoverable either through use or sale) is lower than its carrying amount. Therefore, banks first identify the assets that may be impaired and then estimate the recoverable amount. As for the second approach, we recall that fair value is *the price that would be received to sell an asset or paid to transfer a liability in an orderly transaction between market participants at arm's length at the measurement date*. Hence, the principle relies on the idea of "transaction at arm's length between knowledgeable parties".

As translating such principle in practice may not always be directly feasible, there is an order of preference of acceptable methods to compute the fair value of financial assets and liabilities. This preference system is called the *Fair Value Hierarchy*, from the top to the bottom, and is built on three levels:

- Level 1 is to consider the price of a similar asset traded in an active market; this method of valuation is generally referred to as *mark-to-market*.
- Level 2 is based on the application of a valuation technique (a model) to value the asset; such a model should obtain its inputs among the market expectations regarding interest rates and other market variables that appear to have an impact on the asset or liability value. This method is labeled *mark-to-model*.
- If neither an active market nor any relevant market variable is available, we need to move to Level 3 of the hierarchy, analyzing the features of the financial asset and forming a judgment about the value on the basis of reasonable input. This more subjective procedure is called *mark-to-management*.

The IAS 39 provides also a classification scheme to measure the value of financial assets and liabilities after their initial recognition. The categories are the following four:

- The first category, *financial assets at Fair Value Through Profit or Loss* (FVTPL), is divided in two sub-categories:
  - Financial Assets initially recognized at fair value (with the exception of non-listed equity stock, for which the price cannot be reliably estimated, most financial instruments in a bank Balance Sheet are comprehended in this group).
  - Held For Trading (HFT) assets, namely those assets acquired principally for being sold (and which may even be repurchased in the short term). Such assets may also be part of a broader portfolio where the other assets are treated differently. Financial derivatives may be included in this group with the exception of those derivatives that have a hedging instrument role.
- Loans and Receivables (L&R) are "non-derivative financial assets with fixed or determinable payments that are not quoted in an active market" (IAS 39 §9), namely, with no quoted price on an active market as a reference price.
- Held To Maturity (HTM) are "non-derivative financial assets with fixed or determinable payments and fixed maturity that an entity has the positive intention and ability to hold until maturity" (IAS 39 §9). Therefore, banks have to explicitly state their intention to hold those assets to maturity independently from market conditions, but on the sole basis of corporate financial and economic considerations.
- Available For Sale (AFS) assets, whose residual definition encompasses all those non-derivative assets that have not been included in the previous three categories.

Importantly, IAS 39 (§43) establishes that any financial activity must be initially recorded at its fair value at that date regardless of the specific category to which it belongs.

Table 2.1 links each of the four IAS categories with the valuation criterion to apply.

It's worth mentioning at this stage that, since loans and receivables represent a huge portion of what is regarded as a "standard" bank Balance Sheet, it's not completely true, as sometimes popularized by the press, that overall bank Balance Sheet is recorded "at fair value". Such items under IAS/IFRS are recorded at ACIT even if their initial recognition was at fair value.

In terms of financial statements representation of the value change of financial assets, the approaches are the following:

- FVTPL and HFT financial activities are measured at fair value and any change in their value is recorded in the Income Statement;

Table 2.1   Categories of financial assets and accounting criteria

Categories	Valuation criterion	How to recognize gains or losses
FVTPL	Fair value	Profit & Loss Statement
HFT	Fair value	Profit & Loss Statement
HTM	Amortized cost with impairment test	Profit & Loss Statement
L&R	Amortized cost with impairment test	Profit & Loss Statement
AFS	Fair value with impairment test	Revaluation reserve in the Balance Sheet (Equity) Impairment test results in the Profit & Loss Statement

- HTM assets are valued at historical amortized cost and any impairment loss is recorded in the Income Statement;
- As for L&R, they are measured at amortized cost with impairment test;
- AFS assets are measured at fair value and any revaluation impacts the revaluation reserve. Accumulated revaluation is finally translated in the Income Statement when the revaluated asset is sold.

Despite the framework provided by the IAS/IFRS principle is quite precise, when moving from the general rule to the practical application to bank Balance Sheet items, the areas of ambiguity are numerous. In some jurisdictions, national banking authorities provide additional guidance and clarification on which criteria to use (for example, Table 2.2 shows the criteria released by the Italian Central Bank). Some Central Banks in Europe have, for example, clarified how IAS 39 should be implemented by national banks when dealing with hybrid securities. The base criterion is to make a distinction between "debt securities" and "equity notes". For debt securities the relationship between investors and the bank is assumed to

Table 2.2   Categories of Financial Assets: Examples of what to include

Categories as defined previously	Debt securities (government bonds, certificate of deposits)	Equity stock	Shares in investment funds
FVTPL **HFT**	Included	Included	Included
HTM	Included, if and only if the security is listed, has fixed or determinable payments with a definite life	Not included	Not included
L&R	Included, if and only if the security is *not* listed, has fixed or determinable payments with a definite life	Not included	Not included
AFS	Included	Included	Included

Source: Bank of Italy, Circular no. 262/2005.

be based on a credit scheme, while for equity notes there is an active involvement of investors in the operations of the bank and they are entitled to receive a portion of the bank's results.

Furthermore, in some jurisdictions perpetual bonds cannot be classified in the HTM or L&R categories since they lack the characteristic of a "definite" life.

It's worth mentioning that under IAS 39:

> ... an entity shall not classify any financial assets as held to maturity if the entity has, during the current financial year or during the two preceding financial years, sold or reclassified more than an insignificant (a relevant) amount of held-to-maturity investments before maturity (more than insignificant in relation to the total amount of held-to-maturity investments).

In such case, the rest of the assets in that class must be reclassified as available-for-sale.

Finally, there are restrictions about reclassification patterns. HFT securities, satisfying the necessary requirements, can be reclassified in any of the three classes, while the opposite is not allowed. AFS assets can be moved to L&Rs and HTM, as long as the category specific requirements are satisfied. IAS 39 forbids any other reclassification and prescribes recording the reclassified asset at the fair value as of the reclassification date.

2.1.7 Equity Stakes

With the term *equity stake*, here we will refer to any possible form of ownership of equity capital, no matter what purpose and size of the stake. Apart from IAS 39, other principles touch on the equity stakes accounting: namely, IAS 27 (*Consolidated balance sheet, for a group of entity under the control of the parent company*), IAS 28 (*Associates*), and IAS 31 (*Joint ventures*).

In terms of scope, those accounting principles are applied as follows:

- A controlled entity (subsidiary) is one upon which the parent company can exercise control. According to the definition by IAS 27, control is "the power to govern the operating and financial policies of an entity so as to obtain benefits from its activities";
- According to IAS 31, "a joint-venture is a contractual arrangement whereby two or more parties undertake an economic activity, which is subject to joint control". The key point here is that joint control means that none of the companies can exert a controlling power by itself.
- An associate, under IAS 28, is an entity over which the investor has significant influence and that is not recognized either as a subsidiary or an interest in a joint venture.

Most banks do have a complex web of equity stakes in subsidiaries, joint-ventures, and associates because they carry out operations in different countries and in different sub-business for which a separate *ad hoc* entity is required by

Table 2.3 Equity stakes and accounting criteria

Categories as defined	Accounting category	Valuation criteria	Where to recognize gains or losses
Equity stakes in controlled entity (even joint control)	IAS 27/IAS 31 or FVTPL, HFT, AFS (IAS 39)	IAS 27/IAS 31 Fair value	Income Statement As IAS 39
Equity stakes in associates	IAS 28 or FVTPL, HFT, AFS (IAS 39)	IAS 28 Fair value	Income Statement As IAS 39
Other equity stakes	FVTPL, HFT, AFS (IAS 39)	Fair value	As IAS 39

national regulations (an example might be the bank-assurance business run by banks via *ad hoc* subsidiaries or joint-ventures with insurance companies).

According to IAS/IFRS, banks can exercise discretion in deciding under what IAS to record a specific equity stake (Table 2.3).

IAS 31 establishes that an interest in a joint venture shall follow either the *proportionate consolidation* (which is the favorite method) or the *equity method*. If the former is chosen, only the venturer's share of assets, liabilities, revenues, and expenses are included in the consolidated financial statements. As under IAS 27, financial statements must be subject to adjustments (for instance, intra-group transactions must be eliminated), but under IAS 31 adjustments are proportional to the equity stake.

When accounting for associates (under IAS 28), the *equity method* has to be applied. Under the equity method, the initial recognition of an investment is at its cost and then the carrying amount is modified to recognize the investor's portion in the associate's profit or loss (which is also recorded in the investor's income statement). In case some changes in the investee's equity that has not passed through the investee's income statement took place, further adjustments have to be carried out in order to correct the value of investor's interest in the investee and the investor's equity (directly). Examples of those changes comprehend those related to the revaluation of fixed tangible assets. Finally, in applying the equity method, any distribution received from the investee is subtracted from the value of the stake in the investor's Balance Sheet.

Impairment of those equity stakes not recognized under IAS 39 follows the regime indicated by IAS 36. According to such principle an entity is asked to evaluate at each reporting date whether or not there is evidence that an asset may be impaired and in case such an assessment suggests a positive answer, the entity is required to estimate the recoverable amount of the asset. However, even the concept of impairment signal is different from that derived from IAS 39 (the concept of "breach of a contract" is not adequate in the case of an equity stake). We have to record an impairment loss whenever the carrying amount of an asset is higher than its recoverable amount (recoverable through its use or disposal). The recoverable amount is the greater of: (1) an asset's fair value less costs to sell; and (2) its value in use. Therefore, similarly to what we have already seen, if it's impossible to compute the fair value of an asset, the company is required to estimate its value in use.

2.1.8   Loans and Receivables

IAS 39 (§43) establishes that any financial activity, including L&Rs, must be initially recorded at its fair value at that date. Therefore, if the loan was issued at a fair market rate, the value is given by the loan amount, while if the loan was issued at an interest rate different from the fair market one, fair value must be computed. Moreover, IAS 39 (§11) prescribes the separate recognition of any derivatives embedded in a financial instrument (not only L&R) not carried at fair value (in our case L&R). Embedded derivatives are defined (§10) as components of a combined instrument that also includes a non-derivative host contract. However, as shown in Figure 2.1, to deserve separate recognition, embedded derivatives have to satisfy the following requirements (§ 11):

- the economic characteristics and risks of the embedded derivative are not closely related to the economic characteristics and risks of the host contract;
- a separate instrument with the same terms as the embedded derivative would meet the definition of a derivative (IAS 39 § 9);
- the hybrid (combined) instrument is not measured at fair value with changes in fair value recognized in profit or loss.

In case the requirements are satisfied, embedded derivatives must be segregated from financial assets and the right valuation criteria must be applied to each component separately. It's worth highlighting that derivatives embedded in loans which satisfy the first requirement are rather rare. For example, two popular loan contracts are either (1) a variable rate loan with the maximum interest rate payable established at 6% (a *cap*), or a variable rate loan that gives the borrower the option after one year to convert the variable rate at a predetermined fixed rate (the so-called "swaption"). In both cases, they do not meet the first requirement, regarding the relation of economic characteristics and risks of the two instruments.

The rule concerning disentangling the embedded derivatives applies to financial instruments (including liabilities) and not only to L&Rs. A case in which the risk of the derivative is not closely related to the risk of the *host* financial instruments is the equity conversion or put option in debt instruments such as bonds.

Transaction costs should be considered as well. IAS 39 (Appendix A § AG13) defines transaction costs as "fees and commissions paid to agents (including employees acting as selling agents), advisers, brokers and dealers". Such costs may include those that will not be reimbursed by the client. These are incremental

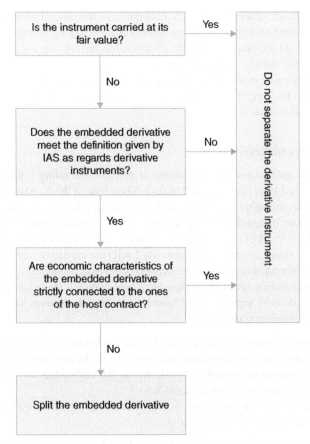

Figure 2.1   Process before deciding to separately recognize the embedded derivative

costs directly attributable to the financial asset or liability (§ 9), in the sense that they would not have been incurred if the entity had not acquired, issued, or disposed of the financial instrument. For that reason, IAS 39 suggests transaction costs to rectify (increase or decrease) the fair value in any case (so, even for L&Rs) except for FVTPL assets for which transaction costs are included in the Profit & Loss statement.

From its very definition, the *amortized cost of a financial asset or financial liability* is, "... the amount at which the financial asset or financial liability is measured at initial recognition minus principal repayments, plus or minus the cumulative amortisation using the effective interest method of any difference between that initial amount and the maturity amount, and minus any reduction (directly or through the use of an allowance account) for impairment or uncollectibility" (IAS 39).

The effective interest rate is the rate used to discount future cash-flows that allows achievement of the same net value as the one initially recorded.

How loans are accounted for

An example of the computations involved in loans accounting may prove useful at this stage. This table shows the features of a loan issued by a bank.

Fixed interest rate loan		
Notional:	130 000	€
Time:	10	years
Type:	Bullet	
Contractual rate	8%	
up-front commission	3250	€
Net issue	126 750	€

In the next table is each expected future cash flow ($130\,000 \times 8\% = 10\,400$).

Time	Cash flows	Discounted cash flows
1	10 400	9595.96
2	10 400	8854.08
3	10 400	8169.55
4	10 400	7537.95
5	10 400	6955.18
6	10 400	6417.46
7	10 400	5921.32
8	10 400	5463.53
9	10 400	5041.13
10	140 400	62 793.84
Total	234 000	126 750

The cash flows are discounted using the "effective rate" obtained from the following formula:

$$\text{Initial Value (net of transaction costs and commissions)} = \sum_{t=1}^{n} \frac{\text{Cash Flow}_t}{(1 + \text{effective rate})^t}$$

Where the net initial value is equal to 126 750 ($= 130\,000 - 3250$), and the cash flows are the ones in table previously. The effective interest rate is equal to 8.38%.

In order to compute the effective interest, we simply multiply the effective rate times the cost at the beginning of the year. The amortized cost is computed by discounting (using the effective rate) at the end of each year the cash flows expected in the subsequent years. In our example the cash flows are always equal to €10 400 with the exception of the final year when the face value of the loan should be added.[2]

Time	Cost at the beginning of the year	Effective interest	Cash flows	Amortized cost
1	126 750	10 620	10 400	126 970
2	126 970	10 639	10 400	127 209
3	127 209	10 659	10 400	127 468
4	127 468	10 680	10 400	127 748
5	127 748	10 704	10 400	128 052
6	128 052	10 729	10 400	128 382
7	128 382	10 757	10 400	128 739
8	128 739	10 787	10 400	129 126
9	129 126	10 819	10 400	129 545
10	129 545	10 855	140 400	0

2.1.9 Impairment Test

Banks shall assess at the end of *each* reporting period whether there is any *objective* evidence that a financial asset or group of financial assets may be impaired. IAS 39 § 59 offers some examples, such as a significant financial difficulty of the issuer or obligor, a breach of contract, or the likely event that the borrower will go bankrupt or activate a financial restructuring process, as examples of events that constitute an objective evidence that the asset may be subject to impairment. In the same paragraph (§ 59), IAS 39 establishes that losses expected as a result of future events, no matter how likely they are, shall not be recognized. Therefore, the only relevant events are those related to *incurred losses* and not *expected losses*. If there's evidence that Loans & Receivables (or HTM assets) must be impaired and the loan is of a significant amount, the entity shall compute the difference between the asset's carrying amount and the present value of estimated future cash flows (excluding future credit losses that have not been incurred) discounted at the original effective interest rate. The value of the asset shall be reduced either directly or through an *allowance* (contra-asset) account (*provisions* in the Income Statement). If, afterwards, when the actual loss occurs, the loss is lower than the amount impaired, any difference will be recorded in the Income Statement. In terms of computation, it is necessary to know not just the recoverable amount, but also the time in which that amount will be recovered.

As a final rule, IAS 39 § 64 provides a sort of decision tree to help assess whether or not to carry out an impairment test:

> "An entity first assesses whether objective evidence of impairment exists individually for financial assets that are individually significant, and individually or collectively

---

[2] For floating rate loans, future cash flows are determined using the last known rate.

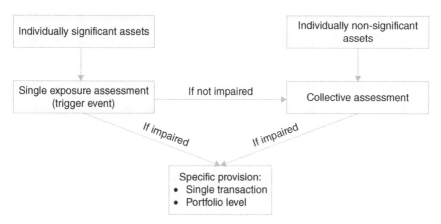

Figure 2.2   Decision tree for the impairment of a financial asset

for financial assets that are not individually significant. If an entity determines that no objective evidence of impairment exists for an individually assessed financial asset, whether significant or not, it includes the asset in a group of financial assets with similar credit risk characteristics and collectively assesses them for impairment. Assets that are individually assessed for impairment and for which an impairment loss is or continues to be recognized are not included in a collective assessment of impairment".

Figure 2.2 shows how the impairment decision tree is structured.

How to conduct an impairment test

To show an example of impairment test, we assume the figures from the case discussed in the previous paragraph.

Time	Cost at the beginning of the year	Effective interest	Cash flows	Amortized cost
1	126 750	10 620	10 400	126 970
2	126 970	10 639	10 400	127 209
3	127 209	10 659	10 400	127 468
Impairment loss				−75 304
				52 164
4	52 164	4371	0	56 535
5	56 535	4737	0	61 272
6	61 272	5134	0	66 406
7	66 406	5564	0	71 970
8	71 970	6030	78 000	0

At the end of year 3, the bank realizes that, due to a problem with the borrower, the loan will not be refunded in total and that the only cash flow it

will receive is equal to 60% of the "notional amount" which means €78 000
(= 60% × €130 000). This remaining cash flow will be paid to the bank after
5 years.

However, time value of money has to be taken into account so that the bank
cannot simply deduct from a current value the amount to be received in five
years from the moment the impairment is conducted. The recoverable amount
estimated (€78 000) should instead be discounted using the original effective
interest rate, which leads to €52 164. The difference between the amortized cost
computed at the end of year 3, had no impairment been recorded (€127 468),
and the discounted recoverable amount is the impairment loss (= €75 304 =
€127 468 − €52 164). In each of the subsequent years, estimated future cash
flows are discounted at the effective rate: in this case there is just one final cash
flow expected.

If in the subsequent year the borrower's financial conditions unexpectedly
improve, a revaluation must be recorded in the Income Statement.

Time	Cost at the beginning of the year	Effective interest	Cash flows	Amortized cost
1	126 750	10 620	10 400	126 970
2	126 970	10 639	10 400	127 209
3	127 209	10 659	10 400	127 468
Impairment				−75 304
				52 164
4	52 164	4371	0	56 535
Reversal of value				71 214
				127 748
5	127 748	10 704	10 400	128 052
6	128 052	10 729	10 400	128 382
7	128 382	10 757	10 400	128 739
8	128 739	10 787	10 400	129 126
9	129 126	10 819	10 400	129 545
10	129 545	10 855	78 000	0

It's worth noting that the reversal of value (€71 214) is lower than impairment
loss, because the bank actually loses the cash flow in year 4. Moreover, reversal
of value is equal to the minimum of the impairment loss and the difference
between the amortized cost, had no impairment loss been recorded (€127 748)
and the amortized cost at that date (€56 535).

2.1.10 Financial Liabilities

Financial liabilities and, specifically, the accounting definition of equity are key
elements for the valuation of banks as we will discuss in the next two chapters.

IAS/IFRS contain many features that have a direct impact on the definition and magnitude of accounting equity (e.g., revaluation reserve due to a higher fair value in AFS financial assets).

The revised IAS 32 introduces criteria to distinguish between financial liabilities and equity. However, especially for banks and other financial companies, the task poses several difficulties.

A financial instrument is a liability when the issuer, due to contractual obligations, is or may be asked to deliver either cash or another financial asset (at unfavorable conditions) to the holder. Alternatively, a financial instrument is a liability if it may be settled in the issuer's own equity, and one of the two following circumstances is met:

It is a non-derivative for which the entity is or may be obliged to deliver a variable number of the entity's own equity instruments; or

It is a derivative that will or may be settled other than by the exchange of a fixed amount of cash or another financial asset for a fixed number of the entity's own equity instruments. For this purpose, rights, options, or warrants to acquire a fixed number of the entity's own equity instruments for a fixed amount of any currency are equity instruments if the entity offers the rights, options, or warrants pro rata to all of its existing owners of the same class of its own non-derivative equity instruments.

Under International Accounting Standards (IAS 32 § 11), an equity instrument is any contract representing a residual interest in the assets of an entity after deducting all its liabilities. So, the problem is to understand what constitutes a financial liability and how to distinguish it from equity when complex securities and hybrid instruments are in place. Moreover, it's worth underlining that the category of the instrument is crucial in order to determine the proper accounting rules to apply with respect to interests, dividends, and gains (losses).

As a general indication of the nature of a financial instrument, the following principles hold:

- If the issuer does not have the "unconditional right to avoid delivering cash or another financial asset", that instrument is considered a liability.
- If redemption of the financial instrument can be imposed, it's appropriate to consider it as a liability.

In Table 2.4, we present some examples of equity, liability, and compound instruments.

Different to what is prescribed for financial assets, IAS 39 distinguishes just two categories in which to record a financial liability:

Financial liability at fair value;
Liability measured at amortized cost.

Table 2.4   Equity or liability classification

Instrument	Cash obligation for principal	Cash obligation for coupon/ dividends	Settlement in fixed number of shares	Classification
Ordinary shares	No	No	N/A	Equity
Redeemable preference shares with 8.7% fixed dividend each year subject to availability of distributable profits	Yes	Yes	No	Liability
Redeemable preference shares with discretionary dividends	Yes	Yes	No	Liability for principal and equity for dividends
Bond convertible into a fixed number of shares	Yes	Yes	Yes	Liability for bond and equity for conversion option
Bond convertible into shares at the value of the liability at the date of conversion	Yes	Yes	No	Liability

Source: Adapted from *Financial Instruments under IFRS*, PricewaterhouseCoopers (2008).

If the purpose is to repurchase the instrument in the near term with the goal of obtaining short-term profits – we are referring to trading liabilities, including non-hedging derivatives if they are at negative values – a financial liability is measured at fair value. The rest of liabilities, which is constituted by the non-trading ones, are carried at amortized cost.

As far as financial liabilities at fair value (FLFV) are concerned, IAS suggests a further segmentation:

> *held for trading liabilities*, for instance obligations to deliver financial instruments, for example money market paper, or other debt instruments that the bank has sold to third parties without owning them ("short" positions);
> financial liabilities for which the bank decided to utilize the *fair value option at inception*.

Therefore, if the purpose is to gain in the short term, the financial liability is included in the definition in (1) (e.g., an obligation to deliver securities borrowed by a short seller). On the other hand, the liabilities in (2) follow the same approach exercised by banks when they use the fair value option for financial assets at recognition. Finally, a key point is that the reclassification of financial liabilities is *not* allowed in any case (IAS 39 § 50).

2.1.11 Hedging

For accounting purposes, hedging operations are limited to offset potential net losses, due to a specific risk, on financial instruments (hedged items) through potential gains on hedging instruments, inversely related to that same source of risk.

Rules prescribed by IAS as regards the accounting treatment of derivatives vary depending on the classification of the derivatives themselves: namely whether they are *trading* or *hedging* derivatives. Under IAS 39, any derivative is presumed to be a trading derivative unless the bank states its *designated* and *effective* hedging capacity.

Moreover, the model as outlined in the IAS framework establishes a different methodology for the recognition of the derivative instrument depending on the *specific risk* that will be covered. As a matter of fact, IAS identifies three main sources of risk allowing for the recognition of the instrument:

Exposures to changes in the fair value of assets or liabilities or irrevocable commitments.

Exposures to variations in cash flows related to assets or liabilities or future transactions.

Exposure to currency exchange risk.

Since the accounting rules for the third category are the same as the ones for the second source of risk, we can treat both in the same way. While at recognition, the hedging instrument is always recognized at fair value in the Balance Sheet, IAS 39 introduces two accounting methods for any measurement of the hedging strategy results after the initial recognition:

Fair value hedge. This approach is taken when the goal is to reduce the exposure of some instruments to specific risk sources. An example of a fair value hedge may be provided by hedge of the exposure to changes in the fair value of a fixed rate debt instrument related to changes in the relevant interest rate curve. As to financial instruments at fair value, changes in fair value related to that specific risk are recognized in the Income Statements where they are offset by changes in the market value of the hedging instruments.

Cash flow hedge or *hedge of a net investment in a foreign entity.* This approach can be applied when the goal is to reduce the variability of cash flows. Such variability is related either to interest rate or to exchange rate movements. An example of a cash flow hedge is provided by the application of a swap to "turn" a variable rate debt into fixed rate liability. The purpose, however, is always to limit the variability of Income Statement results. Therefore, potential gains or losses get recognized in the bank capital, to the extent that they represent an effective hedging strategy, and get reported in the next period in the Income Statement so as to offset profit variability as they occur. As for the portion of gains or losses of the derivative representing an ineffective hedging strategy, this gets recorded immediately in the Income Statement.

Furthermore, IAS 39 does not prescribe any specific closed list of hedging and hedged instruments or risks to cover, but it requires that some specific strict requirements have been met so that an instrument may be classified for hedging purposes. In this way, any earning management strategy is avoided. In fact, from the points discussed so far, you can argue that hedging accounting (fair value hedge) may have an impact on the valuation criteria applied to financial instruments, such as available-for-sale assets (otherwise measured at fair value in the Balance Sheet) and loans and receivables (otherwise measured at amortized cost). Therefore, by applying the hedge accounting framework, a company could implicitly reorganize its financial assets going beyond the few reclassifications explicitly allowed in IAS 39.

Under the fair value hedge, the initial recognition at fair value of the hedged instrument is depreciated over time after the hedging operation has expired. It's finally prescribed that interest rate risk in held to maturity assets cannot undergo fair value hedging accounting.

As far as the cash flow hedge is concerned, the adverse variations in financial flows must comply with two requirements in order to be recognized under that model: (1) variations must be attributed to a specific risk; and (2) variations must have an impact on the Income Statement.

Furthermore, the Cash Flow Hedge also covers a highly probable transaction, namely a *forecast transaction*. The concept of a forecast transaction can be understood via a comparison with a *firm commitment* (that may be subject to a fair value hedge). A firm commitment is an irrevocable and binding commitment to exchange a specified item in a predetermined period at a pre-fixed price. On the contrary, a forecast transaction implies a less binding agreement, in which the agreement may not even exist yet, but the entity foresees they will carry out a specific transaction that will have an impact on the Income Statement. Let's, for instance, consider the case in which a bank decides to assume a specific position on FRAs (forward rate agreements) to keep "fixed" the interest rate on the debt notes it predicts to issue in the short term. We stress here that a mere intention to issue new bonds is not sufficient. Each situation, as well as the elements affecting the completion of the specific transaction, must be carefully and separately assessed (both the past history of the company and the current competitive landscape must be subject to a deep analysis).

The main accounting rules under the cash flow hedge worth knowing when using a bank's financial statements for valuation purposes are the following:

Derivatives must always be measured at fair value;

Gain or losses related to the effective portion of the hedging instrument get recognized in the *hedging reserve* (Equity);

In case of over-hedging, any exceeding portion of gains or losses must be recognized in the Income Statement, while, in case of under-hedging, the entire variation in the derivative value gets recognized in the reserve.

As for the hedging instruments allowed under IAS 39, only derivatives can be utilized as hedging instruments except for the case of hedging against exchange risk: in that case a non-derivative instrument (e.g., held to maturity investments) can also be used. Moreover, hedging instruments can only cover a specific relevant risk, while generic risks do not allow the bank to adopt hedging accounting rules. In any case, a specific set of documents demonstrating how the bank plans to monitor and update its risk positions and how to track the maturity of the hedging instrument has to be realized.

Regarding the initial recognition process, the hedging strategy to be recognized must be *highly effective*. Such effectiveness should be tested via mathematical techniques: the framework does not explicitly mention what sort of techniques should be used and such a decision is left to bank management who should consider the specific nature of the risks involved and the structure of the financial instruments used to hedge the risks. However, in case a bank applies different mathematical techniques in different transactions to show the effectiveness of hedging strategies, such a decision has to be justified.

2.1.12 De-recognition of Financial Assets and Liabilities

In the IAS/IFRS framework, *de-recognition* refers to process of removal of a financial asset or liability from a company's balance sheet. In essence, an entity must de-recognize a financial asset if either the entity's contractual rights to the asset's cash flows have expired or the asset has been transferred (together with the risks and rewards related to the ownership). In case of a financial instrument transferal, if the ownership risks and rewards have not been moved to the buyer, then the selling entity must keep the financial instrument in its statement of financial position and report a liability related to the consideration received. Examples of de-recognition may be provided by many typical financial practices applied by "modern" banks such as securitizations. On the contrary, repurchase agreements fail to meet the de-recognition criteria.

2.1.12.1 De-Recognition of Financial Assets

The de-recognition process can be seen as a five step process, as shown in Figure 2.3. The first step involves the consolidation of the financial statements

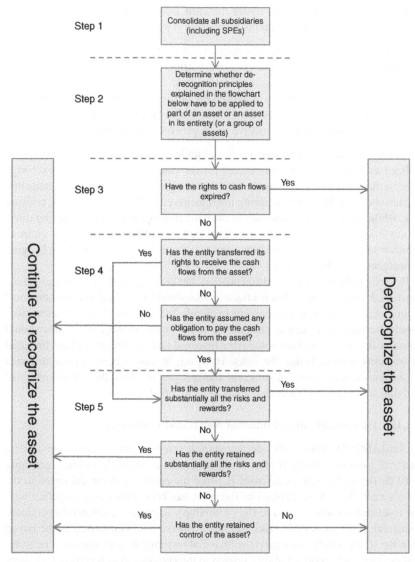

Figure 2.3   Process before deciding to derecognize a financial asset
Source: Adapted from IAS39 § AG36.

because de-recognition must be applied at a consolidated level. Most de-recognition transactions (e.g., securitization) are made via other *ad hoc* entities, usually referred to as *Special Purpose Entities* (SPE). Such entities, in fact, are generally created only for the purpose of separating the transferred assets, so that those assets get formally acquired and the acquisition is funded through capital raised in the market. If the entity is owned by the bank, in the consolidated financial statement the entity must be aggregated and then its assets de-recognized (if the de-recognition requirements are met).

The second step consists of identifying the financial assets to be de-recognized, while the third step consists in testing whether or not the related contractual rights to the cash flows have expired or are forfeited (e.g., in case the debtor pays its obligation, or in case the right under an option expires). The second test or step four in the procedure must be carried out if the answer to the first test has been negative, and it involves questioning whether the entity has transferred the rights to receive cash flows or has assumed any obligation to pay the cash flows from the asset. In case the answer to one of either questions is negative, the asset must be maintained in the Balance Sheet, while if the answer to one of the previous questions is positive some further requirement has to be met in order to proceed with the de-recognition. A typical example in which the entity maintains its right to receive cash flows while entering an obligation to pay these same cash flows is a pass-through arrangement in securitization.

Therefore, if one of either answer turns out to be affirmative, the bank has to perform what is usually referred to as *de-recognition test*, which is made up of the following two questions:

Has the entity *transferred substantially* all risks and rewards of the asset? If the answer is positive the asset should be de-recognized, otherwise the second question applies.

Has the entity *retained substantially* all risks and rewards of the asset? If the answer is negative the asset should be de-recognized.

Let's consider two examples. In case a formal sale has been completed, but the bank has already set the repurchase (higher and fixed) price (so, it's not substantially transferring the risk of holding the asset), the asset must not be de-recognized because bank exposure to the risk factors embedded in the asset have not been substantially eliminated and, as a matter of fact, bank substantially retained those risks. On the contrary, in case of sale of a financial asset together with the acquisition of an option to repurchase the asset at its fair value at a given time, the asset may be de-recognized. The requirement of transfer of risks and rewards has, in fact, been met since the new repurchase price is not fixed (so it doesn't keep the transferor subject to risk movement in the price of the security), but it has been set at fair value and the seller has an option (not an obligation) to repurchase it. Clearly from these two tests it emerges that *securities lending* is not an eligible transaction for de-recognition.

Finally, if the entity has neither transferred nor retained substantially all risks and rewards of the asset, the third test requires us to ask if the *control* has been *retained* by the entity. Control on the transferred asset is defined as the transferee's *practical* ability to sell the transferred asset, which is presumed for those assets "traded in an active market because the transferee could repurchase the transferred asset in the market if it needs to return the asset to the entity" (IAS 30 §AG42). The key question here is, what is the transferee able to do in practice, and not what contractual rights the transferee has.

If an asset (or portion of an asset) is derecognized, IAS39 requires the recognition of the difference between the consideration received and the asset carrying amount in the profit and loss statement. If only a portion of asset has been sold the carrying amount has to be split accordingly.

If the transaction has not passed this test, concerning the substantial transferal of risks and rewards related to the financial asset, only one of two events can occur: either all risks and rewards of ownership have been substantially retained; or only some of the risks and rewards of ownership have been retained.

In the former case, the transaction must be considered a collateralized borrowing and the accounting practice is the following: bank recognizes a financial liability equal to the received consideration while, if the transferee has the right to sell or re-pledge the asset, the asset is reclassified in the statement of financial position under loaned asset, repurchase receivables or pledge securities.

On the contrary, in the latter case, the risk and rewards have not been transferred or retained substantially and the following two situations may emerge:

Control has not been transferred, and we are therefore in a so called *continuing involvement* situation. The accounting treatment in this instance considers that the combined assets and liabilities (which are the results of the transaction) should turn out to represent the entity's net exposure to the financial asset either at fair value or at amortized cost, depending on how the item was previously recognized.

Control has actually been transferred. In that case, the company should de-recognize the financial assets whose control has been transferred and record new assets or liabilities for those rights and obligations that have been originated in the transaction or those ones that have been retained. For instance, if it sells an asset traded in an active market but retains a call option to reacquire the asset at a pre-established price, the transferor de-recognizes the asset and recognizes the call option.

2.1.12.2   De-Recognition of Financial Liabilities

As stated in IAS 39§57, a financial liability is extinguished when the debtor either:

discharges it by paying the creditor, with cash, other financial assets, goods or services; or

is legally released from primary responsibility for the liability either by process of law or by the creditor.

An important point is that IAS 39 establishes a way to distinguish between liabilities that have been subject to *restructuring* and those ones that have been *replaced* by new debt. If the debt terms are substantially different from the previous ones, the exchange has to be accounted by extinguishing the previous debt and by recognizing a new one. More specifically, as a practical rule, terms are regarded as:

> ... substantially different if the discounted present value of the cash flows under the new terms, including any fees paid net of any fees received and discounted using the original effective interest rate, is at least 10 per cent different from the discounted present value of the remaining cash flows of the original financial liability.

That distinction is highly relevant in terms of recognition of gain or losses. In fact, the difference between the book value of the financial liability extinguished or transferred and the consideration paid, including any non-cash assets transferred or liabilities assumed and any costs or fees incurred, shall be recognized in the Income Statement.

On the contrary, any net cash flow related to the restructuring of financial liabilities is accounted as an adjustment to the debt's book value and gets amortized over the liability's remaining life.

Example 2.1 – Repurchase Agreement[3]

The Volumian Bank Corp. agrees to sell a debt security, which is exchanged in an active market and is classified as Held-To-Maturity, at $5M (for sake of simplicity, let's suppose $5M is also its fair value) to the Far-East Bank and agrees to repurchase it at $5.25M after 1 year, for a return of 5%. This transaction clearly does not meet the requirements for de-recognition as all the risks and rewards are retained substantially by Volumian Bank Corp.: as mentioned, the transferor is dealing with a collateralized borrowing transaction.

On the date of transfer, transferor's accounts will be as follows:

Volumian Bank Corp. will recognize a new financial liability for $5M against cash:

Numbers in millions	Debit	Credit
Cash	5	
Repo liability		5

---

[3] The two examples that follow have been adapted from *IAS 39- Derecognition of Financial Assets in Practice*, PricewaterhouseCoopers (October 2008).

and will reclassify the asset:

Numbers in millions	Debit	Credit
Loaned Asset	5	
HTM asset		5

Even though Volumian Bank Corp. will keep reporting the debt security as a Held-To-Maturity financial asset, the instrument will be moved to the *loaned asset* category. The liability will be measured at amortized cost, and the difference between the price at which the security has been sold and the repurchase price (the interest portion) will be accrued as an expense over the term of the agreement using the effective interest rate method.

Numbers in millions	Debit	Credit
Interest expenses	0.25	
Repo liability		0.25

Numbers in millions	Debit	Credit
Cash		5.25
Repo liability	5.25	

On the date of transfer, the transferee's accounts (those of the Far-East Bank) will be as follows:

Numbers in millions	Debit	Credit
Cash		5
Reverse Repo (loan to Volumian Bank Corp.)	5	

Subsequently, the Far-East Bank has accounted this loan at amortized cost.

Numbers in millions	Debit	Credit
Reverse Repo (loan to Volumian Bank Corp.)	0.25	
Interest Income		0.25

Numbers in millions	Debit	Credit
Cash	5.25	
Reverse Repo (loan to Volumian Bank Corp.)		5.25

Finally, it's worth noting that if the repurchase price had been set equal to the market price on the repurchase date, the transaction probably would have met the requirement regarding transferal of risk and rewards.

Example 2.2 – Securitization: The Revolving Structure Case

Middle-Town Bank, one of the biggest banks in the mortgage market, decides to set an SPE that is formed with the sole purpose of buying $500M of mortgage loans and raising funds among investors (beyond servicing the debt).

The SPE issues both senior and subordinated notes, but, while the $400M senior notes get entirely acquired by third-party investors, the $100M subordinated notes are acquired by Middle-Town Bank itself (it was very common for banks in the pre-crisis era, and even today, to invest in subordinated or equity notes issued by "their own" SPE). However, the structure presented here has a peculiarity: each month, after cash gets collected from mortgage debtors, the interest element is transferred to the holders of the notes (issued by the SPE) in the form of interest payments, while the principal gets reinvested in new financial assets of the same type. At maturity, the principal will also be paid back. As usual, subordination principles will be applied in the reimbursement process.

The average rate of default over five years is 10% and the fair value is equal to the carrying value ($500M). Those loans are accounted for under L&R in IAS 39.

So in Step 1, the entity must be consolidated as we assume it meets the definition of control.

Step 2 consists of identifying the assets: these loans should be assessed grouped together.

In Step 3 we will determine that the rights to the cash flows of the portfolio of loans have not expired.

Step 4 consists of asking whether we are dealing with a pass-through arrangement in securitization. In our example for this to be true (and de-recognize the asset) we have to meet three requirements:

Middle-Town Bank (consolidated) is not obligated to pay anything to investors unless it receives payments from the borrowers of the loans (test passed);

The SPE is not allowed to sell or pledge the loans (test passed);

Nevertheless, that transaction fails the third test as Middle-Town Bank retains the control on those assets. In fact, it is not required to remit collected cash-flows without material delay, since the principal does not get reimbursed before the fifth year. In addition, Middle-Town Bank is qualified to reinvest such money in new mortgages and not simply in cash or cash equivalents (test failed).

So, Middle-Town Bank has to continue to recognize the assets on its Balance Sheet. On the transfer date, Middle-Town Bank will record as follows:

Numbers in millions	Debit	Credit
Cash	400	
Senior notes issued		400

Specifically, these subordinated notes are intercompany debt/credit and, according to international accounting standards about consolidation, we know that such an item will be eliminated. Finally both the loans and the liability will be carried at amortized cost.

2.2 THE US GAAP FOR BANKS

Like with IFRS, US GAAP distinguish among different categories of financial instruments and establish accounting rules specifically applicable to each category. For sake of simplicity, we will just focus on Marketable securities, Loans and Loan Commitments, as reported in Table 2.5.

Marketable securities may be classified into four sub-categories: trading, available-for-sale, held-to-maturity securities, or the fair value option (option can be applied to marketable securities, loans, and loan commitments). The bank management intent is the relevant criterion to classify securities in each category.

While trading securities are usually assumed to be held with the aim of short term reselling (within some hours or days), FASB staff clarified that "at acquisition an enterprise is not precluded from classifying as trading a security it plans to hold for a longer period". Both AFS and trading securities are reported at fair value, but, while for the former any change in value goes through AOCI (accumulated other comprehensive income) net of tax in shareholder's equity, changes in the latter's value are reported in the income statement. Changes in AFS go through an Income Statement instead if the instrument has been sold or if other-than-temporary impairment has been recognized. For HTM securities only impairments get recorded in the Income Statement.

According to US GAAP, corporate and mortgage loans may be classified either as held-for-sale or held-for-investment (but the fair value option, as prescribed by FAS 159, can also be applied). Figure 2.4 shows the classification criteria according the US GAAP. Reporting a loan as held-for-investment implies that the bank is able and has the willingness to hold it until a predictable date or maturity: then, for example, a generic phrase such as "until the market recovers" doesn't constitute a foreseeable future. On the other hand, held-for-sale loans are the ones held with the purpose of selling them: for that reason, due to the principle of

Table 2.5 Financial Instrument Accounting under US GAAP

Category	Classification and standard	Comment	Balance Sheet value	P&L Accounting
Marketable Securities Accounting	Trading Securities (FAS No. 115)	Intention is to hold for purpose of near-term selling or desire is to use fair-value accounting	Fair value	Marked-to-market
	Available-for-Sale Securities (FAS No. 115)	Default Category; held for an indefinite period of time	Fair value; changes in fair value recorded in AOCI net of tax in shareholders'equity	Marked-to-market through AOCI (not income statement), unless there is an other-than-temporary impaired. All, or a portion of, unrealized holding gain or loss that is deemed to be hedged by a fair value hedge is to be included in earnings during the hedge period
	Held-to-Maturity Securities (FAS No. 115)	Must have a positive intention and ability to hold to maturity; classification not available for equity securities	Carried at amortized cost. Amortized cost is the net present value of the debt security's future cash flows discounted at its interest rate on the initiation date	Record interest revenue. Not marked-to-market, unless impaired
	Fair-Value Option for Financial Assets and Liabilities (FAS No. 159)	Instruments selected on an instrument by instrument basis for this treatment	Fair value	Marked-to-market

(continued)

Loan Accounting	Held-for-Sale Loans	Intention to sell	Carried at lower of cost or fair market value ("LOCOM")	If the loan's fair value is lower than the loan's balance sheet carrying amount, the loan is written down to fair market value through a valuation allowance and the loss is recorded in earnings (the valuation allowance is a contra-asset account to the held-for-sale asset). If there is a subsequent recovery in the loan's fair value, the loan may be written back up to where it would have been without the write-down (adjusted carrying amount)
	Held-for-Investment Loans (FAS No. 65)	Must have intention and ability to hold for a foreseeable future or until maturity. Company cannot intend to "hold until market recovers"	Carried at amortized cost and not marked-to-market	Interest income recorded based on effective interest rate on loan's initiation date multiplied by amortized cost. Evaluate for impairment and take charge if it becomes probable that the holder "will be unable to collect all amounts due according to the contractual terms"
	Fair-Value Option for Financial Assets and Liabilities (FAS No. 159)	Loans selected on a loan by loan basis for this treatment	Fair value	Marked-to-market

Loan Commitment Accounting			
Derivatives: Loan Commitments related to Origination of Mortgage Loans to be Held-for-Sale (FAS No. 133)	Loan commitments relating to the origination of mortgage loans held-for-sale are required to be accounted for as derivatives under FAS No. 133	Fair value	Marked-to-market
Loan Commitments related to Loans to be Held-for-Sale (other than Commitments related to the Origination of Mortgage Loans)	Intention to sell	Carried at lower of cost or fair market value ("LOCOM") or FAS No. 5 Contingent Loss Approach (allowance for bad debts)	Marked-to-market
Loan Commitments related to Loans to be Held-for-Investment (other than Commitments related to the Origination of Mortgage Loans)	Must have intention and ability to hold for a foreseeable future or until maturity. Company cannot intend to "hold until market recovers"	FAS no. 5 Contingent Loss Approach (allowance for bad debts)	Marked-to-market
Fair-Value Option for Financial Assets and Liabilities (FAS No. 159)	Loan commitments selected on a loan by loan basis for this treatment	Fair value	Marked-to-market

Source: FASB; JP Morgan (2008).

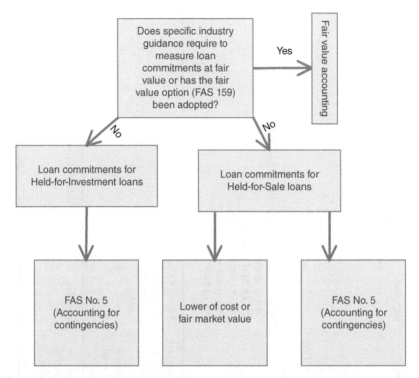

Figure 2.4 How loans are accounted for in the US GAAP framework

conservatism, US GAAP prescribes to account for those loans at the lower of cost or fair market value: in case the loan, after having been written down, recovers its value, it shall be written back up to its carrying amount (the one it would have had in normal circumstances).

Had no specific fair value treatment been required to or opted for by the bank, a loan commitment gets classified depending on the bank intent to sell or hold the underlying loan. In case they refer to held-for-sale loans, accounting rules for loan commitments may either follow the "lower of cost or fair market value" rule or what is prescribed by FAS 5 (accounting for contingencies). In this last case, a contingent loss is recognized (in the income statement) if it's both probable and measurable. Held-for-investment loans are instead recorded only according to FAS 5.

As briefly mentioned, FAS 159 grants the option to record most of financial assets and liabilities (some exceptions, for example, are given by investments in consolidated subsidiaries or pension assets and obligations) at fair value. Any change in fair value, from one period to the next one, is recorded in the income statement. Moreover, gains or losses related to the adoption of the FAS 159 standard for securities already accounted for in another sub-category go directly to impact shareholders' equity (as adjustment to retained earnings).

2.2.1   Reversal of Impairment

Impairment tests must be carried out for AFS, HTM or non-marketable securities. According to FAS 115, if impairment is considered "other-than-temporary", loss must be recorded in the income statement. The phrase "other-than-temporary" was chosen because FASB didn't want to restrict loss recognition just to "permanent impairments", but the unwelcome consequence is that subjectivity becomes a dominant factor to determine what the meaning of "other-than-temporary" is in practice. Nevertheless, as a general rule, if, after quarterly testing the security (test is performed at an individual-security level), fair value of the investment is less than its cost and that situation doesn't appear to be temporary, the investment book value gets impaired to equal fair value and any difference is recognized in the income statement. As regards AFS, if a portion of the impairment is already gone through AOCI, that same portion has to be moved back to the Income Statement.

2.2.2   Transfer among Different Categories

Although reclassification of financial securities is not prohibited under US GAAP, it is somehow discouraged. Once a transfer has occurred, all the assets shall be reported at fair value but the treatment of any recognized gain or loss depends on the specific category. For instance, in case of transfer out from the trading category, any unrealized gain or loss has to be recorded in the income statement. In case of transfers out from the AFS category, applicable accounting rules depend on the new category. If AFS securities are transferred to trading securities, any unrealized gain or loss (which for AFS is recognized in AOCI) gets moved to the Income Statement. On the other hand, for AFS that are classified as HTM, the unrealized gain or loss amount stays in AOCI while it gets amortized into earnings using the effective interest method.

2.3   PROFIT & LOSS STATEMENT

Banks, as non-financial companies, may choose one of the several formats available to present the balance sheet and the income statement. Here, we will refer to an Income Statement organized "per margin" and, consequently, to a "per margin analysis". Following IAS 7, we present the structure of a bank's Profit & Loss Statement where group income and expenses are defined by nature.

In the first row, the entity accounts for positive and negative interest on several Balance Sheet items issued to (received by) retail customers other banks and financial institutions, namely cash and cash equivalents, held-for-trading assets, held-to-maturity assets, available-for-sale financial assets, loans and assets at fair value, as well as held-for-trading liabilities and liabilities at fair value. Therefore, net interest income (the first margin in the list) is the direct result of *volumes* and *composition* of those assets and liabilities as well as applied *interest rates*.

	Time T	Time T-1

Interest and similar income
Interest and similar expense
Net interest income
Provision for credit losses
Net interest income after provision for credit losses
Commissions and fee income
Commissions and fee expenses
Net commission and fee income
Dividends and similar income
Net trading Income
Fair value adjustments in hedge accounting
Gains (losses) on disposal or repurchase of:

a) loans and receivables
b) Available for sale assets
c) Held to maturity assets
d) financial liabilities

Gains (losses) on financial assets and liabilities designated at fair
    value through profit and loss
Operating income
Net impairment losses on

a) Available for sale assets
b) Held to maturity assets
c) other financial activities

NET OPERATING PROFIT (LOSS) from financial activity
Payroll costs
Other Administrative expenses
Provisions for risks and charges
Amortization, depreciation and impairment losses on intangible
    and tangible assets
Operating costs
Profit (loss) of associates
Net valuation at fair value of tangible and intangible assets
Gains (losses) on disposal of investments
Impairment of goodwill
PROFIT (LOSS) BEFORE TAX
Income tax for the period
NET PROFIT (LOSS)
Gains (losses) on assets classified as held for sale, after tax
PROFIT (LOSS) FOR THE PERIOD

Then, leaving the typical format of Income Statement per margin, we have entered provisions for credit losses because it is really important in order to analyze consistently the net result of that portion of operating activities. In practice, we can have banks posting very high interest income (e.g., on loans), but if the amount of provision is very high as well, the sole information about the gross interest income might be misleading for assessing the quality of the bank strategy and positioning (and hence of its value).

The second margin, net commission and fees, includes income and expenses for provided and received services. Those services, depending on the richness of businesses the bank is running, may include underwriting and placement of securities, brokerage, transaction advisory, asset management services, and guarantee services: these are all commonly charged a fee or commission.

Operating income is then obtained by aggregating the first two margins with some more items, which are linked to the typical operating activity of a bank but that produce neither interest nor commissions. For instance, dividends (whatever the classification, financial assets or associates) from equity stakes in other companies represent an important part of the banking business today and are included in operating income.

To complete the picture of a bank's financial operations, we further consider the net impairment losses and we obtain net the operating profit from financial activity.

Other non-financial items have then to be considered: payroll costs, other administrative expenses, provisions for risks and charges, amortization, depreciation and impairment losses on intangible and tangible assets. In the bottom rows, extraordinary items (e.g., gains or losses on disposal of investments and impairment of goodwill) are reported and, adding/subtracting them, profit (loss) before tax if finally obtained.

2.4   MAJOR DIFFERENCES BETWEEN IAS/IFRS AND US GAAP

	IAS/IFRS	US GAAP
PPE		
Valuation	Both revaluation cost and historical cost	Only historical cost
Impairment	If cost method is chosen impairments are recognized in the Income Statement; if revaluation is chosen impairment is accounted for as reversal of revaluation unless it exceeds former write-up, in which case excess impairment is recorded in the Income Statement	Impairment is recognized in the Income Statement

(*continued*)

	IAS/IFRS	US GAAP
INVESTMENT PROPERTY		
Valuation	Investment property may be accounted for by cost (and depreciation) method, or by fair value method with changes taken to income	Investment property must be accounted for by cost (and depreciation) method
INTANGIBLES		
Valuation	Both revaluation cost and historical cost. Revaluation model can be applied when an active market on which the intangible is traded does exist	Only historical cost
Internally generated intangibles	Research cost are expensed while development costs may be capitalized had proper criteria been met	Both research and development costs are expensed. Different rules apply to computer software and web site development
Advertising	All costs in advertising shall be expensed	In some specific cases, capitalization of advertising costs is permitted
Amortization	Indefinite useful life assets are not amortized	Same as IAS
IMPAIRMENT TEST		
Procedure	One step approach: if carrying amount exceeds the recoverable amount, an impairment loss is recognized	Two step approach: carrying amount is first measured against the undiscounted cash flows arising from the utilization of the asset for those assets held to be used or fair value less costs to sell for assets held for sale; Second, the impairment loss is equal to the carrying amount less the asset fair value (less cost to sell if the asset is held for disposal)
Reversal of impairment loss	Permitted for any intangible except from goodwill	Prohibited by US GAAP

	IAS/IFRS	US GAAP
Impairment of goodwill	The test is performed at CGU level. 1 step approach: If the carrying amount of the CGU exceeds the recoverable amount an impairment loss is recognized	The test is performed at Reporting Unit level. Two-step approach: First a comparison is carried out between the carrying amount of the RU and its fair value. If the latter is higher than the previous, the implied fair value of goodwill is measured and an impairment loss is computed

FINANCIAL INSTRUMENTS

	IAS/IFRS	US GAAP
Fair value option	Option to recognize any financial asset or liability at fair value through profit or loss	In an effort of convergence with IFRS, the fair value option has been adopted
Impairment	Impairment of financial securities has to be accounted for when "loss events" are of objective evidence of impairment	Impairment of debt and equity instruments is only recognized when reduction in the fair value is regarded as non-temporary
Reversal of impairment	Reversals of impairment losses are allowed by IASs for loans and receivables, HTM and AFS debt securities where specific criteria met	Reversal of impairment losses is banned for HTM and AFS assets. Reversals of impairment losses on loans are accounted for in the income statement
Disposal of meld-to-maturity financial assets, before maturity	If held-to-maturity securities are sold, securities of that same category are forbidden to be recorded as HTM for next two years	If held-to-maturity securities are sold, securities of that same category are banned to be recorded as HTM type of assets thereafter
De-recognition	De-recognition of financial assets is based on an assessment of the transfer of risks and rewards of ownership of an asset. Only in case that test is not conclusive, an evaluation of the transfer of control takes place (secondary test)	De-recognition of financial assets is based on loss of control

(*continued*)

	IAS/IFRS	US GAAP
What they mean for control	*Control* refers to the idea of the "transferee's *practical* ability to sell the asset unilaterally without any restriction"	Loss of control requires legal isolation from transferor, transferee ability to pledge or sell the asset, and absence of repurchase obligation by transferor
Hedging of part of term	Hedging for a portion of term of hedged item is allowed	Hedging for part of term of hedged item is never allowed
Hedging a portion (Cash Flow Hedge)	Hedging of part of cash flows of hedged item is allowed	Hedging of part of cash flows of hedged item is forbidden
Hedging effectiveness	Hedging effectiveness is never presumed	Hedging effectiveness can be presumed in some specific circumstances
Non-derivative instrument w.r.t. currency risk	Permitted to hedge foreign currency risk	Allowed to hedge currency risk linked to an investment in a foreign organization or a firm commitment (fair value hedge)

2.5 EXAMPLE OF IAS/IFRS APPLICATION

We propose here a brief analysis of the Income Statement and of the "Statement of Financial Position" (Balance Sheet) of Deutsche Bank, a leading German investment bank with a strong private client base. Financial statements have to be read in the context of company's strategy. The bank affirms that one of its goals is to take "full advantage of the synergy potential between the two mutually reinforcing businesses", namely commercial and investment banking. With more than 100 000 employees, Deutsche Bank is a market leader with 3078 branches worldwide: from Europe to North America and Asia, Deutsche Bank competes and is firmly established in 72 countries.

The financial statements refer to 2011, a year in which the economic and financial environment recorded a relatively favorable first half, but a significant downturn in the second half as the European sovereign debt crisis worsened and economic activity declined.

In 2011, despite of the challenging environment, Deutsche Bank managed to strengthen its capital position and liquidity reserves, reckoning that it was "well prepared for further potential challenges caused by market turbulences and stricter regulatory rules".

Before describing the reports, we stress that analysts comparing several banks need to assess management's reporting choices and how those choices have affected results. For example, managers can organize the acquisition of equity stakes in a manner which might help them managing their "accounting results". Some banks in fact, try to avoid the use of equity method (for associates) since that method is regarded as a source of a higher variability for the bank results (results of the associates get proportionately included in the investor's profit or loss). A critical eye on reported figures is key to understanding the bank, and to performing an accurate and reliable valuation.

INCOME STATEMENT

in €M	2011	2010
Interest and similar income	34 878	28 779
Interest expense	17 433	13 196
Net interest income	17 445	15 583
Provision for credit losses	1839	1274
Net interest income after provision for credit losses	15 606	14 309
Commissions and fee income	11 544	10 669
Net gains on financial assets/liabilities at fair value through profit or loss	3058	3354
Net gains (losses) on financial assets available for sale	123	201
Net income (loss) from equity method investments	−264	−2004
Other income (loss)	1322	764
Total non-interest income	15 783	12 984
Compensation and benefits	13 135	12 671
General and administrative expenses	12 657	10 133
Policyholder benefits and claims	207	485
Impairment of intangible assets	0	29
Total noninterest expenses	25 999	23 318
Income before income taxes	5.39	3975
Income tax expense	1064	1645
Net income	4326	2330

Starting with the analysis of the Income Statement, at first glance it is striking that interest income increased by an impressive 21.2% despite the fact that, as mentioned, 2011 was overall a difficult year with one of the worst financial crises ever looming in Europe and the US. Such an extraordinary result derives from the fact that Postbank, a retail commercial bank, was consolidated in 2011 (according to IFRS 3). Excluding Postbank, net interest income in 2011 was down versus 2010, due to the disappointing results in CB&S (Corporate Banking & Securities), the investment bank division. Generally speaking, higher costs of funding associated with higher spreads and lower net interest income on trading positions were behind the poor CB&S performance.

Net interest income was also impacted by the accounting treatment of some hedging instruments.[4] Furthermore, it's worth recalling that under IFRS, interest and similar income earned from trading instruments and financial instruments designated at fair value through profit or loss (e.g., coupon and dividend income), and the costs of funding net trading positions are part of net interest income.

The increase in provisions for loan losses was also driven by Postbank acquisition and, as it is stated in the annual report, without Postbank a decrease in provisions should have been reported.

As to the trading activities, nothing relevant can be noticed at a first glance except what stated by Deutsche Bank itself: "our trading activities can periodically shift income between net interest income and net gains (losses) on financial assets/liabilities at fair value through profit or loss depending on a variety of factors, including risk management strategies".

The consolidation of Postbank also impacted positively fees for other customer services and brokerage fees. However, underwriting and advisory fees (that refer to corporate and investment banking activities) decreased by 17% given a reduced number of deals following the challenging macroeconomic and financial conditions.

Net gains from financial assets available for sale, although equal to €123M, suffered from impairments on Greek government bonds for a consideration of €527M.

As for non-interest expenses, two aspects are worth noting. First, while Deutsche Bank claimed to have paid lower performance related compensations in 2011, which had a negative effect on the item compensation and benefits, that item experienced an increase in 2011 due to the consolidation of Postbank. Second, "General and Administrative expenses" is a comprehensive item, and the recommendation would be to identify in detail its main components by analyzing their magnitude and evolution one by one.

	2011	2010
IT costs	2194	2274
Occupancy, furniture and equipment expenses	2072	1679
Professional service fees	1632	1616
Communication and data services	849	785
Travel and representation expenses	539	554
Payment, clearing and custodian services	504	418
Marketing expenses	410	335
Consolidated investments	652	390
Other expenses	3805	2082
Total general and administrative expenses	12 657	10 133

---

[4] As it should be already clear, "when derivative transactions qualify as hedges of interest rate risks for accounting purposes, the interest arising from the derivatives is reported in interest income and expense, where it offsets interest flows from the hedged items. When derivatives do not qualify for hedge accounting treatment, the interest flows that arise from those derivatives will appear in trading income." (Deutsche Bank, Annual Report 2012).

In this case, by reading the notes to the Income Statement, it comes up with the useful information that the major contributors to the increase in G&A expenses are the specific charges in CB&S (€655M litigation-related expenses). Whether such expenses can be considered an extraordinary non-recurring item or not is a relevant question. The answer might actually impact, as we are going to see, the valuation process (e.g., the Price/Earnings multiple normalization, or the business plan forecasts).

At the bottom of the Income Statement, we also find policyholder benefits and claims, which are insurance charges, offsetting related gains on financial assets/liabilities at fair value through profit or loss.

In order to allow readers to further analyze its results, Deutsche Bank, in line with other diversified banks, also provides readers with a further segmentation of results associated with the different business areas. The accuracy and structure of such segmentation may lead the valuator to the decision of using a *Sum Of Parts* framework, namely a valuation of the entire bank as the sum of the values of each and every business unit valued independently.

ASSETS (in €M)	31 DEC 2011	31 DEC 2010
Cash and due from banks	15 928	17 157
Interest-earning deposits with banks	162 000	92 377
Central bank funds sold and securities purchased under resale agreements	25 773	20 365
Securities borrowed	31 337	28 916
Financial assets at fair value through profit or loss		
Trading assets	240 924	271 291
Positive market values from derivative financial instruments	859 582	657 780
Financial assets designated at fair value through profit or loss	180 293	171 926
Total financial assets at fair value through profit or loss of which €87 billion were pledged to creditors and can be sold or repledged at December 31, 2011	1 280 799	1 100 997
Financial assets available for sale of which €9B were pledged to creditors and can be sold or repledged at December 31, 2011	45 281	54 266
Equity method investments	3759	2608
Loans of which €3 B were pledged to creditors and can be sold or repledged each year ending December 31, 2011	412 514	407 729
Property and equipment	5509	5802
Goodwill and other intangible assets	15 802	15 594
Other assets	154 794	149 229
Assets for current tax	1870	2249
Deferred tax assets	8737	8341

ASSETS (in €M)	31 DEC 2011	31 DEC 2010
TOTAL ASSETS	2 164 103	1 905 630
LIABILITIES AND EQUITY (in €M)	**31 DEC 2011**	**31 DEC 2010**
LIABILITIES		
Deposits	601 730	533 984
Central bank funds purchased and securities sold under repurchase agreements	35 311	27 922
Securities loaned	8089	3276
Financial liabilities at fair value through profit and loss		
Trading liabilities	63 886	68 859
Negative market values from derivative financial instruments	838 817	647 195
Financial liabilities designated at fair value through profit or loss	118 318	130 154
Investment contract liabilities	7426	7898
Total financial liabilities at fair value through profit or loss	1 028 447	854 106
Other short-term borrowings	65 356	64 990
Other liabilities	187 816	181 827
Provisions	2621	2204
Liabilities for current tax	2524	2736
Deferred tax liabilities	1789	2307
Long-term debt	163 416	169 660
Trust preferred securities	12 344	12 250
TOTAL LIABILITIES	2 109 443	1 855 262
SHAREHOLDERS' EQUITY		
Common shares, no par value, nominal value of €2.56	2380	2380
Additional paid-in capital	23 695	23 515
Retained earnings	30 119	25 975
Common shares in treasury, at cost	−823	−450
Accumulated other comprehensive income, net of tax	−1981	−2601
Total Shareholders' Equity	53 390	48 819
Non-controlling interests	1270	1549
TOTAL EQUITY	54 660	50 368
TOTAL LIABILITIES AND EQUITY	2 164 103	1 905 630

As far as Deutsche Bank's balance sheet is concerned, it closely follows the model suggested by IAS/IFRS. The increase of 14%, compared to December 2010, was primarily due to derivatives and interest-earning deposits with banks. Deutsche Bank, in fact, reported that moving US dollar, euro, and pound sterling yield curves as well as currency exchange rates accounted for most of the change in derivative value. On the other hand, the increase in deposits with other banks was a direct consequence of the strategy aimed at enhancing the liquidity position of the bank. Loan amount was stable during the year.

Some of the major movements that occurred on the asset side have been as follows:

- The decline in equity securities available for sale was primarily driven by the application of equity method accounting for the Group's stake in Hua Xia Bank from February 2011;
- Within the unamortized intangible asset class, it's worth mentioning two of the main items: Retail investment management agreements and trademarks. The former is an intangible asset specific to the financial industry and refers to contracts that provide Deutsche Bank with the right to manage several mutual funds for a determined period. However, since those contracts may be easily extended (which means at minimal cost) and they have been renewed smoothly several times in the past, these agreements are not expected to have a foreseeable limit on the contract period, so they are intangibles with an indefinite life;
- In 2011, Deutsche Bank classified several "disposal groups" within the Corporate Banking & Securities division and the Asset & Wealth Management division as held for sale. A disposal group (according to IFRS 5) is a group of assets, sometimes with some associated liabilities, that an entity is willing to dispose of in a unique transaction. To classify an asset as held-for-sale, some criteria has to be met, for instance an active program to find a buyer must be begun and with a high level of probability the sale will be completed within 12 months from the date of reclassification. However, once classified in that way, the following accounting rules apply: disposal groups held for sale are not depreciated; they get reported at the lower of carrying amount and fair value less costs to sell, and show up as a separate item in the Balance Sheet. Impairment must be carried out both when the assets get reclassified and subsequently. One example can be that of Deutsche Bank that classified its investment in BHF-BANK AG as a disposal group within the Group Division Corporate Investments held for sale because of exclusive sale negotiations initiated with Liechtenstein's LGT Group.

As for the liability side, negative market values from derivatives increased by €192B, mainly due to similar reasons as derivatives in the asset side. Change in negative market values of derivatives accounted for 75.6% of the total change in liabilities.

When bank financial statements are analyzed it is always good practice to split liabilities and assets by maturity. Clearly banks are involved in the maturity transformation business so that they borrow short-term (on demand) funds to issue long-term loans. Therefore, we can expect a certain maturity mismatch. Nevertheless, it is up to the bank's management to maintain a certain position in terms of liquidity and reduce the maturity mismatch while still taking care of the profitability for shareholders. The magnitude of the maturity mismatch should be assessed, as far as possible, from the financial statements notes and the other information released by the bank to investors.

Dec 31, 2011 in €M.	On demand	Due within 3 months	Due between 3 and 12 months	Due between 1 and 5 years	Due after 5 years
Non-interest bearing deposits	99 047				
Interest bearing deposits	163 620	277 462	30 600	21 736	16 008
Trading liabilities	63 886				
Negative market values from derivative financial instruments	838 817				
Financial liabilities designated at fair value through profit or loss	99 182	45 211	6204	6695	9189
Investment contract liabilities	604		840	1338	4643
Negative market values from derivative financial instruments qualifying for hedge accounting	452	135	11	1018	3170
Central bank funds purchased	2866	2050			
Securities sold under repurchase agreements	24 781	4975	1022		
Securities loaned	7643	38			
Other short-term borrowings	48 879	15 471	1330		
Long-term debt	3608	9691	26 100	83 610	68 256
Trust preferred securities	167	3163	5966	6359	
Other financial liabilities	143 375	3788	345	660	47
Off-Balance Sheet loan commitments	87 433				
Financial guarantees	23 684				
Total	1 607 273	359 592	69 615	121 025	108 142

To conclude the overview of the main aspects that a valuator should look at when dealing with bank financial statements, the last table represents the maturity analysis carried out by Deutsche Bank on its own financial liabilities in 2011. We notice that almost 87% of all Deutsche Bank's financial liabilities have a maturity lower than 3 months and that 71% of them are on-demand items. A comparison of such structure with that of similar financial institutions would yield important information to the analyst, conveying insight about possible changes in the funding strategy of the bank.

3

The Regulatory Capital for Banks

One of the key aspects that sets the valuation of financial firms apart from the valuation of non-financial companies is the heavy regulation of the capital structure. The presence of specific and detailed capital requirements – defined at international level and enacted by the national banking authorities – affects not only the way banks manage their operations but also how much equity they should retain to meet the relevant requirements. This means that compliance with capital regulations – more than managerial discretion – defines how much income or cash is actually "freely" distributable to bank shareholders. Therefore, when applying valuation approaches like the DDM or the DCF, income, dividends, and cash flow forecasts should take into account how regulatory capital will evolve. Analogously, adjustments to multiple valuations of banks may be appropriate when the capital is significantly distant – either in excess or in deficit – from the level that regulators and investors consider adequate. This is why the regulation of capital is paramount for bank value and valuation.

This chapter begins by examining the main features of the relevant capital requirement regulation, and of the capital structure and asset base definitions according to the Basel II framework. It then looks at how management can actively work towards a capital structure assumed to be adequate by both regulators and investors. The last part presents the main changes expected to be introduced by the forthcoming Basel III framework.

3.1 REGULATORY CAPITAL REQUIREMENTS

Banking regulations can vary widely across nations and jurisdictions, but everywhere a certain form of regulation is actually in place. The rationale behind regulating banks is that, because of their interconnectedness and the reliance that the national (and global) economies hold on banks, it is important for regulatory actors to maintain control over the practices of these institutions. The main bank regulatory framework is international in nature and promoted via subsequent frameworks (so called Basel I, II, and III) by the Basel Committee on Banking Supervision.

The first international regulatory capital accord, usually referred to as Basel I, came into effect in 1992, four years after its first publication in 1988. The logic underlying those rules was to link the amount of capital that banks were required to maintain to the risks of their assets: the higher the risks, the higher the capital to maintain. Another goal was to level the international playing field so

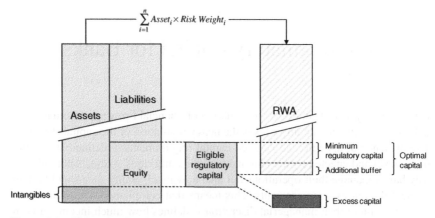

Figure 3.1   The optimal and excess capital estimation

as to avoid regulatory competitiveness. In particular, at the time US banks were concerned about the unfair advantage Japanese banks had, as the latter competed with much lower capital to assets ratio.[1] The core principle of this framework was that regulatory capital had to be maintained over the minimum required level, namely 8% of the Risk-Weighted-Assets:

$$\frac{RC}{\sum A_t \cdot RW_i} \geq 8\% \tag{3.1}$$

where RC is the regulatory capital, A_i is the value of each asset i held by the bank, and RW_i is the risk-weighted coefficient associated to asset i. The processes leading to the minimum and optimal capital estimations for a bank (and hence to the quantification of the excess capital, if any) are shown in Figure 3.1. The rest of this chapter is devoted to showing how each of these elements can be computed.

3.1.1   Definition of Capital According to Basel I and II

As for the regulatory capital, namely the numerator in the ratio mentioned previously, a financial compromise was achieved, even though it was not supported by a strong analytical rigor. The Basel Committee tried to harmonize the national definitions of its members (especially Germany and France) into a unique set of rules. It identified that not all the instruments had the same capacity to absorb losses and, based on this reasoning, capital instruments were divided into two categories: *Tier 1* (meeting German demands for narrow definition of banking

---

[1] Pettway R.H., Kanedo T. and Young M.T. (1991) International bank capital standards and the costs of issuing capital securities by Japanese banks, *Journal of Banking & Finance* **15**, 559–580.

capital) and *Supplementary Capital*, Tier 2, and 3 (where Tier 3 was introduced in 1996) satisfying French requests.

According to initial Basel capital requirements, Tier 1 capital had to be at least equal to 50% of the total minimum requirement for regulatory capital, which means 4% of RWA. Tier 1 capital can be further divided in *Upper* and *Lower Tier 1*. *Upper Tier 1* comprises paid-up share capital, disclosed reserves (e.g., share premium reserve), and retained earnings. In order to be included, disclosed reserves have to be immediately and unconditionally available to cover losses. *Lower Tier 1*, which was initially constrained to a maximum of 15% of the total Tier 1 capital, is made of innovative capital (any extra innovative capital will be considered in Tier 2).

Innovative capital was admitted in the computation of Tier 1 by the Bank of Regulatory Settlements after the amendment in 1998. Innovative capital has to meet the following requirements: it has to be unsecured, permanent, callable at the initiative of the issuer only after a minimum of 5 years, junior to all general and subordinated creditors and useful for absorbing losses on a going-concern basis (that is before bankruptcy occurs). As a final point, goodwill has to be directly deducted from Tier 1 capital.

As for Tier 2 capital, it was limited to 100% of the total Tier 1 amount. Tier 2 and Tier 3 included revaluation reserves and hidden reserves, general credit risk reserves, hybrid capital instruments, medium to long-term subordinated loans (lower Tier 2) and short-term subordinated loans (Tier 3).

Hidden or undisclosed reserves are special reserves that don't show up in the Balance Sheet and they have to meet the same requirements that apply to Tier 1. For revaluation reserves, namely the reserves created after the revaluation of assets at their market value, there is a prudential deduction of 55% of the difference between the market value and the recognized historical cost. Finally, hybrid capital is a source of capital sharing both debt and equity features. Usually, the definition is country specific and set by national regulators. However, as a general requirement, hybrid capital instruments have to meet the following criteria:

- they have to be fully paid up, unsecured, subordinate to the bank's entire debt;
- redeem is only allowed conditional to a national supervisor's prior authorization;
- they could participate in losses without forcing the bank into liquidation (that's the main difference with subordinated debt);
- any periodic remuneration, that couldn't be waived or reduced, can be deferred if the bank's profits don't allow the full payment (so also in cases where the bank makes profits, which are not considered sufficient).

The only instrument originally available as lower Tier 2 was subordinated debt. Subordinated debt, in order to be relevant for regulatory purposes and be admitted in the Lower Tier 2:

- has to be unsecured with a minimum original term of 5 years;
- its redemption, in a default situation, has to be subordinated to all other creditors;

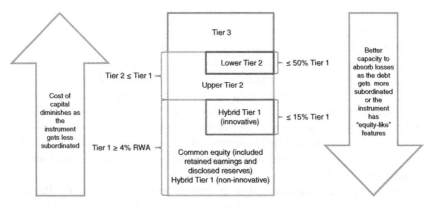

Figure 3.2 Capital structure under Basel II

- has to share the first two characteristics of hybrid capital instruments. In the last five years, it cannot be considered in Tier 2 for more than 80% of the original amount. Finally, subordinated debt does not participate in losses without forcing the bank into liquidation.

Tier 3 was first introduced in 1996 and it could only be used as "coverage" for market risk (which also became part of the regulatory framework in 1996). It is mainly composed of short term subordinated debt with the same features of the subordinated debt in Tier 2, apart from the original two-year term and the fact that there had to be a "lock-in" clause allowing the bank to avoid principal or interest payments if, due to these disbursements, the minimum capital ratio is not maintained. However, Tier 3 couldn't exceed 250% of the amount of Tier 1 capital used to cover the market risk.

Investments in non-consolidated banks and financial institutions are deducted from total capital. Figure 3.2 shows the main quantitative relations between the different tiers of regulatory capital, while Figure 3.3 shows the composition of each tier.

3.1.2 The Risk-Weighted Assets

One of the original shortcomings of Basel I was that capital regulation initially only considered credit risk as a source of risk in the banking business, simply because credit risk was perceived to be the major reason for banks' failures in the past. Capital requirements were subsequently extended to market risks (1996) and to operational risks (2004).[2] A second major flaw was associated with the fact

---

[2] For further details about capital requirements and risks, see Resti and Sironi *Risk Management and Shareholders' Value in Banking: From Risk Measurement Models to Capital Allocation Policies*, John Wiley & Sons, Inc., 2007.

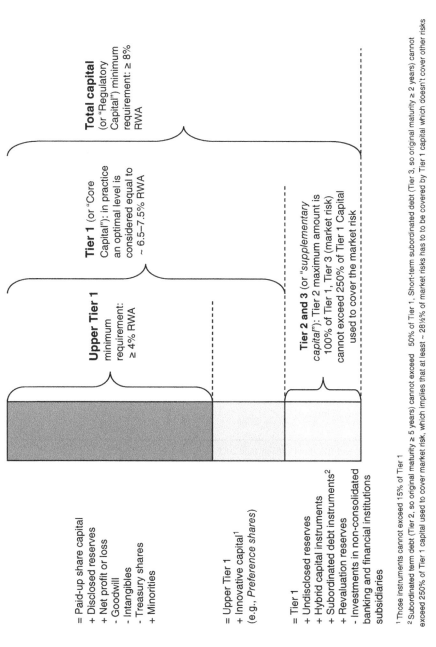

Total capital (or "Regulatory Capital") minimum requirement: ≥ 8% RWA

Tier 1 (or "Core Capital"): in practice an optimal level is considered equal to ~ 6.5–7.5% RWA

Upper Tier 1 minimum requirement: ≥ 4% RWA

Tier 2 and 3 (or "*supplementary capital*"): Tier 2 maximum amount is 100% of Tier 1, Tier 3 (market risk) cannot exceed 250% of Tier 1 Capital used to cover the market risk

= Paid-up share capital
+ Disclosed reserves
+ Net profit or loss
- Goodwill
- Intangibles
- Treasury shares
+ Minorities

= Upper Tier 1
+ Innovative capital[1]
(e.g., *Preference shares*)

= Tier 1
+ Undisclosed reserves
+ Hybrid capital instruments
+ Subordinated debt instruments[2]
+ Revaluation reserves
- Investments in non-consolidated banking and financial institutions subsidiaries

[1] Those instruments cannot exceed 15% of Tier 1

[2] Subordinated term debt (Tier 2, so original maturity ≥ 5 years) cannot exceed 50% of Tier 1, Short-term subordinated debt (Tier 3, so original maturity ≥ 2 years) cannot exceed 250% of Tier 1 capital used to cover market risk, which implies that at least ~ 28½% of market risks has to to be covered by Tier 1 capital which doesn't cover other risks

Figure 3.3 Regulatory capital composition under Basel II

Table 3.1   Coefficients under Basel I and Basel II

	Basel I	Basel II simplified standardized	Basel II standardized based on external ratings	
SECURITY				
OECD Government/central bank (Non-OECD)	0 (100)	0		
AAA to AA−			0	
A+ to A−			20	
BBB+ to BBB−			50	
BB+ to B− (& Unrated)			100	
Below B−			150	
Other public (supervisor's discretion)	0–50	0		
Claims on MDBs	20	0		
Most OECD Banks & Securities firms	20	20	< 90 days	others
AAA to AA−			20	20
A+ to A−			20	50
BBB+ to BBB− (& Unrated)			20	50
BB+ to B−			50	100
Below B−			150	150
Residential Mortgages−fully secured	50	35	35	
Retail Lending (consumer)	100	75	75	
Corporate & Commercial RE	100	100		
AAA to AA−			20	
A+ to A−			50	
BBB+ to B− (& Unrated)			100	
Below B−			150	

Sources: BIS (1988) and BIS (final version June 2006).

that the assets were weighted according to the average credit risk of the debtor category. This was a potentially misleading way to solve the risk-weighting issues that led to regulatory arbitrage: for example, banks used to lend money to very risky debtors, belonging to "safe" categories. Doing so, banks could both increase their lending capabilities with the same amount of capital and increase their ROE, because the riskier the debtor the higher the return required by a bank for the loan granted: the 2004 regulatory reform attempted to hinder the regulatory arbitrage phenomenon. The risk-weighting coefficients under Basel I are shown on the left side of Table 3.1.

Table 3.1 shows how risk weights were assigned to assets. The criteria were based on *liquidity* considerations (the more liquid the assets, the less the risk weight to apply, e.g., cash has a 0% weight), on the *debtor type* (e.g., governments

Table 3.2   Conversion factors for off-Balance Sheet items

Conversion factor (%)	Examples of off-Balance Sheet exposures
0	Commitments unconditionally cancellable or automatically cancellable due to deterioration in a borrower's creditworthiness
20	Commitments with an original maturity up to one year
50	Commitments with an original maturity greater than one year
100	General guarantees of indebtedness (including standby letters of credit serving as financial guarantees for loans and securities) and acceptances; Sale and repurchase agreements and asset sales with recourse

or financial institutions, or individuals), and on the debtor's *country of residence* (OECD or non-OECD). The borrower's individual creditworthiness was not taken into direct consideration.

Off-Balance Sheet items such as loan commitments and Over-The-Counter (OTC) derivatives were covered by the framework as well. They were included on the basis of their "loan equivalent exposure". The loan equivalent exposure was simply computed by multiplying the nominal value by a credit conversion factor, ranging from 0%, for those commitments that could be cancelled at any time without prior notice, to 100% for irrevocable standby letters of credit. Table 3.2 shows the risk-weights for off-Balance Sheet items.

Computing the Regulatory Capital Ratio: An Example

The table that follows is a stylized balance sheet of a bank.

ASSETS		LIABILITIES	
Loan to Greece	30	Deposits	89
Residential Mortgage	40	Innovative Capital	6
Loan to GE	30	Common Equity	5

As for the assets, assuming that we derive from the Basel framework that the Loans to Greece have a RW equal to 0% (as Greece is a OECD country), the residential mortgage portfolio of 50%, and the Loans to General Electric of 100% (as it is a corporate issuer), the first step is to compute the RWA for the bank which are equal to 50.

The second step is to quantify the regulatory capital for the bank. The common equity is entirely eligible as regulatory capital while innovative cannot exceed 15% of the Tier 1 capital. As a consequence, the maximum Tier 1 capital would be 5.88 (= 5/85%) including 0.88 (= 5.8 × 15%) of innovative capital.

Finally, the regulatory capital ratio for the bank is obtained by dividing the regulatory capital by the RWAs, and it is in this case 11.76%.

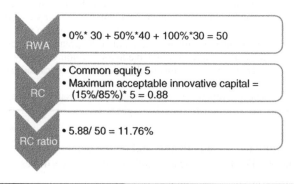

3.2 BASEL II

The New Basel Capital Accord (2004) based its foundation on three equally important pillars: (1) minimum capital requirements; (2) regulatory supervision; (3) market discipline and transparency.

For valuation purposes, of specific importance are the understanding and modeling of the first pillar, namely the *minimum capital requirements*, and we shall devote our attention specifically to this.

Considering the regulatory capital ratio presented in the previous section, both the numerator, namely the definition of eligible regulatory Capital and its "Tiers", and the coefficient (8% in the case of the RC over RWAs ratio) have been confirmed in the Basel II framework. On the contrary, the denominator ($\sum_{i=1}^{n} RW_i * A_i$) went through substantial revisions especially with regards to the computation of the risk-weights. It's worth underlining that while the Basel Committee provides general frameworks for banks' capital requirements, the definition of the details (which may matter a lot) are left to the national regulators, usually the Central Banks. Therefore, the valuator willing to model precisely the capital evolution for a bank should have a look at national regulators' guidelines.

The key innovation of Basel II was the approach to the estimate of the RWAs. The paradigm shift consisted in moving towards an analytical *credit rating* system for the risk level associated to loans and assets. According to the new regulation, the *grade* on the debtor's creditworthiness to repay both the interest and the principal amount should be assigned either under a Standardized Approach (SA) carried out by external rating agencies (i.e., Standard's & Poor, Moody's, Fitch), or under an Internal-Rating Based Approach (IRBA) operated by the banking institution itself. To run the latter approach a bank must comply with specific technical requirements using models validated by the *national* regulator.

The Standardized Approach allows more granularity in grading the risks for each asset. But, despite such improvement, some grey areas remain. For example, as for claims on sovereigns (government and central banks), at national discretion a lower risk weight may be applied to banks' exposures to their sovereign of incorporation if denominated and funded in domestic currency. Also, national supervisors may overlook the rating agencies grades and recognize the country risk scores assigned by Export Credit Agencies (ECAs), for instance, according to the following scheme:

ECA risk scores	0–1	2	3	4–6	7
Risk weight (%)	0	20	50	100	150

Claims on banks can apply one of the two strategies allowed. Under the first, claims on banks will be assigned a risk-weight a notch below that assigned to claims on the sovereign of that country. Alternatively, risk weights are based on external credit assessment of the banking institution itself, distinguishing between originally short-term loans and all the other types of loans. Table 3.1 doesn't consider the possible preferential treatment that can be granted to claims in domestic currency. Claims on domestic Public Sector Entities (PSEs) will be risk-weighted at national discretion, according one of the two approaches available for claims on banks.

As for corporates, national supervisors may increase the standard risk weight for unrated claims if the latter is not considered sufficient, based on historical default data. Risk-weights on non-performing loans will be 150, 100 or even 50%, conditional on national supervisors' approval, if the *specific* provisions represent less than 20% of the outstanding amount of the loan, more than 20% or more than 50%, respectively.

At this stage, it is worth mentioning that some rules apply in order to take into account guarantees. Personal guarantees can be considered in the computation only if they are accepted by national regulators and they must be issued by a government, bank, or corporate whose rating is, at least, equal to A-. The guarantee is subject to a "haircut" if a maturity mismatch exists (the guarantee expires before the loan is completely repaid) or a currency mismatch (guarantee and loan are denominated in different currencies). As for real guarantees, we face the option between two approaches: the simple approach can be used only for instruments like cash, gold, or qualified debts and it implies a substitution of the risk-weight of the borrower with that of the instrument. Under the comprehensive approach, which is allowed also for listed stocks, the guarantee is reduced by a haircut suggested by the national authority.

Claims on Multilateral Development Banks (MDBs), such as the World Bank Group, the European Investment Bank (EIB) or the Asian Development Bank (ADB), are eligible for a 0% risk weight, while the risk weight for claims on other MDBs will be 100%. The standard weight for claims on corporates and mortgages secured by commercial real estate is 100%. Low exposure (< €1M) sufficiently diversified retail lending is subject to a 75% risk weight, unless national regulators find this coefficient too low, based on the observation of past defaults in their country. The coefficient applied on claims secured by residential real estate (allowed *only if* the housing finance is provided for residential purposes) is 35%, conditional on the evaluation from national regulators, who can actually increase it again on the basis of previous default experiences. National supervisors may apply a 150% or higher risk weight reflecting the higher risks associated with other alternative asset classes, such as venture capital and private equity investments.

As for the Internal-Rating Based Approach (IRBA), the external valuator usually has little visibility about its applications in practice; therefore we will just sketch the two possible ways to carry it out. The first one is the "Foundation Approach", which according to the Committee's intention should be used by less sophisticated banks. The second one is the "Advanced Approach". The difference mostly relies on the fact that, while under the Foundation Approach banks are required to estimate just the *Probability of Default* (PD) of the borrower and the other parameters are set by regulators, under the Advanced Approach banks will also estimate *Loss Given Default* (basically depending on collateral), the expected *Exposure At Default* and the duration of the facility.

3.2.1 Does Basel II Work?

Following the financial crisis, which was originated or magnified by an overestimation of risks held by banks, many have questioned whether the Basel framework is doing a proper job. For example, a study carried out by IMF[3] suggests the following:

- RWAs are primarily driven by the regulatory framework enacted in their home jurisdiction.
- After a decade marked by an increase in total assets, RWA density (defined as RWA over Total Assets) decreased.

---

[3] Vanessa Le Leslé and Sofiya Avramova (2012) *Revisiting Risk-Weighted Assets* "Why Do RWAs Differ Across Countries and What Can Be Done About It?", IMF Working Paper.

Table 3.3   Minimum, median, and maximum risk weights attributed to categories of credit risk

	Mortgages (%)	Corporates (%)	Institutions (%)	Other retail (%)
IMF estimates	5–20–53	32–59–76	n/a	n/a
Barclays	7–15–49	33–55–89	n/a	n/a
BBVA	8–15–23	37–52–78	4–16–27	14–33–48
BNP	6–13–25	27–54–75	n/a	10–38–156
KBW	6–18–53	26–55–158	6–19–34	7–36–64
Average	*6.4–16.2–40.6*	*31–55–95.2*	*5–17.5–30.5*	*10.3–35.7–89.3*

Source: V. Le Leslé and S. Avramova (2012) *Revisiting Risk-Weighted Assets* "Why Do RWAs Differ Across Countries and What Can Be Done About It?", International Monetary Fund Working Paper.

- Regulatory capital attributed to all the categories of credit risk are in general lower than expected (one of the main correct critics against the IRB Approach is that it is exploited to "save capital").

The data shown in Table 3.3 supports the points made. The IRB Approach actually allows banks to "save" huge capital, by applying lower risk-weights than it appears they should have. It is fair to say that among the Committee's intentions, there was also the idea to push for increasing modeling sophistication by awarding savings in capital requirements.

"Red Flags" in the Assessment of RWAs

Below we report four "red flags" for valuators and financial analysts assessing, on the basis of public data, RWA quality.

- *"Too variable" RWAs*: while RWAs tends to vary with economic cycle, if there have been no substantial changes in the business mix, roller-coaster patterns are worth a more careful look.
- *Banks with a much lower RWA density* (the ratio between RWA and Total Assets) than their peers, and peers should be banks with similar business models in the same jurisdiction, therefore facing comparable risks, deserve further scrutiny.
- *A strong risk-weighted capital ratio* associated with really poor leverage ratio (as defined under Basel III), may indicate a situation of financial fragility.

"Cherry picking" the most favorable approach depending on the specific risk to cover and the tendency to mix different methodologies without proper justification may raise doubts about the quality of the bank risk management and true solidity.

How to Compute the RWAs

The implications of moving from Basel I to II are worth a practical example, because such regulatory changes have affected dramatically the industry over last decade. Let us assume that the balance sheet of a bank comprises the items in the table below.

ASSETS (in thousands)	
Cash	4000
Long term loan to Greece (government)	2500
Loan to Russia (government)	2500
Loan to Froes & Co. (rating A+)	250
Loan to John Bank (rating AA−)	1200
Consumer lending	450
Residential Mortgages-fully secured	5000

Cash gets a 0% weight under both sets of rules. The loan to Greece would have received a 0% weight under Basel I capital accord (as Greece is an OECD country), and a 100% weight under Basel II (as Greek debt has been rated B-, there actually would have been a time period in which 150% would have been the right coefficient to use, namely the stage when Greek debt was rated "selective default"). The loan to Russia would receive a 100% weight (as a non-OECD country) under Basel I, and a lower risk-weight (50%) than Greece under Basel II. The loan to Froes & Co would receive a 100% weight under Basel I and a 50% weight under Basel II, while the loan to John Bank, which is established in the US, will receive a 20% risk weight under both Basel I and Basel II (given the AA-rating). Consumer lending and Residential Mortgages-fully secured will receive a 100 and 50% risk-weight under Basel I, while they will receive 75 and 35% respectively under Basel II.

Therefore, the computation of RWAs under Basel I and II would be respectively:

$$\text{RWAs under Basel I} = 0\% * 4000 + 0\% * 2500 + 100\% * 2500 + 100\% * 250 \\ + 20\% * 1200 + 100\% * 450 + 50\% * 5000 = 5940$$

$$\text{RWAs under Basel II} = 0\% * 4000 + 100\% * 2500 + 50\% * 2500 + 50\% * 250 \\ + 20\% * 1200 + 75\% * 450 + 35\% * 5000 = 6202.5$$

Risk-weights under Basel II appear more granular and try to reflect more accurately debtors' creditworthiness.

3.3 THE REFORM OF BASEL III

The level and quality of regulatory capital, the high leverage, and the lack of liquidity that many banks showed during the financial crisis raised concerns about the effectiveness of the Basel II framework. In particular, many commentators blamed the apparent pro-cyclicality of the measures required by Basel II for being one of the main reasons why the financial crisis became so severe.

The newly introduced banking regulatory standard, and specifically the Basel III framework, comprehensively covers the main aspects of financial regulation: quality of the bank regulatory capital, financial leverage, structured finance, liquidity risk, connection between prudential rules, and economic cycle. Since the scope of the regulation is too broad to be covered in a few pages and the purpose of this chapter is to give some insights on how to analyze capital requirements, here we will just focus on how to model Regulatory Capital under the new rules of Basel III, and we will just briefly analyze the recently introduced "long-term" liquidity ratio.

According to the Basel Committee, during the financial crisis banks were suffering from an excessive on- and off-balance sheet leverage accompanied by a significant erosion of capital.[4] Therefore, the Basel Committee introduced a more restrictive definition of regulatory capital, while maintaining the minimum total capital ratio equal to 8%.

Beyond setting Common equity Tier 1 to a minimum of 4.5% and Tier 1 Capital to a minimum of 6%, the Committee eliminated Tier 3 Capital to allow that market risks could be covered by the same capital (in terms of quality) as the other risks. Furthermore, the "Tiers" as previously defined have been modified in order to include or exclude some instruments.

3.3.1 New Definition of Capital

The sharp distinction between Tier 1 and Tier 2 capital reflects the distinction between "going concern capital" (all those instruments that can cover losses when the bank is still solvent), and "gone concern capital", namely those instruments capable to cover losses in case of bankruptcy.

Specifically, Common Equity Tier 1 consists mainly of:

- Common shares meeting the criteria for bank classification;
- Share premium;
- Retained earnings, accumulated comprehensive income, and other disclosed reserves.

To be eligible to enter this category, an instrument must represent the most subordinated claim in liquidation of the bank, must have no maturity and has to be entitled to discretionary dividends.

---

[4] Strengthening the resilience of the banking sector (see *Consultative Document*, 2009, BIS).

Additional Tier 1 capital consists of both the instruments that meet the specific eligibility requirements and the share premium on those instruments. The criteria are the following:

- They have to be subordinated to the subordinated debt of the bank;
- They shall not have a fixed maturity date, and neither step-up features nor other incentives to redeem should be embedded;
- Banks must have full discretion at all times to cancel dividends/coupons with no effect for their stakeholders, except for common equity shareholders.

Unlike Common Equity Tier 1 instruments, they may be callable at the initiative of the issuer only after a minimum of five years and with a prior supervisory approval.

Tier 2 capital consists of only unsecured subordinated debt and the stock surplus on the latter. With an original maturity of at least five years and no step-ups or other incentives to redeem, Tier 2 capital instruments must not have any "credit-sensitive" dividend, which is a dividend that is periodically reset based on whole or on a part of the banking credit standing. Moreover, it may be callable, with supervisor approval like additional Tier 1, only after a minimum of five years and on the initiative of the issuer.

It's worth noting that the treatment of minorities has been subject to an important change with Basel III. While they were fully included in the computation of Tier 1 capital under the Basel II framework, with Basel III any minority interest exceeding a subsidiary's regulatory capital requirement (on a pro-quota basis) should be deducted from consolidated common equity as recorded in the bank group's Balance Sheet. For example, let's suppose we face the following simplified situation in which Bank Alpha has an 80% equity stake in Bank Beta.

Assets of Bank Alpha		Liabilities of Bank Alpha	
Loans	1000	Deposits	600
Majority Stake in Small	80	Common Equity	480

For sake of simplicity, let us assume that common equity of Bank Beta is 100 and minorities are equal to 20. If the capital requirement for Bank Beta is 60, the minorities that can be considered in the computation of capital ratios for Bank Alpha are just 12, that is 20% of 60. Therefore, the Consolidated Common Equity results in being 492, instead of 500, as it would be under Basel II. Obviously, the 20% equity stake will enter the computation only for 20% of the 7% (4.5% as a minimum requirement + 2.5% as a conservation buffer, as will be explained later) of RWAs when CET1 of Big Bank is computed, or 8.5% when Tier 1 capital is calculated and 10.5% for the total capital ratio (we are not taking into account any anti-cyclical buffer).

Finally, goodwill, other intangibles, and investments in own shares must be deducted from Common Equity Tier 1. The composition of the regulatory capital according to the most updated Basel III version is shown in Figure 3.4.

3.3.2 Change in RWA Computation

As for RWA, we can see that under Basel III, there was no change to the banking book treatment of non-financial loan exposure. In fact, Basel III reform strengthened the numerators, but the change in the method to compute the denominator was limited. Nevertheless, it is worth mentioning that RWA will increase as a consequence of the implementation of the new capital regulation. The following two capital requirements will be introduced for those banks with a validated internal model of market risk calculation:

- A Stressed VaR, which is an additional capital requirement measuring losses in periods of stress.
- An Incremental Risk Charge, trying to capture the credit risk of trading positions.

Finally, as regards OTC derivatives, the following two measures have been introduced:

- Effective Expected Positive Exposure (EEPE), to be computed both under a base and a stressed scenario.
- Credit Value Adjustment (CVA), as an additional capital requirement aimed at measuring the counterparty's credit deterioration.

3.3.3 New Coefficients

Moving from the Basel II to III framework, Common Equity Tier 1 will move from a minimum of 2% (50% of the minimum Tier 1 which is equal to 4%) of RWA to a minimum of 4.5%. In addition, a "non-mandatory" capital conservation buffer equal to 2.5% of RWA, made of Common Equity, has to be added as a cushion against financial distress. Those banks that don't meet the capital conservation buffer requirements will be only subject to constraints on the distribution of dividends. On the contrary, the Tier 1 minimum level has been increased from 4 to 6%, but the actual minimum becomes 8.5% when we add the conservation buffer. Finally, the new "variable" countercyclical buffer requirement has been introduced to reduce growth in period of "hot" expansion (by increasing the requirement) and increase loan growth in periods of crisis (by reducing the requirement). It varies from 0–2.5% according to national authority purposes. Considering also the entire possible value of this last buffer, our Tier 1 minimum ratio becomes 11% and the new actual total capital ratio 13%. The countercyclical buffer is composed of common equity Tier 1, even if the Committee does not exclude alternative forms of capital, which should be available to cover losses "on a going concern basis".

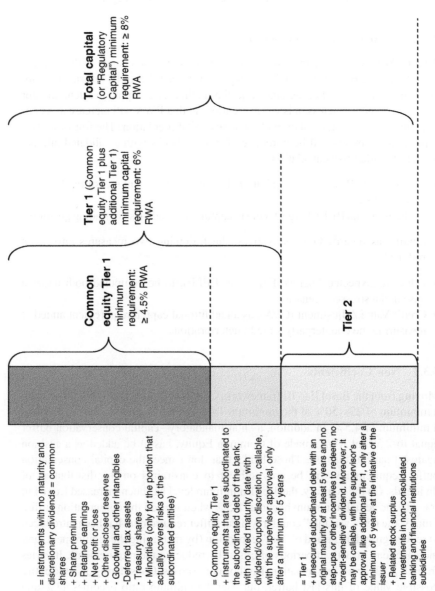

Figure 3.4 Regulatory capital composition according to Basel III

Table 3.4   Minimum percentage of risk-weighted assets for Basel capital ratios

Type of requirement	% of risk-weighted assets	Basel 2 (%)	Basel 3 (%)
Common equity	a. Lower limit	2.0	4.5
	b. Conservation buffer		2.5
	d. Total (a + b)		7.0
Tier 1 capital ratio	c. Lower limit	4.0	6.0
	e. Total (c + b)		8.5
Total capital ratio	f. Lower limit	8.0	8.0
	g. Total (f + b)		10.5
Additional	h. Countercyclical buffer		0–2.5
macroprudential	i. Additional requirement for		to be defined
requirements	systemic banks		

Source: Resti and Sironi (2010), *Risk Management and Shareholders' Value in Banking*, based on Basel Committee on Banking Supervision.

As shown in Table 3.4, global systemically important banks will likely be subject to additional common equity Tier 1 requirements based on a "bucketing method". The latter will take into consideration size, interconnectedness, complexity, cross-jurisdictional activity, and substitutability of the bank itself. The requirement ranges from 1–3.5%, depending on the "bucket" to which the bank belongs (the BIS Committee affirms that today no bank falls in the 3.5% bucket, but most of the systemic banks fall into the 2.5% bucket, that is the one right below).

3.3.4   Leverage Ratio

One of the most interesting and discussed innovations introduced with Basel III is the *Leverage Ratio*. The purpose of this ratio is still undefined: it's not clear whether it will be used as a complementary mandatory requirement or simply to measure the "temperature" of the economic cycle, therefore setting the countercyclical buffer at an adequate level. However, in both cases, it is useful to know how it is computed and the minimum requirement. As for the calculation, it is simply the ratio between Tier 1 (computed under the new set of rules) and Total Assets, both on- and off-Balance Sheet items, after intangible assets are deducted from the latter (to make them comparable to the numerator). The ratio is currently a minimum of 3%.

The leverage ratio is strongly reliant on the utilized accounting standards: it is usually relatively lower if IFRS rather than US GAAP is used: under IFRS netting conditions are stricter and what is commonly presented in the Balance Sheet is the gross replacement value of derivatives (paradoxically this is so even if positions are held under master netting agreements with the same counterparty).

3.3.5   Liquidity Ratios

Previous Basel frameworks did not consider the possibility that a banking institution, especially one of the large international banks to which the standards were specifically addressed, could ever suffer from lack of liquidity. Moreover, at the time there were strong confidence and trust relationships among the largest participants in the inter-banking market. However, following the financial crisis it became urgent to address the liquidity risks as well via regulation. As discussed in the first chapter, maturity transformation (funding the long-term loans banks grant through short-term deposits) is a key job for banks as any major hindrance in the inter-banking funding channels process may have systemic consequences. No wonder that, for the first time with Basel III, two liquidity ratios were introduced among regulatory requirements. The first one ("Liquidity Coverage ratio") is designed for banks to ensure an adequate level of liquidity sufficient to survive for a short time period (30 days), while the second one ("Net Stable Funding ratio") is designed to encourage a higher portion of investments in more liquid assets. In this section, we will briefly linger on the second one.

The *Net Stable Funding Ratio* is defined as the ratio between stable funding resources (*available* stable funding) over the medium term needs of the banks (*required* stable funding): this ratio must be higher than 100%. Stable funding resources are considered the ones that will not be subject to "panic runs" during a period of financial stress. Mostly they are the capital and liabilities with effective maturities of 1 year or greater, and specifically the portion of deposits that would be expected to be maintained by the institution for an extended period during an idiosyncratic stress event. Each of these items is assigned a specific "stability coefficient", obviously higher for capital (both Tier 1 and 2) for which the coefficient is 100% than for "stable" or "less stable" deposits. The same logic applies also to the *Required Stable Funding*, the denominator. Each item is assigned a specific "liquidity coefficient": the more liquid or easy to liquidate the asset, the lower the coefficient to apply.

The Net Stable Funding Ratio is of importance within a bank valuation process because when modeling the forecast financial statements internal Balance Sheet consistency should meet also the associated requirements.

3.4   MANAGING THE REGULATORY CAPITAL

Banks manage their operations to meet each of the minimum capital requirements at least. In practice, banks do not simply fulfill the required capital ratios, but they consistently tend to maintain an additional capital buffer, which grants them both a greater economic and financial resilience, and some flexibility to support new corporate strategies. From a managerial point of view, the appropriate regulatory capital should be seen as the sum of: (1) the minimum amount of capital required by regulation; and (2) the additional buffer, which represents the safety margin

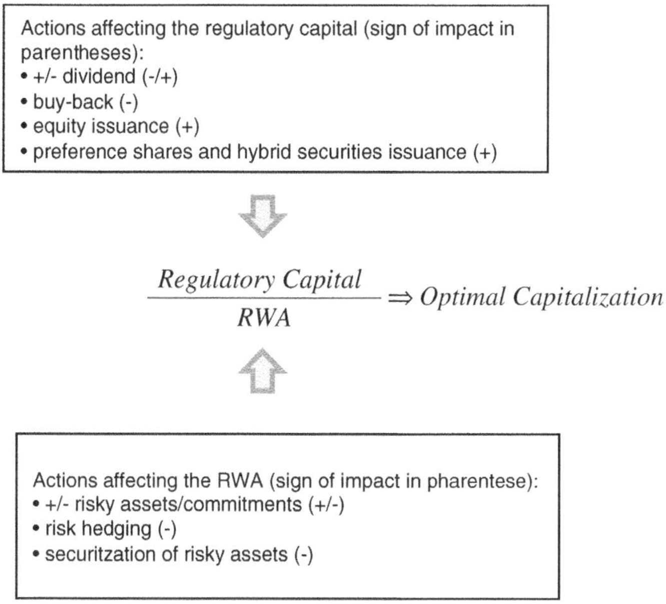

Actions affecting the regulatory capital (sign of impact in parentheses):
• +/- dividend (-/+)
• buy-back (-)
• equity issuance (+)
• preference shares and hybrid securities issuance (+)

$$\frac{Regulatory\ Capital}{RWA} \Rightarrow Optimal\ Capitalization$$

Actions affecting the RWA (sign of impact in pharentese):
• +/- risky assets/commitments (+/-)
• risk hedging (-)
• securitzation of risky assets (-)

Figure 3.5   The levers to manage a bank's capitalization

to support bank strategies or expectations, and importantly, the expectations of investors. The latter plays a key role in influencing how much capital banks hold internationally, because institutional investors and equity research analysts tend to have precise views about what is the right equity capital amount given the current market conditions. Market opinion therefore drives the regulatory capital as much as the regulators do.

If actual level of capital falls short of the regulatory requirements or is below what the market considers appropriate, the bank management can attain or restore the physiological level by intervening on the elements that define the numerator and/or the denominator of the relevant capital ratios. As far as the denominator is concerned, management could reduce the risk of bank investments by hedging some risks, terminating risky loans, or by "disposing of" some granted risky loans via securitization. The interventions that affect the numerator are the dividends cut and the issuance of securities eligible to be included in the regulatory capital. If the latter action is chosen, the securities' type and design should take into account the related costs and agency problems. By issuing common shares, all the ratios – from CET1 to Total Capital – are impacted, while with more senior claim instruments only the less core Tier levels are affected. For example, during the financial crisis banks in a "deficit capital" situation mostly preferred to issue hybrid securities rather than common equity in order not to dilute their shareholders' positions.

In the opposite situation, if the current regulatory capital is higher than the level required by regulation and investors, the bank has "excess capital". Such *surplus* if not justified by managerial concerns (e.g., pessimistic outlook about market conditions) or corporate strategy (e.g., planned M&A transactions) may result in an inefficient capitalization. This is because the extra capital is somehow "unemployed" because against it no assets with an adequate risk/return profile have been created by the bank. It can be assumed that the excess capital is invested in safe assets with a low or null return: as a consequence, the profitability for shareholders is diluted. In such a situation, the surplus capital could be returned to shareholders via dividends or buybacks. Bank management can also increase the risk/return profile of the assets in Balance Sheets as reflected on the RWA. The financial and operating "levers" for management that can be used to optimize a bank's capital structure are shown in Figure 3.5.

4

Assessing and Preparing the Business Plan for a Bank

Amedeo Giammattei

Forecasting bank earnings may appear to be something of a lottery with so many uncertain line items.

Stephen Frost, The Bank Analyst's Handbook

The purpose of this chapter is twofold: we will first present a framework to analyze the business plan of a bank from a valuation perspective, and we will then provide guidelines for preparation of the business plan itself. As a matter of fact, the business plan is the fundamental input of the valuation process. Assessing its sustainability and highlighting areas of potential inconsistency might have a critical impact on the final valuation and requires not only strong judgment but also a solid method.

If the business plan already exists and is available to the analyst, there are three broad categories of checks that can be performed:

- *Status quo analysis*: establishes whether the current value of some key on- and off-Balance Sheet items requires potential adjustment. Areas that are particularly critical for banks include asset quality, toxic and illiquid assets, goodwill, and capitalization.
- *Internal consistency*: assessment of the forecasts included in the business plan to make sure they are internally coherent, that is, there is consistency between historical performance and projected performance, the expected evolution of P&L items and that of Balance Sheet items, asset side and liability side, financial forecasts, and operating forecasts;
- *External consistency*: assessment of those elements that are not under direct control of the company management but can have a significant impact on the expected performance of the bank; that is, macro scenarios and competitive dynamics. One additional action, which has to be considered in assessing the credibility of the business plan, is a comparison with market consensus whenever available.

4.1 *STATUS QUO* ANALYSIS

While a lot of attention is generally placed on forecasts, a key part of the business plan evaluation process is the analysis of the current financial position of the bank. The analyst must investigate whether the value of some key on- and off-Balance Sheet items needs to be adjusted to better reflect the current situation and expected evolution of the business. Such adjustments might include:

- Additional write-offs on the loan portfolio as a result of an inadequate reserve policy, in the light of the expected evolution of the portfolio and of the macroeconomic outlook (*asset quality*).
- Additional trading losses from toxic assets as a result of under-reserving, taking into account the likelihood and the size of future write-downs (*toxic* and *illiquid assets*).
- Additional impairments on the value of goodwill due to expected underperformance of subsidiaries (*goodwill*).
- The need for a rights issue or shrinking the RWAs given higher projected capital requirements imposed by market expectations or regulators (*capitalization*).

An important point is that the valuation of each of these items is intrinsically related to expectations and forecasts. For this reason, any consideration has to be performed in connection with examination of the business plan as a whole.

4.1.1 Asset Quality

As discussed in the previous chapters, one of the largest risks for a bank is that of a borrower defaulting on a loan, that is, credit risk. Assessing the quality of the customer loan portfolio is, therefore, extremely important. Such analysis should be performed mainly along two dimensions: composition of the portfolio and level of reserves.

As far as composition is concerned, it is important to segment the loan portfolio in terms of quality and analyze the proportion of "non-performing" loans (NPLs). A key metric, from this perspective, is the NPL ratio, that is, the percentage of non-performing loans on the total loan portfolio. NPLs can be further split into bad loans, doubtful loans, restructured positions, and overdue positions.[1] Although

---

[1] Although there exists no universally acceptable classification of non-performing loans, here we refer to the one applied the most in practice, recalling however that specific classification rules, in particular delinquency periods and judgmental factors permitted for classification purposes, vary across countries. Depending on how serious collection problems are, loans may be segmented into different classes. When debt is considered uncollectible and there are no chances for a possible recovery or interest and/or principal are overdue by more than 1 year, a loan is defined a *bad* loan (relative provision for loan losses is suggested to be equal to 100%). When the risk of default is high, but default is not a certain event yet (doubtful) or the loan is past due by more than 180 days, loans are classified as *doubtful*. *Substandard loans* are those overdue by more than 90 days from the due date but still there are chances of reimbursement. Finally, from the definition given by BIS, we know that a loan is "a restructured troubled loan when the lender, for economic or legal reasons related to the borrower's financial difficulties, grants a concession to the borrower that it would not otherwise consider".

some non-performing loans will be upgraded to performing, a high percentage of them will eventually be written-off. Thus, the NPL ratio provides valuable insight regarding probable levels of future write-offs.

In terms of reserve adequacy, the coverage ratio (impairment allowance/gross loans) is indicative of how much the bank has provisioned against its portfolio of problematic loans. It should be computed separately for each type of non-performing loan (bad, doubtful, restructured, and overdue). Low ratios suggest that banks may be forced to build their reserves in the future, which will increase impairment charges and reduce earnings. An additional ratio that can provide further insight on reserve adequacy is given by the proportion of impairment allowance over net write-offs. This ratio captures how many years of net write-offs banks' reserves represent. Hypothetically, the bank would be able to operate for this number of years (without adding to its reserves) before it would be forced to take a charge against its equity capital. Collateral, the *borrower's pledge* of specific *properties* to *secure* repayment of loans, is playing a growing role in the coverage ratio structure.

Banks' loan mixes should be taken into account when determining appropriate reserve levels. Banks with riskier loan portfolios will likely have higher levels of net write-offs and NPLs and should, in turn, have higher reserve levels. A number of additional loan portfolio characteristics, such as sector and geographic concentration, should be considered as well. A diversified portfolio is likely to experience smoother loss trends, which reduces the amount of reserves that are necessary.

Finally, benchmarking the historical levels of the NPL ratio and of the NPL coverage ratio against direct competitors can be useful in understanding whether the bank being valued is adequately reserved.

4.1.2 Toxic and Illiquid Assets

The term *toxic* is used to designate those assets for which there is no longer a functioning market and, therefore, it is difficult to estimate their value. Such assets include manly different types of asset-backed securities (ABS) like collateralized debt obligations (CDO) and mortgage backed securities (MBS). Typically for these assets, banks disclose the net exposure and the cumulative write-downs. However, it is crucial to assess the potential size and likelihood of further charges.

Depending on their classification, toxic assets can be found in the loan portfolio in financial assets at FVTPL, HTM, AFS, and off-Balance Sheet. As a result, they can be measured both at fair value and at amortized cost with impairment tests. In both cases, there is high uncertainty around their actual value given that even when valued at fair value, they are often treated as level II or level III assets. Nonetheless, benchmarking against peers the percentage of write-downs on the total gross exposure (which can be inferred by summing up the net exposure and the cumulative write-down) can be helpful to understand if the bank is under-reserving.

4.1.3 Goodwill

Goodwill purchased as part of a business combination is not amortized, but is tested for impairment annually (or more often if events or changed circumstances indicate evidence of a possible impairment loss). Impairment is recorded if the carrying amount of the cash-generating unit (CGU) to which goodwill has been allocated is below its realizable value. The recoverable amount is the higher of the CGU's fair value, less any costs to sell, and its related value in use. Value in use is equal to the present value of the estimated cash flows for the years of operation of the cash-generating units, including those deriving from its disposal at the end of its useful life.

It is clear that the determination of the amount of any impairment is strongly linked to the company estimate for the value in use. This, in turn, relies on the business plan forecasts for the specific CGU. As a result, the bank is not obliged to take the write-down if it can demonstrate that there is a robust business plan underlying the value in use. Therefore, when it comes to goodwill evaluation it is important for the analyst to assess that:

- The current value of goodwill on-Balance Sheet is consistent with the projected performance illustrated in the business plan.
- The underlying business plan is robust enough and not too ambitious.

Otherwise, additional impairment losses will have to be accounted for and so will their impact on earnings. However, it is important to remember that goodwill impairment does not have any direct impact on the bank level of capitalization, as intangibles are already deducted from regulatory capital.

Additional signals of potential future impairment losses on goodwill are a significant modification of the company strategy, often accompanied by a top management change, and the need of deleveraging or making disposals. In the first case, it is easier for the new management to acknowledge that previous acquisitions did not pay off as expected. In the second case, reducing the book value of the assets to be disposed makes them more attractive to potential investors.

4.1.4 Capitalization

The concept of adequate level of capitalization for a bank has been evolving rapidly in the past 20 years. On the one hand, regulators have been refining the set of rules defining capital requirements (e.g., Basel I, Basel II, and Basel III) and, at the same time, the number of subjects having a word on the matter has increased (BIS, EBA, national supervisors). On the other hand, market expectations have often anticipated the need for more stringent rules and have, in many cases, set the "new standard" in terms of capital adequacy.

Therefore, in this context, it appears increasingly difficult to establish univocally whether a bank is solid enough in terms of capitalization. Nonetheless, it is absolutely necessary for the analyst to assess thoroughly the current capital position of the bank being valued. In addition, this exercise has to be performed not only on the bank as-is but also after potential adjustments deriving from the analysis on the three areas discussed before (asset quality, toxic assets, and goodwill).

From a practical standpoint, the bank capital position will have to be assessed under a number of increasingly stringent constraints:

- Current regulatory framework (e.g., Basel II).
- Expected regulatory framework (e.g., Basel III).
- Market expectations and peer benchmarking.
- Stress tests (e.g., EBA stress tests).

Whenever the bank being valued appears undercapitalized, and there are no measures in the business plan to address the issue effectively, it is legitimate to anticipate the need of a rights issue or the implementation of a deleveraging program (i.e., shrinking the RWAs). In both cases, it is important to estimate what the impact would be on the final valuation.

4.2 INTERNAL CONSISTENCY

A second area of investigation on the business plan is the assessment of *internal consistency*. The analyst should check the forecasts and question the connections among the different elements of the plan (e.g., P&L and Balance Sheet projections, operating forecasts). Such connections should be easily understandable and justifiable in terms of "what drives what and why". Those which are not need to be highlighted and further investigated.

The set of checks that can be performed to assess internal consistency can be segmented into four main categories:

- Consistency between forecasts and historical data.
- Consistency between P&L items and Balance Sheet items.
- Consistency between the asset and liability sides of the Balance Sheet.
- Consistency between financial and operating forecasts.

For the analysis to be performed properly, it is important to be familiar with the key dynamics of a bank business model, the structure of a bank financial statement and the basic concepts behind the forecasting model of a bank. While the first two elements were treated in previous chapters, a review of the key notions underlying forecasting will be presented for each category of checks in the next paragraphs.

4.2.1 Historical versus Projected Performance

A first set of considerations around the business plan internal consistency concerns the relationship between historical data and forecasts. The aim is to understand whether projected performance is or is not in line with historical performance, what the underlying reasons are for that, and if such reasons are sensible and robust. Generally, it is expected that under many metrics – for example, cost of funding, increase in capital requirements, and cost of risk – the post crisis performance of banks will be significantly worse than the pre-crisis one. So care should be taken in comparing historical with future financial performance.

In the following paragraphs, three different methodologies of assessment are presented. The three approaches are not alternatives, in fact they are mutually reinforcing.

4.2.1.1 Express P&L and Balance Sheet in Percentage Terms

One way to analyze the evolution of historical and projected financials is to express both the P&L and the Balance Sheet in percentage terms and question any significant variation. As for the P&L, each item should be expressed as a percentage of total income (in some cases, it can be helpful to use also total assets as denominator to have a reference external to the P&L itself). Some typical elements that need to be investigated are:

- How is the revenue mix evolving?
- If the proportions of net interest income, net commission income, and other income are changing, what is the reason for that? Is it a strategic choice affecting the business model or is it due to external factors (i.e., macroeconomic environment)?
- Is the cost income ratio expected to move significantly? What is the rationale behind such evolution?
- Similar considerations can be made for extraordinary items and tax expenses.

As for the Balance Sheet, each item should be expressed as a percentage of total assets. Areas that need to be looked into typically are:

- How is the asset mix evolving?
- If the proportions of net loans, trading assets, and other assets are changing, what is the reason for that? Is it a strategic choice affecting the business model or is it due to external factors (i.e., macroeconomic environment)?
- Similar considerations can be made for the liability side.

4.2.2 ROE Framework

ROE is arguably the most common measure of bank performance. To highlight the different components of performance, a number of frameworks have been developed breaking up ROE into a set of indicators. From a financial analysis perspective, the accuracy and reliability of these frameworks have been debated. In particular, the main criticisms refer to a lack of risk sensitivity on elements like capitalization, funding and asset quality. However, in this case, the idea is to apply the ROE framework over time (both on historical and projected financials) to identify potential areas of discontinuity in the performance and, therefore, flag elements which require further investigation.

The ROE framework proposed here is based on the following equation:

$$ROE = \frac{NI}{PBT} \times \frac{PBT}{OI} \times \frac{OI}{TI} \times \frac{TI}{NII} \times \frac{NII}{TA} \times \frac{TA}{Shareholders\ Equity} \qquad (4.1)$$

The variables used in the ROE framework are the following:

- *Net Income (NI)/Profit Before Tax* (PBT): highlights the impact of tax expenses on the net result. There is a limited possibility for the bank to control such a ratio.
- *PBT/Operating Income* (OI): highlights the impact of extraordinary items on PBT.
- *OI/Total Income* (TI): the level of this ratio is mainly driven by the impact of impairment charges on the loan portfolio and operating expenses. It is important to analyze the two components separately (through asset quality ratios and cost income).
- *TI/Net Interest Income* (NII): influenced by the level of specialization of the bank. It highlights the impact of commission and trading income on total income.
- *NII/Total Assets* (TA): approximation for the net interest margin (which is computed only on interest bearing assets and liabilities).
- *TA/Shareholders' Equity*: proxy for the level of financial leverage (does not include off-Balance Sheet obligations).

The ROE framework analysis, complemented with the other methodologies presented in this chapter, is an important element to assess the level of sustainability of the projected profitability of the bank.

4.2.3   P&L and Balance Sheet Drivers

A third way to assess potential inconsistencies in the projections compared to historical data is to look at the evolution of the key P&L and Balance Sheet drivers (e.g., net interest margin, cost of risk, cost income ratio, tax rate, customer loans growth, loans to funding ratio). Any abrupt jump in growth rates and margins should be highlighted and further investigated. Also in this case, an explanation should be found either in the set of management actions announced with the business plan or in the expected evolution of the macroeconomic and competitive outlook.

4.2.4 P&L versus Balance Sheet

P&L and Balance Sheet evolution should follow some patterns that derive from the fundamental business model of a bank. As a matter of fact, profitability is mainly driven by volumes, margins, and risk taken (for a given level of efficiency and leverage). If we take, for instance, a simple retail bank involved in deposit taking and loan making, profitability will be mainly a result of:

• The average balance of interest earning assets and interest bearing liabilities.
• The Net Interest Margin (NIM) influenced by the level of riskiness of the portfolio, the macroeconomic environment and competitive dynamics.
• The quality of the loans made and the reserving policy of the bank.

Finally, Balance Sheet size and the quality of the assets will determine the regulatory capital requirements and, in turn, how much the bank needs to retain in the business or distribute as dividends.

Therefore, when checking for consistency between the evolution of P&L and Balance Sheet items, it is important to assess the robustness of the relationship between volumes, margins, and risk taken underlying projected performance. The following subsections highlight some elements that require careful investigation.

4.2.4.1 Net Interest Income (NII)

As previously mentioned the level of NII is mainly driven by two variables: the evolution of volumes (interest earning assets and interest bearing liabilities) and NIM. The first level of considerations refers to the consistency between the expected growth rate for volumes and for NII, given the expected evolution of NIM provided in the business plan. The second level of considerations concerns the drivers of NIM evolution. As anticipated, NIM might vary based on interest rate movements, competitive dynamics, and risk taken. While the first two drivers will be analyzed in depth in the section on external consistency, it is worth spending some time here on the third driver. Assuming no significant change is expected as for interest rates and competitive pressure, a higher NIM implies the bank is increasing the level of riskiness of its credit portfolio. As a result, this should be reflected in the evolution of the cost of risk, the NPL ratio, and the coverage ratio.

4.2.4.2 Net Fee and Commission Income (NFCI)

As for the NII, the level of NFCI is also driven by volumes and margins. However, in this case, volumes might refer to a number of Balance Sheet and off-Balance Sheet items (e.g., customer loans, customer deposits, assets under management, capital markets volumes). Which items are more relevant in driving NFCI will very much depend on the business model of the bank being evaluated: customer loans and deposits for commercial banks, capital markets volumes for investment banks, all the items for universal banks. Once again, it is important to check for consistency between the expected growth rate of volumes and of NFCI, given the expected evolution of margins.

4.2.4.3   Cost of Risk

Cost of risk is defined as the ratio of net impairment charges over average customer loans. Intuitively, all else being equal, the ratio should increase the higher the portion of NPLs on the total loan portfolio increases and the stricter the reserve policy of the bank. Therefore, one should check that the cost of risk, the NPL ratio, and the coverage ratio move in the same direction. An additional element to be considered is the relative weight of different NPL categories. It can be the case, for instance, that while the NPL ratio stays constant, the relative weight of bad loans to less risky categories of NPLs increases. Also in this case, the cost of risk should increase.

4.2.5   Asset Side versus Liability Side

A third set of considerations around the business plan internal consistency concerns the relationship between the asset side and the liability side of the Balance Sheet. The goal is to assess whether the projected evolution of assets and liabilities results in sustainable funding structure, leverage position, and capitalization.

4.2.5.1   Funding Structure

The assessment of the sustainability of the funding structure relies mainly on the following elements:

- *Loans to direct customer funding ratio*: expresses the percentage of customer loans funded by customer deposits and securities issued to customers. A value significantly above 1 should be flagged as a potential source of liquidity risk. As a matter of fact, customer funding is expected to be more stable than wholesale funding, given wholesale funding providers are more sensitive to the credit risk profile of the institutions to which they provide funds.
- *Net interbank position*: is computed as the difference between due *from* banks and due *to* banks. It is another measure of reliance on wholesale funding: when negative, it means that the bank being evaluated is a net borrower and therefore exposed to the fluctuations of the wholesale funding market.
- *Maturity profile*: while a carry trade of short-term funding to invest in higher yield long-term lending is part of the core business of a bank, high reliance on short-term borrowings and a significant maturity mismatch are both elements to be accounted for when evaluating the sustainability of the funding structure.

- *Liquidity position*: sustainability of business plan forecasts with respect to assets and liabilities evolution requires the presence of an adequate liquidity buffer which can be measured as (liquid assets – liquid liabilities)/liquid liabilities). An additional ratio that should also be monitored is the percentage of liquid assets over total liabilities.
- *Access to capital markets*: even if not related to consistency between assets and liabilities, the ability to access the capital markets of a specific bank has proved to be a significant constraint on funding decisions during the crisis. As a result, it should be included as an additional element to consider when evaluating the sustainability of the funding structure.
- Under the proposed Basel III framework, two further specific ratios will have to be taken into account, namely the *Net Stable Funding Ratio* (NSFR) and the *Liquidity Coverage Ratio*. The former seeks to calculate the proportion of long-term assets which are funded by long term, stable funding (customer deposits, *long-term* wholesale funding, and equity). The latter requires a bank to hold sufficient high-quality liquid assets to cover its total net cash outflows over 30 days.

4.2.5.2 Leverage Position

Projections of assets and liabilities imply a certain level of leverage that can be measured as the ratio of total assets over equity. This is a critical indicator of bank performance and should be carefully monitored. On the one hand, leverage might boost profitability in the upswing in the way it functions as a multiplier (as indicated in the ROE framework presented previously). On the other hand, it has a significant impact on solvency risk, that is, it increases the chance for a bank to fail as a result of unexpected losses. Therefore, high levels of leverage, similar to those reported before the recent financial crisis, should raise questions about the sustainability of the Balance Sheet structure. In fact, most banks have recently committed to deleveraging plans reporting regularly to stakeholders the results of such process.

An additional element to be considered is the impact on leverage of off-Balance Sheet items, such as the nominal value of derivatives embedded in structured products or in the trading book. Although disclosure on this aspect is generally limited, it is important to try and gather as much information as possible on this point.

4.2.5.3 Capitalization

The evolution of the capitalization level of a bank is determined by the amount of regulatory capital and risk weighted assets (RWAs) that the institution is projected to have in the business plan. The analysis has two goals: first, to assess whether the bank is expected to stay adequately capitalized going forward; second, to verify that the assumptions underlying the evolution of capital and RWAs are robust.

As for the first goal, the same considerations presented in the previous section apply. However, it is important to keep in mind that regulatory capital requirements are constantly evolving and projected capitalization levels should be compared with expected minimum capital ratio at each point in time.

As for the second goal, that is, assessing the reliability of the assumptions underlying the evolution of capital and RWAs, the analysis should focus on the drivers used to project capital and RWAs. The regulatory capital available at each time changes mainly as a result of retained earnings. Therefore, the two drivers to be monitored are profitability and dividend payout. As far as profitability targets are concerned, all the methodologies presented in this chapter can be used in the assessment of their reliability. As for dividend payout ratio, the main way to assess the sustainability of the policy adopted by the bank is to look at where it stands compared to industry levels. Therefore, this topic will be analyzed in more details in Section 4.3 on external consistency.

RWA's evolution has to be consistent with the projected amount of risk taken by the bank to operate its business going forward. Although imprecise, total assets can be taken as a proxy of risk taken. Therefore, an initial check that can be performed on RWAs is to look at the evolution of the ratio of RWAs over total assets. If the ratio decreases significantly it is important to understand the reasons. Possible explanations could be the adoption of an internal rating based (IRB) approach for the measurement of credit risk (which is able to provide a more precise measure of risk compared to the standardized approach), a change in the business mix of the bank, the implementation of a process of de-risking on the asset portfolio, the improvement of asset quality, and so on.

A second approach that can be used to analyze the evolution of RWAs is to evaluate separately each different component. The possibility of performing a detailed analysis very much depends on the level of disclosure provided in the business plan. However, it is important to have an idea about the main drivers underlying the calculation of RWAs. For this purpose, we provide a brief summary by risk category here:

- *Credit risk*: different risk weights are applied to the loans in the loan book according to the respective credit rating (standardized approach) or probability of default (IRB approach).
- *Market risk*: a multiple is applied on market value at risk. Additional charges based on stress testing might be imposed.
- *Counterparty risk*: net counterparty exposure is treated similarly to the loan book.
- *Operational risk*: computed as percentage of historical revenues.

4.2.6   Financial versus Operating Forecasts

A final set of considerations around the business plan internal consistency refers to the relationship between financial and operating forecasts. In particular, there are two elements that shape this relationship in a relevant way: *efficiency* and *productivity*.

Efficiency

The evolution of operating expenses in the income statement should be supported by actions announced with respect to administrative expenses and staff expenses. A decrease of the former could be driven by cost control actions such as centralization of procurement, optimization of IT platform, and streamlining of activities. The impact of these actions is hard to estimate and, as a result, is difficult to check for consistency with respect to this category of expenses. On the other hand, a reduction in staff expenses implies either a lower number of employees or a lower cost per employee. These are indicators that can be easily computed and, therefore, should be very carefully analyzed. The goal is to understand whether the targets set by the bank in terms of headcount and average salary are achievable and sustainable.

Productivity

Business plans generally embed targets with respect to the increase of productivity. These are generally expressed in terms of ratios per employee and per branch (e.g., total income per employee, total loans per employee/branch, total customers per employee/branch). On the other hand, what is generally underestimated is the fact that productivity gains require investments. Such investments include branch upgrading, personnel training, IT platform innovation, build-up of multichannel systems for customer interaction, and so on. In addition, banks might achieve productivity gains by re-designing the branch network or rationalizing positions, that is, re-deploying employees to customer-facing activities. The main goal is to check that there is an adequate explanation for the projected increase in productivity.

In conclusion, efficiency and productivity are the two main elements explaining the evolution of the cost income ratio. As a result, when looking at the ratio it should be possible to understand what is driving a potential reduction/increase and why.

4.3   EXTERNAL CONSISTENCY

So far we have seen how to check that business plan forecasts derive from a solid and reliable basis (*status quo* analysis) and that the projected evolution of the different components of the plan is internally coherent. A final area of investigation refers to the external consistency of the plan, that is, the fact that future macroeconomic trends and expected developments in the competitive landscape are properly reflected. Another important point is to establish whether the targets set in the business plan are above or below market expectations. This can be verified by comparing such targets with market consensus, whenever the latter is available.

4.3.1 Macroeconomic Outlook

The performance of a bank is highly affected by the evolution of some macroeconomic variables such as real GDP growth, inflation, and interest rates. In the following, we report three important examples of elements that are clearly impacted by macro trends.

4.3.1.1 Net Interest Income

Interest rate levels drive both loan yields and cost of funding. Banks determine both the "mark-up" and the "mark-down" over the prevailing interest rate respectively for loans and deposits. Assuming that interest-earning assets re-price faster than interest-bearing liabilities, rising interest rates will positively impact NII and vice versa, declining interest rates will negatively affect NII.

The slope of the yield curve has a relevant impact of NII as well. As a matter of fact, most banks make money by borrowing at the short end of the curve and lending at the long end. Therefore, NIM usually increases when the curve steepens and decreases when it flattens.

4.3.1.2 Loans Growth

Loan demand is influenced by GDP growth, interest rate movements, and inflation. While GDP expansion has a positive effect on loans growth, rising interest rates typically reduce demand for loans (incentives to invest are lower when the cost of borrowing is higher). Moreover, rising rates, especially when experienced during the latter stages of economic expansion, are often accompanied by inflation. This is driven by capacity constraints coupled with low unemployment during times when demand for goods and services is growing rapidly. Increasing inflation results in a monetary constraint and GDP expansion slows, further reducing the demand for loans.

In extreme cases, it may be difficult to understand whether a decrease in GDP is driving loan reduction, or whether restrictions in credit granting criteria may cause a decrease in GDP, as many commentators argue may have been the case for certain European countries in the latest financial crisis.

4.3.1.3 Equity

Interest rate movements also have an impact on the value of a relevant portion of banks' assets. The value of securities (which generally account for a large portion of a bank's assets) for instance, declines when interest rates rise. In most cases (unless the securities are classified as held to maturity), unrealized security losses flow through to the banks' shareholders' equity.

The considerations made previously for NII, loans growth, and equity highlight the importance of analyzing the assumptions related to the macroeconomic outlook underlying the business plan. One way to model the uncertainty embedded in macroeconomic forecasts is to build a set of scenarios, which reflect different potential evolutions of the macro picture and assign a probability to each scenario. When the bank being valued provides a business plan based on different scenarios, there are two key questions that one should ask:

- Are the main potential macro scenarios correctly reflected in the business plan?
- Is the probability assigned to each scenario credible?

As for the first question, companies generally provide three different scenarios: a base case, an upside case, and a downside case. Although this approach might seem reasonable, it is important that each scenario is based on solid views of what is the most likely macroeconomic output (base case), what could go better than expected (upside case) or what could go wrong (downside case). In addition, once the different scenarios have been defined in terms of macroeconomic drivers' evolution, their impacts on forecasts need to be reflected in a consistent way throughout the different components of the plan.

As for the second question, establishing probabilities to be assigned to the different scenarios is clearly not an exact science. However, in this case it is important to evaluate whether they are conservative enough and, if this is not the case, what would be the impact on forecasts of more prudent assumptions.

It must be noted that Basel III will render the correlation between equity and external environment even more important as any movements in equity will directly impact Core Tier 1, whilst this was not always the case under Basel II.

Additionally, banks have historically classified a large portion of their non-loan assets as Held-To-Maturity in order to minimize equity volatility: different accounting practices should be taken into account for the purpose of the valuation of banks.[2]

4.3.2 Competitive Dynamics

The expected evolution of the competitive landscape plays an important role in shaping business plan projections. In order to form a judgment around the potential

---

[2] For instance, in 2011 the European Banking Authority (EBA) has asked banks to report the Core Tier 1 ratio calculated by marking to market all government bonds, which has highlighted a meaningful reduction in equity for many European banks and led to a wave of capital strengthening initiatives.

impact of competitive dynamics on expected performance it is critical to analyze the following three elements:

- The strategic positioning of the bank in question to understand its main strengths and weaknesses compared to peers.
- The evolution of competitive pressure as a result of expected changes in the competitive landscape (e.g., as a result of consolidation).
- The expected performance of peers to be used as a reference to check the reliability of business plan assumptions.

Competitive pressure has an impact on three main dimensions of the plan: volumes, margins, and payout ratio.

Volumes

Macroeconomic trends drive the evolution of volumes at an aggregated level. For instance, one can assume that total customer loans for a given country will move in line with expected GDP growth (although we have seen that interest rates and inflation play an important role as well). The fact that the growth rate of a given bank's portfolio of customer loans is above or below such a level depends on the expectation that the bank will be or will not be able to increase its market share. Therefore, especially in case of market share gains, it is important to understand what potential sources of competitive advantage could justify such process or, alternatively, if the bank is simply giving away margins in exchange for volumes.

Margins

As for volumes, margins are also determined by a combination of macroeconomic trends and competitive pressure. If we take, for example, the net interest margin, it is driven by a mark-up and a mark-down applied by the bank on the prevailing interest rates. Both the mark-up and the mark-down are the results of strategic decision and competitive pressure. It is clear that higher competition should lead to lower margins and vice versa. Therefore, given a certain view on the competitive landscape evolution, one should be able to judge if a margin's evolution is consistent with such view or not. Moreover, if projections assume a simultaneous increase in market share and in margins (above competitors' levels) this should be flagged and further investigated.

Payout Ratio

The payout ratio determines the portion of earnings distributed out as dividends. It has a critical impact on valuations carried out applying multiples on expected values of equity or tangible equity. In fact, a lower payout ratio will increase the base of the valuation (i.e., the book value or tangible book value). As a result, it is important to check that the dividend policy assumed by the company is consistent with industry levels, that is, it is not significantly below peers and in line with what is demanded by investors.

4.3.3   Business Plan versus Market Consensus

An important reference for the evaluation of a business plan is the comparison of the main targets with market consensus, that is, with the expectations on the bank's future performance published regularly by research analysts. Such information is generally available only for listed companies.

The possibility of identifying which targets are above or below expectations can be a very useful tool to highlight areas that require further investigation. In particular, whenever there is a significant delta between the plan and market expectations it is essential to understand the underlying reasons. On the one hand, market expectations are formed on public information, therefore it could be the case that they do not account for the impact of future actions that the bank is going to implement but has not yet disclosed. On the other hand, there could be a difference between what the market expects in terms of macroeconomic outlook or competitive dynamics and the assumptions of the plan. If this is the case, and especially if the plan proves to be less conservative than what the market expects, it is important to estimate what the impact on the final valuation would be should the market assumptions hold.

Generally, however, it can be expected that banks' business will lag behind consensus in period of economic downturn, and will be more aggressive than consensus in periods of economic upturn, mainly because consensus is updated far more often than business plans.

4.4   THE FORECASTING MODEL OF A BANK

The main factors shaping the evolution of a bank's business are volumes, margins, and risk. These elements, in turn, determine the amount of retained earnings a bank is able to generate and, as a result, its capital evolution. In order to build a solid forecasting model, it is crucial to move from the evolution of volumes and risk taken (Balance Sheet) and then forecast earnings (P&L) by applying the correct level of margins on estimated volumes. At this point, it is possible to model those Balance Sheet items that are linked to the P&L, that is, equity, minority interests, and associates. Finally, the entire model has to be checked through a careful analysis of resulting ratios, making sure in particular that capital ratios meet regulatory requirements.

4.4.1   Balance Sheet

The Balance Sheet is the starting point of the forecasting model. The different items to be modeled can be broken down into four categories:

- Assets
- Liabilities
- Items that depend on P&L evolution
- Balancing items

4.4.1.1   Assets

One of the most important items to be forecasted among the assets of a bank is the amount of gross loans to customers. This is generally the largest component of interest earning assets and an accurate estimate is paramount to model net interest income properly. The evolution of loans is generally estimated in two steps:

- Forecast the growth rate of loans at an aggregated level (generally by country) by looking at macroeconomic trends (e.g., GDP growth, inflation, monetary policy).
- Forecast the growth rate for the bank's loan portfolio by assuming a certain evolution of the bank's market share (increasing market share means bank's growth rate above industry level and vice versa).

The second item to be modeled thoroughly is the impairment allowance on loans to customers. The value of this item moves according to the following rule: opening balance + loan loss charges (P&L item) – write-off net of recoveries – unwinding of the discount rate. The key drivers in this case are the NPL ratio, the cost of risk, the net charge off (write-off less releases over gross customer loans), and the coverage ratio. In particular, the latter should converge to a constant long term level – however, historically reduction in coverage ratios can be expected and is observed in recessionary periods, when banks tend to utilize any extra provisions taken in a more benign period.

As for other assets, they are generally assumed to grow in line with gross customer loans, unless management envisaged significant changes in the business mix of a bank (e.g., a reduction in prop trading books). However, there are some relevant exceptions

- *Goodwill*: its value depends on specific transactions and impairment charges; therefore, it is incorrect to apply a growth rate to goodwill.
- *Fair value items* (i.e., trading portfolio): in the short term their value depends on capital market volatility, while in the long term their growth rate should converge with that of accrual items (e.g., loans).

- *Cash and reserve deposits*: they are generally modeled as a constant percentage of deposits although their value might also change as a result of movements in central bank reserve requirements.
- *Due from banks*: as will be discussed later on, this is one of the items that can be used as a balancing item for the Balance Sheet.

4.4.1.2 Liabilities

Customer deposits are a very important element to model on the liability side, as they generally account for a large part of interest-bearing liabilities. There are generally two alternatives to estimate deposit evolution:

- Estimate a growth rate with a method similar to the one applied for customer loans, that is, starting from the growth rate for the aggregated level of deposits (by country) and then establishing the individual bank's deposit growth rate based on market share considerations. In this case, it is important to check *ex-post* that the resulting ratio of loans to deposits is actually sustainable at any point in time.
- Fix a target loans to deposits ratio and apply it to the amount of customer loans previously estimated. In this case, it is crucial to verify that the resulting level of deposits is actually achievable given market and competitive dynamics.

The estimated growth rate of customer deposits is generally applied to other liabilities to model their expected evolution. There are generally two exceptions to this rule:

- *Long term debt*: the value is generally rolled forward as it is assumed to be refinanced, unless there are specific indications that this will not be the case.
- *Due to banks*: as it will be discussed later on, this is one of the items that can be used as balancing item for the Balance Sheet.

4.4.1.3 Items that Depend on P&L Evolution

The main items whose evolution depends on P&L movements are shareholders' equity, minority interests, and associates. In order to model them properly, it is important to reflect accurately the relationship that links them to the P&L.

Shareholders' equity evolution is mainly impacted by the amount of retained earnings generated by the bank, that is, the difference between reported earnings and dividends paid. Reported earnings come directly from the P&L. On the other side, dividends paid are the result of the payout ratio applied on earnings. Such a ratio can be estimated based on company targets and peer analysis, always considering regulatory constraints on capital. Other elements affecting shareholders' equity evolution are capital increases, capital reductions, and asset revaluation.

In general, these items are not embedded in forecasts unless there is a specific indication from company management.

4.4.1.4 Balancing Items

For the balance sheet to balance at any point in time, it is important to choose a balancing item, otherwise called "the plug". The most common alternatives are the following:

- *Due from banks* (on the asset side). This is generally the choice if the bank has an excess of deposits compared to the amount of loans to customers.
- *Due to banks* (on the liability side). This is generally the choice if the bank has a deficit of deposits compared to the amount of loans to customers.

In both cases, it is assumed that the balancing item of the Balance Sheet is the net interbank position.

4.4.2 P&L

Once the amount of volumes and risk taken has been estimated, it is possible to model the P&L and project earnings. The main items that require in-depth modeling are:

- Net interest income
- Net fee and commission income
- Net trading income
- Operating expenses
- Impairment charges

In addition, there are other items of the P&L that might require the attention of the analyst on a case by case basis. We provide some indications on those elements in the subsection 4.4.2.6 "Other Items".

4.4.2.1 Net Interest Income

Net interest income is generally the main component of banks' total revenues. It is the result of interest income minus interest expenses. Interest income is estimated by applying the appropriate interest rate on each category of interest-earning assets (previously forecasted). The appropriate level of interest rate is generally computed by identifying the reference benchmark (e.g., Libor, Euribor), forecasting its evolution based on macroeconomic trends (or available public estimates), and finally applying the expected spread (or mark-up) the bank is able to charge to its customers. Such spread is impacted by several factors and in particular by the level of competition in the market. As for interest expenses, a similar approach can be followed. In this case, for each category of interest-bearing liabilities, the appropriate interest rate will be computed by applying a mark-down on the reference benchmark. At the end of the forecasting process, it is important to check the reasonableness of the assumptions made by looking at the resulting evolution of the net interest margin.

The projections of net interest income are obviously highly sensitive to all macro and micro assumptions made, but it is worth highlighting at least that:

• On the asset side, whilst banks have the ability to re-price the loan portfolio and hence, in theory, can make assumptions on spread that are seemingly insensitive to risk free rates, the re-pricing effort is limited by the duration of the loans (i.e., how quickly can the loan book be re-priced to reflect external shocks?);
• On the liabilities side, mark-down is limited the most by:
  ○ The level of risk free rates. In the current low rate environment mark-down cannot exceed the risk free rate, and hence it is usually very low;
  ○ The competition for deposits, which for instance, in the current environment of low liquidity for banks means that often banks may have to accept even negative mark-downs in certain instances.

4.4.2.2 Net Fee and Commission Income

Net fee and commission income comes from a number of different sources that should be identified and modeled separately. We report here the most relevant:

• *Commercial banking fees*: can be modeled as a given percentage of the total amount of loans and deposits.
• *Asset management fees*: can be modeled as a given percentage of the total amount of asset under management.
• *Investment banking fees*: driven by capital markets volumes, margins, and market share.

4.4.2.3 Net Trading Income

Net trading income is generally the most volatile component of banks' revenues. In the short term, gains, and losses from trading activities will reflect capital market volatility. However, in the long term, it is reasonable to assume reversion to normalized capital gains.

These normalized capital gains may most likely be lower than pre-crisis levels, as a result of regulators throughout the world requiring – particularly to commercial banks – a reduction in the proprietary trading activity.

4.4.2.4 Operating Expenses

As for the estimate of operating expenses, a certain cost to income ratio or cost to assets ratio is generally applied respectively on forecasted revenues and total assets. The cost : income ratio tends to be more cyclical than cost : assets as revenues are generally more volatile than total assets. As a result, the definition of the appropriate level of cost income ratio to be used should take cyclicality into consideration.

Operating expenses – compared to other P&L items – are under more strict control of the management. Therefore, other than the ratios mentioned previously, absolute costs are equally and increasingly important, with banks announcing credible and substantiated plans to cut costs in order to offset declining revenues/increasing capital requirement.

4.4.2.5 Impairment Charges

As for impairment charges, the most relevant component is given by loan loss provisions. These are estimated when modeling the evolution of the impairment allowance on customer loans. The key drivers are the expected level of NPL ratio and the desired level of coverage ratio.

From the outside, the estimate of impairment charges is one of the most difficult tasks and hence sensitivities around impairment losses are important.

4.4.2.6 Other Items

Other P&L items to be modeled include income from associates, tax expenses, and minority interests. While the modeling for these elements is in line with that for industrial companies, it is important to underline the relevant impact of tax rate on the final estimate of net earnings. As a result, it is crucial to carefully account for the geographical breakdown of profits and specific situations such as goodwill amortization, loss making subsidiaries, gains on disposal of fixed assets, and tax loss carried forward.

4.4.3 Checking Forecasts

Once the forecasting process is completed, it is essential to check that overall the model produces forecasts which are sensible, achievable, and sustainable from a business perspective. This check is generally performed by looking at the evolution of key ratios related to growth, profitability, risk, and capital adequacy as already described previously in this chapter. Considerations based on the analysis of ratios allow fine-tuning of the assumptions of the model. A number of iterations are generally necessary before getting to a satisfactory result.

The checks over the reliability of such ratios should be done in at least two ways:

- Comparing them with the banks' historical performance, while acknowledging that many ratios have muted because of regulatory changes *in primis*, but also because of cyclical and long-term changes in the industry profitability;
- Comparing them with other banks' similar ratios, acknowledging that managers tend to align their results and projections to what other peers are doing;

Table 4.1   The main ratios for analyzing a bank's business plan

Ratio	Definition
Return on equity	$\dfrac{\text{Net income}}{\text{Total equity capital}} = \dfrac{\text{Net income}}{\text{Total assets}} \times \dfrac{\text{Total assets}}{\text{Total equity capital}} =$ ROA × equity multiplier
Return on assets	$\dfrac{\text{Net income}}{\text{Total operating income}} \times \dfrac{\text{Total operating income}}{\text{Total assets}} =$ Profit margin × Asset utilization
Asset utilization	$\dfrac{\text{Total operating income}}{\text{Total assets}} = \dfrac{\text{Interest income}}{\text{Total assets}} +$ $\dfrac{\text{Noninterest income}}{\text{Total assets}} =$ Interest income ratio + Noninterest income ratio
Overhead efficiency	$\dfrac{\text{Non interest income}}{\text{Non interest expense}}$
Cost-income	$\dfrac{\text{General administrative costs} + \text{other operating expenses}}{\text{Operating income}}$
Net interest margin	$\dfrac{\text{Interest income} - \text{Interest expense}}{\text{Investment securities} + \text{Net loans and leases}} =$ $\dfrac{\text{Net interest income}}{\text{Earning assets}}$
Net interest income to operating income	$\dfrac{\text{Net interest income}}{\text{Operating income}}$
Cost of risk	$\dfrac{\text{Impairment losses}}{\text{Average balance of net loans to customers}}$
Spread	$\dfrac{\text{Interest income}}{\text{Earning assets}} - \dfrac{\text{Interest expense}}{\text{Interest-bearing liabilities}}$
Non-performing Loans	$\dfrac{\text{Gross non-performing loans}}{\text{Total gross loans}}$
NPL coverage ratio	$\dfrac{\text{Loan loss provisions}}{\text{Gross non-performing loans}}$
Equity and deposits to net loans	$\dfrac{\text{Equity and deposits}}{\text{Net loans}}$
RORAC	$\dfrac{\text{Net income}}{\text{Risk-based capital requirement}}$
RAROC	$\dfrac{\text{Revenues} - \text{Expenses} - \text{Expected losses} + \text{Income from capital}}{\text{Capital at risk}}$
RARORAC	$\dfrac{\text{Revenues} - \text{Expenses} - \text{Expected losses} + \text{Income from capital}}{\text{Risk-based capital requirement}}$

Given the limitations of each method singularly taken, both should be used simultaneously in order to achieve meaningful results.

An additional sophistication of the model is the production of multiple scenarios based on different sets of macroeconomic and competitive assumptions. By assigning a probability to each scenario it is possible to blend them and provide a final set of forecasts. However, the availability of different scenarios is generally a useful tool to express the potential volatility of results going forward.

Whilst the public availability of such scenarios is usually limited, the high volatility of business plan drivers over the course of the latest financial crisis has, on the one hand, made such scenario simulations more and more important, and on the other, has pushed banks' top management to disclose key sensitivities to the market in a more consistent manner.

To conclude this chapter, in Table 4.1 we define the main ratios for assessing a bank's business plan.

5
Bank Valuation

In line of principle, banks are valued using the same valuation methods applied to non-financial companies. However, the specific economics of banks make some approaches more suitable than others, or require specific adjustments to reflect the peculiarities of the financial sector. Going forward we will assume that the reader is already familiar with the most common corporate valuation techniques – namely Discounted Cash Flow, Dividend Discount Model, and Multiples – as presented by the main finance and valuation textbooks. Our focus will be on the problems and solutions to be dealt with when such valuation models are applied to financial institutions. The chapter begins by highlighting what sets financial institutions apart in the realm of company valuation, and then presents, one by one, the main approaches used in practice.

5.1 WHY BANK VALUATION IS DIFFERENT

The nature, systemic importance, and complexity of banks' operations make them unique organizations. This is reflected in the peculiar financial structure of banks, which differs substantially from that of non-financial companies. There are at least three aspects of banks' financial structures that have an impact in terms of valuation.

First, banks are highly levered entities: an equity/total asset ratio as low as 5% is the norm rather than exception in the industry. For non-financial companies such degree of leverage is rare and sustainable only on a short-term basis (it is usually adopted in extraordinary circumstances such as leveraged buy-out transactions).

Second, the core business for banks is to transform money collected from clients into financing products for other clients. In a way, a bank's job is to process financial resources and risks: therefore, debt is a raw material rather than a source of capital. Such a feature is strikingly different from that of non-financial companies: for them financing and investment decisions can be made independently. As a consequence, economic capital is more narrowly defined for banks and comprises only equity and quasi-equity financing.

Last, the capital of banks is heavily regulated by national and international authorities. Banks are left with little freedom on the (minimum) capital that has to be held to counterweight the assumed level of risky assets. This element affects both the dividend policy and the recourse to the capital markets, and implicitly determines the cash flow amount that can be distributed to shareholders at a given moment.

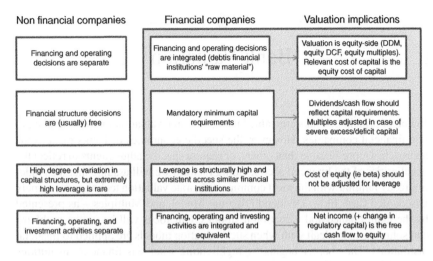

Figure 5.1 Valuation implications of the difference between non-financial and financial companies

Each of those elements has clear consequences in terms of banks' valuation (Figure 5.1). The high level of leverage coupled with the evidence that financing is a *core operation* for banks, implies that the focus of bank valuation is mostly or solely on the equity. Hence, while for non-financial companies the valuation can be approached indifferently from the "asset-side" or from the "equity-side"; the natural approach for financial companies is the latter. Therefore, when valuing a bank, the Discounted Cash Flows technique based on the discounting of Free Cash Flow from Operations (of Free Cash Flow to the Firm) using a Weighted Average Cost of Capital should be discarded. Similarly, the asset-side multiples based on the Enterprise Value (EV) of the company – such as EV/Sales, EV/EBITDA, and EV/EBIT – are not appropriate valuation approaches when dealing with banks. On the contrary, the Dividend Discount Model, the Discounted Free Cash Flow to Equity Model, the Equity Excess Return Models, and the equity-side multiples are appropriate valuation techniques.

The interconnections and substantial equivalence of operating, financing, and investment decisions of banks points toward a cash flow to equity measure which differs from the one typically used for non-financial companies. In practice, the investment and financing components are assumed as "embedded" in the net income of banks and are not computed separately, except for the investment in regulatory capital.

Finally, the high level of leverage, which tends to be homogeneous across banks operating with similar business models, implies that beta adjustments, which are usually applied for nonfinancial companies are, in fact redundant. We will analyze each of these aspects in rest of the chapter.

When approaching the valuation the analyst has first to decide what method(s) to apply. The decision depends on several factors including the purpose of the valuation (i.e., M&A deal vs. investment recommendation/decision), the nature and complexity of the financial institution, the availability of both internal and macro data, and the time and resources the analyst can invest in the process. Relative valuation is usually the quickest approach, while the preparation of the forecasted results (and the cost of capital estimation) necessary to perform DCF or DDM tends to be rather time-consuming. The recommendation of using at least two approaches – preferably a relative valuation one and one based on the discount of future results – applies to all companies, and this is even more compelling when dealing with the valuation of financial institutions. In fact, the complexity and the opaqueness associated with most assets in the balance sheet of financial companies make the valuation, especially from outside, particularly difficult and the use of two methodologies may at least contribute to challenging the valuator's assumptions, thus improving the accuracy of the outcome.

In general, we can group the valuation techniques for banks and other financial companies into three main "families" (Figure 5.2). The first one comprises the methods based on the discounting of future expected results – being the forecasted results either dividend, equity cash flows, or excess returns. The second one includes all the techniques based on multiples. Multiples can be used to derive the value from comparables companies via direct comparison, via regression, or via quantification of the multiple fundamentals. Finally, valuation can be performed by aligning the book value of each asset and claim to the market value: eventually, the value of the equity will be computed as the difference between the market value of the assets and of the liabilities. On the basis of the business model of the

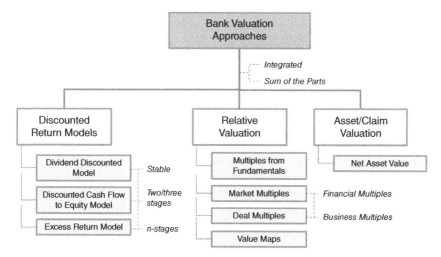

Figure 5.2   The choices in bank valuation

bank and of the granularity of the operational data, the valuator has also to decide whether to carry out the valuation of a bank as an integrated entity or as the sum of the values of its single business segments (see Section 5.5).

5.2   DISCOUNTED RETURNS MODEL

The basic principle that the Discounted Returns Model is based on is that the value of each and every asset is equal to the present value of the streams of results they will generate in future. The present value should be obtained using an appropriate discounting factor (cost of capital) coherent with the level of risk associated to the expected future results. As said, for banks and most financial companies the relevant capital is the equity capital and, therefore, to estimate its value, the relevant streams of results are, depending on the model adopted, the dividends, the cash flows to equity, or the equity excess returns. Each of the three measures has its own features but for all of them the practical quantification of the cost of capital is the same. We will therefore introduce first the peculiarities of the cost of capital estimation for financial institutions, and then present separately the Dividend Discount Model, the Discounted Cash Flow Model, and the Excess Return Model.

5.2.1   The Cost of Capital for Financial Institutions

The approach commonly used to estimate the cost of capital for valuation purposes is the Sharpe–Lintner *Capital Asset Pricing Model* (CAPM). Although more sophisticated cost of capital approaches do exist (i.e., the Fama–French "three factors" model and the Arbitrage Pricing Theory Model) and can be applied to banks, the CAPM is usually an efficient choice when dealing with the valuation of banks.[1]

Therefore, for valuation purposes, we can assume that the expected cost of capital (k_{ei}) or expected return $E(r_i)$ for company i is:

$$k_{ei} = E(r_i) = r_f + \beta_{im} \times [E(r_m) - r_f] \tag{5.1}$$

where r_f is the expected return of a risk-free asset, $E(r_m)$ the expected return on the market portfolio, and β_{im} is the sensitivity of bank i shares to the systematic market risk.

In practice, the empirical strategies to determine the return of the risk-free asset and the market portfolio return are identical to the ones used for non-financial companies. The risk-free rate is usually reflected adequately in the yield of liquid

---

[1] For example, Schuermann and Stiroh, analyzing the returns of US banks from 1997–2005, show that the market factor (hence, the CAPM) clearly dominates in explaining bank returns, followed by the Fama–French models, and other models based on bank-specific factors (*Visible and hidden risk factors for banks*, Federal Reserve Bank of New York, 2006).

long-term (i.e., 10 years) government bonds, while the return of a large stock index (e.g., S&P500, FTSE, DAX) is a natural proxy of the market return.

Similarly, the choices related to the computation of bank betas do not differ from the ones related to non-financial companies: (1) the analyst should define the length of the estimation period – usually from 2–5 years – also on the basis of consideration about the inclusion of structural changes (if any) in the risk profile of the bank; (2) the return interval which may be daily, weekly, or monthly; and (3) the market index to be used in the regression. Furthermore, as with non-financial companies, it is advisable to estimate the beta as an "industry beta" rather than as the historical beta of the bank analyzed (if listed). This is because using the average beta from a panel of homogenous banks – in terms of size, geographical coverage, and business model – should capture more effectively the actual risk of the industry/segment the bank is operating in. In statistical terms, the average across a number of regression betas has a significantly lower standard error than the estimation of a single bank's beta.

Moving to what is peculiar of the financial industry, a notable difference from other companies is the treatment of leverage. While the standard procedure for non-financial companies involves a "de-levering" and "re-levering" process – via the famous "Hamada formula" – financial companies usually do not require such an adjustment. This is the consequence of banks' very nature: leverage is structurally high in this industry and the degree of leverage variation among similar banks tends to be negligible. Therefore, there is usually no need to specifically adjust the bank cost of capital to factor its peculiar degree of leverage.[2] Practically, this implies that the observed betas can be used as they are for the CAPM application as long as the sample of comparable banks has been defined consistently. Such consistency should be preferably verified along three dimensions: size, geography, and business model/risk profile. It would be, for example, a mistake to use a large investment bank beta to estimate the cost of capital of a small commercial bank, as the associated levels of risk are likely to be substantially different.

Figure 5.3 shows the evolution of the beta coefficients for three samples of US banks: large investment banks, large pure commercial banks, and small banks. Apart from the common peak during the most critical phase of the recent financial crisis, the beta of large investment banks has been historically higher than the other banks' one. This is consistent with the business model of investment banks whose risk profile tends to be higher than the one of commercial banks. Smallish US banks showed a very low sensitivity to market as measured by beta during the 1990s when their business was mostly regional and so, at least to a certain extent, unrelated to the wider market movements. With the subsequent regulatory changes they progressively expanded the geographical coverage and the degree of

---

[2] Stever (2007), for example, provides evidences that asset riskiness (beta) rather than leverage affects bank beta (*Bank size, credit and the sources of bank market risk*, BIS Working Papers no. 238).

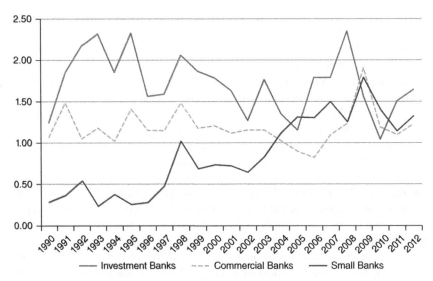

Figure 5.3   Beta levels of three samples of US listed banks

portfolio/business diversification: eventually they appear to converge on the level of large commercial banks.[3]

It is worth mentioning that, in line of principle, the beta of a large well diversified commercial (or mostly commercial) bank is expected to be close to 1, as the risks of the wider economy/financial market are likely to be well mimicked by the portfolio of loans and financial assets held by the bank.[4] Therefore, when dealing with the bank beta estimation, it is worth considering "adjusting" the observed beta to somehow let them converge towards 1.[5] The formula is the following:

$$\text{Adjusted beta} = \text{Observed beta} \, (0.67) + 1.00 \, (0.33) \qquad (5.2)$$

To conclude, Table 5.1 presents the CAPM cost of capital estimates for large samples of banks from various countries. The take-away is that banks' cost of equity capital varies significantly across countries and periods, depending on factors such as the level of the risk-free rate, the equity risk premium, and the impact of regulations (the introduction of the Basel II framework seems to have played a specific major role here). Importantly, the country averages as presented in

---

[3] Further to this, Stever (2007), highlights that small banks appear to be able to secure loans with lower credit risk (either due to their superior knowledge of borrower risk or borrower preference for small banks) but at the cost of less diversity in their loan portfolio; as a consequence small banks tend to report a lower beta than the larger ones (op. cit.).

[4] Furthermore, in some countries, banks and financial institutions represent a large chunk of the national stock market capitalization: as a consequence the bank beta is almost the market beta with itself, hence equal (or close) to 1.

[5] Such adjustment relies on the evidences provided by Blume, M. (1975) in, Betas and Their Regression Tendencies, *Journal of Finance*, 30, June, 785–795.

Table 5.1   Average cost of equity (and its determinants) across countries

Country	Period	Cost of Equity (mean of estimates)	Standard deviation	Risk-free rate	CAPM beta
Canada	1990–2000	10.7	0.8	5.0	1.0
	2001–2009	5.7	1.0	2.4	0.6
France	1990–2000	11.1	1.4	4.7	1.0
	2001–2009	7.5	2.8	2.6	0.8
Germany	1990–2000	12.2	2.7	4.1	0.9
	2001–2009	9.3	3.9	2.5	0.7
Japan	1990–2000	11.8	3.3	2.6	0.9
	2001–2009	11.4	4.1	1.4	1.1
United Kingdom	1990–2000	9.9	2.2	4.3	1.0
	2001–2009	6.7	2.7	2.3	0.8
United States	1990–2000	10.7	2.2	3.4	1.1
	2001–2009	7.5	2.8	2.1	0.8

Source: King, M.R. (2009), The cost of equity for global banks: a CAPM perspective from 1990 to 2009, *BIS Quarterly Review.*

the table conceal considerable variation across individual banks, and the standard deviation of the estimates has increased over time. From a valuation point of view, these evidences highlight how paramount the definition of the comparable sample and of the CAPM parameters is.

5.2.2   The Dividend Discount Model

The principle the Dividend Discount Model (DDM) is based on is rather straightforward: the value of shares depends on the expected dividends the shareholders will receive in future. In practice, depending on the availability of data, on the purpose of the valuation, on the company or market circumstances, the stream of future dividends considered may differ significantly. As a bare minimum, the dividends per share expected over the next period (DPS_1) – which are also equal to $DPS_0 \times (1 + g)$ where g is the dividend growth rate, and to the product of current earnings (EPS0), the growth rate, and the payout ratio – have to be factored in the valuation. Often, the valuation requires the explicit forecast of dividends over a longer time horizon. Although there are several possible forecasting strategies, the three most popular ones are presented in Table 5.2.

In all the three cases, we assume that the cost of equity (k_e) has been estimated using the CAPM as discussed in the previous paragraph.

Then the most appropriate version of the DDM has to be chosen. In case the financial institution is in a stable growth state – meaning that the bank is expected to grow at a rate (g_s) that is positive but less than or equal to the growth rate of

Table 5.2 The three main DDM approaches to valuing banks

DDM design	Formula	Forecasting effort
One-stage (Gordon Growth Model)	$P_0 = \dfrac{DPS_1}{k_e - g_s} = \dfrac{DPS_0 \times (1 + g_s)}{k_e - g_s}$ $= \dfrac{EPS_0 \times \text{payout ratio} \times (1 + g_s)}{k_e - g_s}$	+ Only g_s has to be estimated
Two-stages	$P_0 = \displaystyle\sum_{t=1}^{n} \dfrac{DPS_0 \times (1 + g_x)^t}{(1 + k_e)^t}$ $+ \dfrac{\dfrac{DPS_0 \times (1 + g_x)^n \times (1 + g_s)}{k_e - g_s}}{(1 + k_e)^n}$	++ Apart from g_s, the number of years (n) of extraordinary growth, and the extraordinary growth rate (g_x) itself have to be estimated
Year-by-year	$P_0 = \displaystyle\sum_{t=1}^{n} \dfrac{DPS_t}{(1 + k_e)^t} + \dfrac{\dfrac{DPS_n \times (1 + g_s)}{k_e - g_s}}{(1 + k_e)^n}$	+++ Apart from g_s and n, the year-by-year DPS over the explicit forecast period have to be estimated

the whole economy it is operating in – the one stage DDM approach can be used. Clearly, if there seems to be no growth opportunities at all for the bank ($g_s = 0$)[1] than the DDM relation becomes as follows:[6]

$$P_0 = \frac{DPS_0}{k_e} = \frac{DPS_1}{k_e} \tag{5.3}$$

In case the financial institution is expected to experience a constant higher than normal growth phase of n years, the dividends per share should grow at such extraordinary growth rate (g_x) and eventually converge on the stable growth rate. The analyst should use this approach when quantitative and qualitative elements support the view that the financial institution can actually perform better than the whole economy, at least for a certain (visible) period of time.

Finally, when the growth pattern for the bank is expected to be more articulated changing year-by-year, a greater effort in terms of forecasting and modeling is required. Dividends per share have to be estimated punctually for the "explicit forecast period" as an output of the interplay between the forecasted Balance Sheet and Income Statement.

---

[6] A no growth situation also implies that, there are no equity re-investments and therefore that all the available cash flow is distributed to shareholders.

As for the practical "ingredients" of the method, we saw that the cost of capital can be estimated using the CAPM, and that the stable growth rate should be in line with (and not higher than) the whole economy long term expected growth rate, which can be obtained (for most countries) by national governments or international organizations (e.g., Monetary Fund, the World Bank, OECD), by international financial institutions, or by specialized information providers. As a rule of thumb, a long-term growth rate in the 1–4% range is considered fair by most analysts, but it is always useful to back-up this element with estimations by independent parties (especially because even a few decimals in such percentage may have a significant impact of the valuation outcome). It is also worth underlining that according to the economic theory,[7] given certain assumptions (mainly, the absence of population growth), the sustainable growth rate of the economy should equal the risk-free rate. Therefore, the latter can be taken as an indication of the maximum level of the long-term growth rate.

The current dividend per share (DPS_0) is easily observable in most situations, so the analyst should just check whether such dividend level is consistent with the past behavior of the bank and with the industry trends. In case the current dividends appear anomalous (e.g., a one-off jumbo dividend), in the sense that they are not in line with the historical ones and/or with competitors' payout policy, it is advisable to compute "normalized" dividends that are the dividends the bank would be expected to pay in a "normal" situation. Fortunately or not, the concept of "normality" in assessing corporate or market features is mostly left to analyst's judgment. One approach to normalizing dividends is to consider either the historical company average payout ratio, or the current industry average payout ratio, and to apply it to the company's expected earnings.

Alternatively – and this applies also to financial companies that tend to have very low or no dividends at all – the analyst has to work directly on the expected earnings or dividends. If the financial company is listed and adequately covered by equity research analysts, the consensus numbers could be used to quantify the expected dividends. In many cases, financial institutions themselves provide investors with the guidance about future dividends and growth. Otherwise, the expected dividends can be modeled by forecasting the bank financials. It is worth highlighting when working on a bank's fundamentals, that an essential relationship does exist between growth, payout ratio and ROE, so that:

$$g = (1 - \text{payout ratio}) \times \text{ROE} \tag{5.4}$$

Growth rate is in fact the product of the earnings reinvested in the bank and the return they can generate. In Figure 5.4 we assume that the bank's ROE stays constant at 20% while the *retention rate* (= 1-payout ratio) moves from 70 to 11%.

---

[7] See, for example, Ramsey, F.P. (1928), A mathematical theory of saving, *Economic Journal*, 38, 152, 543–559; and, Cass, D. (1965), Optimum Growth in an Aggregative Model of Capital Accumulation, *Review of Economic Studies*, 32 (3), 233–240.

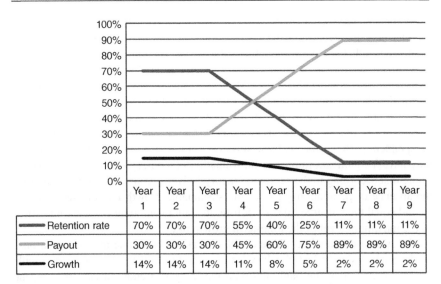

	Year 1	Year 2	Year 3	Year 4	Year 5	Year 6	Year 7	Year 8	Year 9
Retention rate	70%	70%	70%	55%	40%	25%	11%	11%	11%
Payout	30%	30%	30%	45%	60%	75%	89%	89%	89%
Growth	14%	14%	14%	11%	8%	5%	2%	2%	2%

Figure 5.4 The relationships between payout, retention, and growth

In the first three years we have an extraordinary growth (14%), while in the three subsequent years (the transition period) we observe a decay of the growth rate as a consequence of increased dividends paid out. Eventually, from the seventh year we move to a stable growth phase with a limited growth (2%), and a low retention of earnings (11%).

Considering that $ROE_1 = Net\ Income_1/BV_0$, if we know or have forecasted the earnings and/or the growth,[8] the payout ratio can be easily estimated using the previous equation. Once the payout ratio is computed it can be applied to the expected earnings to get the future dividends. Depending on the information we have or we can estimate reliably, the formula's elements can be used interchangeably.

Finally, a key aspect of banks' valuation, which sets this apart from the valuations of other non-financial companies is the treatment of the excess (deficit) capital, if any. This entity can be quantified as:

$$Excess\ (deficit)\ capital = (Optimal\ Tier\ 1\ capital - Actual\ Tier\ 1\ capital)$$
$$\times RWA \qquad (5.5)$$

In case the excess or deficit capital is significantly different from zero, the valuation should incorporate such element because it may have a severe impact

---

[8] To be more precise, if the current earnings (E_0) are known, we need just one of the two elements: either the growth rate (g) or the expected earnings (E_1). This is because the two are linked via the basic relation $= \frac{E_1 - E_0}{E_0}$.

on the intrinsic value of the bank. From a practical point of view, there are two possible strategies. The first one is to add the current excess/(deficit) to the value obtained running a DDM which assumes a balanced capital structure for future dividends:

$$Equity\ value = Excess\ (deficit)\ capital + DDM\ valuation \qquad (5.6)$$

In other words, the *Excess (deficit) capital* is treated as a lump sum which will not affect the bank in future. Alternatively, the DDM assumes that future dividends (in one or more years) will be increased in case of excess capital and decreased in case of deficit capital till the bank capital eventually converges on the optimal level. However, the two situations are not symmetric. While an excess capital situation does not usually raise any concern (except potentially for shareholders since their returns are somehow diluted) and can be dealt with over time, severe deficit capital situations tend to be urgent because of possible solvency concerns and supervision authorities' sanctions. Therefore, deficit capital situations should be addressed quickly, and from a valuation point of view, this implies that the equity value should embed the capital shortage as a one-off current charge. This is apparent also from Figure 5.5 where the capitalization rates of a large sample of

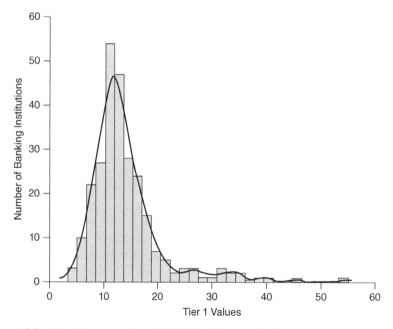

Figure 5.5   Tier 1 (as percentage of RWA) for European banks

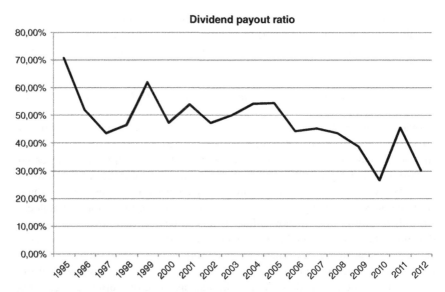

Figure 5.6   Evolution of the payout ratio of the 30 largest global banks

European banks are shown: while the cases of low capitalizations (left tail of the distribution) are limited, the situations generously above the average are numerous (right tail).

In general, DDM has historically been amongst the favorite approaches for bank valuation because banks (along with utilities) tend to meet the two main conditions that make DDM valuations particularly accurate: namely, a high payout ratio and stable/visible expected results. Following the financial crisis, this appears no longer true with banks' dividends that tend now to be extremely erratic. Figure 5.6 shows the payout ratio for the 30 largest global financial institutions: while in the decade 1995–2005 the ratio was mostly above 50%, since the initial eruption of the financial crisis in 2007 the ratio has drifted downwards.

Still, with due caution, DDM is likely to remain a key approach for the valuation of banks. As mentioned, potentially this approach can effectively be applied also to financial companies that have a low payout ratio or pay no dividend at all. In this case, the analyst has to determine what the payable dividend would be, given the relationships between payout ratio, ROE, and growth. But in such circumstances, the use of the equity cash flow method would generally prove more appropriate.

Figure 5.7 shows the share price and the dividend per share of large US banks sample: there is a rather clear relationship between the two as the price is a function of the dividend.

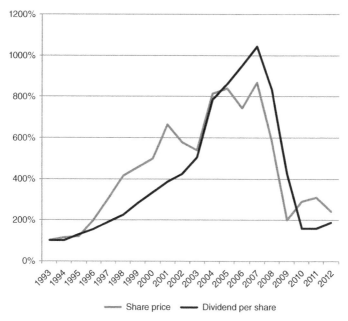

Figure 5.7   Share price and dividend per share evolution for large US banks
Source: data from SNL.

The H and Three-Stages Models

The H DDM model is structured as a two-stage model, but instead of assuming a constant growth rate over the initial period, it considers that the growth rate will decay linearly over time to reach the stable growth phase. The assumption of the H model is therefore that the high initial growth rate (g_i) will decline after the extraordinary growth phase which is assumed to last 2H years. The value per share of the H DDM can be written as follows:

$$P_0 = \frac{DPS_0 \times (1 + g_s)}{k_e - g_s} + \frac{DPS_0 \times H \times (g_i - g_s)}{k_e - g_s} \qquad (5.7)$$

If, for example, the current dividend per share at a bank is €0.80, the cost of capital is 10%, the stable growth rate is 2%, the initial high growth rate is 12%, and the extraordinary growth rate is expected to last 6 years, then the value per share is:

$$P_0 = \frac{0.80 \times (1 + 2\%)}{10\% - 2\%} + \frac{0.80 \times (6/2) \times (12\% - 10\%)}{10\% - 2\%} = €13.20 \quad (5.8)$$

While the H model has the advantage of following a growth decay that looks more "natural" than a sudden drop (like the one assumed in the two-stage model), its implicit assumption is that the payout ratio is constant through both growth phases - and this is inconsistent given the relationship between payout ratio and growth.

An alternative approach is the three-stages DDM framework. When the bank is expected to grow at a sustained rate (g_x) for a certain number of years ($n1$ years), and after that the growth will slow down (g_m) for a further period of time ($n2$ years) to eventually converge (after $n1 + n2$ years) on the stable growth rate (g_s), the following model can be used:

$$P_0 = \sum_{t=1}^{n1} \frac{DPS_0 \times (1 + g_x)^t}{(1 + k_e)^t} + \sum_{z=1}^{n2} \frac{DPS_0 \times (1 + g_x)^{n1} \times (1 + g_m)^z}{(1 + k_e)^{n1+z}}$$

$$+ \frac{\dfrac{DPS_0 \times (1 + g_x)^n \times (1 + g_m)^z \times (1 + g_s)}{k_e - g_s}}{(1 + k_e)^{n1+n2}} \qquad (5.9)$$

5.2.3   The Cash Flow to Equity Model

As mentioned, due to bank peculiarities, the definition of banks' Free Cash Flow to Equity (FCFE) is different from the one used in nonfinancial companies for at least two reasons. First, financing and investments are key elements of bank core activity and cannot be effectively disentangled from the bank's comprehensive income. The implication is that the Net Income can be assumed, to start with, as a gross proxy of the free cash flow available to shareholders. Second, the strict banking capital regulations imply that if there is an expansion of the risky assets base, the net income generated cannot be freely distributed to shareholders but a portion (or all) of it has to be retained by the bank in order to meet the regulatory capital requirements. Furthermore, if the earnings are not enough a capital increase has to be planned. Specularly, a contraction of the bank risky assets may free up a portion of the capital, thus increasing the cash flow freely distributable to shareholders. In other terms, from the shareholders' point of view, the only investments that matters and has to be accounted for is the equity investment/(divestment) done to comply with prudential regulation in association with any foreseeable change in equity capital (i.e., capital raise, buy-backs). At time t, the FCFE for bank valuation is therefore:[9]

$$FCFE_t = Net\ Income_t \pm Equity\ Investment\ in\ Regulatory\ Capital_t$$

$$\pm Planned\ Change\ in\ Equity\ Capital \qquad (5.10)$$

---

[9] Under the US GAAP, the definition of the FCFE should be complemented by adding the bank Other Comprehensive Income (OCI) so that $FCFEt = Net\ Income_t \pm Equity\ Investment\ in\ Regulatory\ Capital_t + OCI_t$. The main (noncash) items included in OCI are net unrealized gains and losses on certain investments, net unrealized gains and losses on hedging activities, adjustments to pension liabilities, and foreign-currency translation items. Apart from the historical and current level of FCFE, when preparing the cash flow forecast for the bank valuation is usually advisable to assume future OCI as null, because the erratic nature of the related items make their estimation questionable and on average they should be equal to zero.

where the *Equity Investment in Regulatory Capital* is the difference between the total equity capital held by bank at time $t-1$, and then to be held by the bank at time t on the basis of the target Tier 1 ratio and of the expected RWA. For banks expanding their RWA base, the sign of such difference is negative implying that the Net Income should be netted of the mandatory equity investment, the opposite is true for banks shrinking their RWA. *Change in Equity Capital* refers, as mentioned, to the planned (if any) capital increases or reductions.

In defining how much equity capital the bank has to invest to comply with capital regulation, it is advisable to use not just the minimum level of capital indicated by the national authority but rather a "market" level that is the threshold investors consider appropriate given the specific market conditions – in fact, a certain buffer above the minimum capital requirements is usually expected and the buffer may depend on the country and on the macro-financial circumstances. Such a market level should therefore be identified considering the analysts' opinion and the average degree of capitalization similar banks have at the time the valuation is carried out. While there is no formal algorithm to estimate "the optimal capitalization" it is essential (especially when a bank appears relatively under-capitalized) to understand what market expectations are and to factor in such considerations.

In depth analyses and detailed forecasts are needed when computing the FCFE for bank valuation, because the evolution of the RWA has first to be forecasted punctually. The equity valuation of a financial institution, depending on the specific growth pattern, can be estimated using one of the three main approaches as seen previously for the DDM (Table 5.3).

Both the DDM and the Cash Flow Model estimate the equity value as a function of the discounted stream of cash flow available to shareholders. What are the differences between the two then? The FCFE defined as net income minus the required investment in regulatory capital is, in fact, the maximum earning dividend

Table 5.3   The three main Cash Flow to Equity approaches to value banks

Model design	Formula
One-stage	$Equity\ Value_0 = \dfrac{FCFE_1}{k_e - g_s}$
Two-stages	$Equity\ Value_0$ $= \displaystyle\sum_{t=1}^{n} \dfrac{FCFE_0 \times (1 + g_x)^t}{(1 + k_e)^t} + \dfrac{\dfrac{FCFE_0 \times (1 + g_x)^n \times (1 + g_s)}{k_e - g_s}}{(1 + k_e)^n}$
Year-by-year	$Equity\ Value_0 = \displaystyle\sum_{t=1}^{n} \dfrac{FCFE_t}{(1 + k_e)^t} + \dfrac{\dfrac{FCFE_{n+1}}{k_e - g_s}}{(1 + k_e)^n}$

that a bank can distribute at a given time. If the bank policy is to return all the distributable income to shareholders, then the yearly dividends are equal to FCFE, and the equity valuation using the two valuation approaches is identical.

In practice, financial institutions (along many non-financial companies) do usually pursue a "dividend smoothing" policy, which implies that dividends actually paid may be lower than the ones potentially distributable. Such a prudential approach aims at piling up cash reserves that can be used in years with less rosy results, thus keeping the dividends constant in the medium term. Alternatively, tax reasons or managerial strategies (e.g., planned acquisitions) may lead the bank to pay dividends lower than the potential ones. As a consequence, the DDM valuation of financial companies with a somehow conservative dividend policy will be lower than the one obtainable by applying the equity cash flow model. In cases of banks paying higher dividends than the current results would allow (typically, to satisfy shareholders or to convey positive signals to the financial market), the reverse situation would apply.

The DCF approach also consents modeling the equity change associated with the rebalancing of the regulatory capital structure directly. Similar to what was seen for the DDM, in practice the current excess/(deficit) can be added to the value obtained running the DCF:

$$Equity\ value = Excess\ (deficit)\ capital + DCF\ valuation \qquad (5.11)$$

Alternatively, and in a more intuitive way than when dealing with DDM, the excess capital is added to the expected equity cash flow either as a one-off or by spreading it over more years.

To conclude, while in practice the DDM is used widely to value financial institutions, the equity cash flow approach is rarely applied. In most cases, the bank DCF valuation is more costly in terms of analyses and forecasting effort. In fact, in order to compute the FCFE, not only the estimation of future net income is required, but also an in depth forecast of RWA structure and evolution is necessary. For banks with relatively high payout policies the DDM is therefore generally recommended. On the contrary, when current and expected dividends do not appear to reflect adequately the profitability of the bank, and when there is substantial excess capital to be embedded in future cash flows, the use of the DCF approach tends to be more accurate.

5.2.4   The Excess Return Model

Although excess return models are run in many ways,[10] they are all based on the principle that the corporate value is equal to the sum of the invested capital at the time of the valuation and of the present value of the excess returns expected to be generated in future – the excess return being the difference between the return

---

[10] For example, the Economic Value Added or EVA® by Stern Stewart is a popular excess return valuation framework.

on invested capital and the cost of capital itself. Since we assume an equity-side valuation for financial institutions, the value can be written as:

$$Equity\ Value_0 = Equity\ Capital_0 + \sum_{t=1}^{\infty} \frac{Excess\ Return_t}{(1 + k_e)^t} \qquad (5.12)$$

where *Equity Capital* is the amount of equity capital currently invested in the financial institution, and k_e is the usual cost of equity. The *Excess Return* at time *i* can be alternatively defined as:

$$Excess\ Return_t = (ROE_t - k_e) \times Equity\ Capital_{t-1} \qquad (5.13)$$

or

$$Excess\ Return_t = Net\ Income_t - (k_e \times Equity\ Capital_{t-1}) \qquad (5.14)$$

Excess return models may be applied on the basis of the growth pattern and data available according to the three designs already presented for DDM and DCF. In Table 5.4, BV is the Book Value of the Equity or Equity Capital, g_s is the stable growth rate, ROE_x is the Return on Equity in the extraordinary growth phase. Again the difference between the two-stage and a year-by-year model relies on the fact that for the former, a unique constant growth rate is assumed for the first stage, while for the latter *ad hoc* forecasts of the ROE (or net income) are made on a yearly basis for the explicit forecast period, and beyond that a Terminal Value is estimated and discounted. In practice, it's not uncommon to assume that in the stable growth phase the ROE will converge on the cost of capital (i.e., $ROE_s = k_e$) because in the long-term, with the erosion of any competitive advantage, it's unlikely or extremely difficult for a bank to be able to generate a return significantly higher than the cost of capital. In such case, the Terminal Value is assumed equal to zero.

The Excess Return Models are frequently used in practice because ROE is a profitability measure that is easily available in the banking industry because it is widely assumed as a key performance measure and often banks communicate to

Table 5.4 The three main excess return approaches to valuing banks

Model design	Formula
One-stage	$Equity\ Value_0 = BV_0 + \dfrac{Excess\ Return_1}{k_e - g_s}$
Two-stages	$Equity\ Value_0 = BV_0 + \sum_{t=1}^{n} \dfrac{(ROE_x - k_e) \times BV_{t-1}}{(1 + k_e)^t} + \dfrac{\frac{(ROE_s - k_e) \times BV_n}{k_e - g_s}}{(1 + k_e)^n}$
Year-by-year	$Equity\ Value_0 = BV_0 + \sum_{t=1}^{n} \dfrac{(ROE_t - k_e) \times BV_{t-1}}{(1 + k_e)^t} + \dfrac{\frac{(ROE_s - k_e) \times BV_n}{k_e - g_s}}{(1 + k_e)^n}$

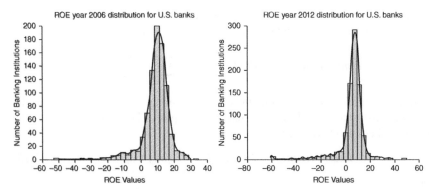

Figure 5.8   The ROE distribution of the listed US banks

investors what their target ROE is. Moreover, ROE makes comparisons among homogeneous banks possible, and allows us to draw insights and to support forecasts about the expected level of profitability banks will converge on. Such a level should be intended to be a long-term sustainable one, and it should not be based solely on the observed current ROE but should be integrated with the analysis of historical trend and a forecast of future industry dynamics. Figure 5.8 shows a comparison of the ROE distribution for all the listed US banks in a pre-crisis versus a "crisis" year. In 2006 the mean ROE was 9.5% (std. dev. 7.9) while in 2012 the mean ROE was only 5.5% (std. dev. 10.7): whether the long-term ROE will recover and return to the pre-crisis level is a judgment to be left to valuator knowledge and analysis.

Finally, similarly to what happens for non-financial companies, excess return measures can be used to structure remuneration packages by linking, for example, the spread $ROE-k_e$ achieved by the management in a certain period to a variable compensation. Similar to what was discussed when we introduced other discounted results approaches, if there is substantial current excess/(deficit) capital at the bank, such a value should be added to the value obtained running the model:

$$Equity\ value = Excess\ (deficit)\ capital + Excess\ return\ valuation \quad (5.15)$$

If such approach is followed, the ROE used to estimate the excess return should be computed consistently: ROE should be netted of the effect of excess capital. In fact, the stable presence of the excess capital may compress the ROE because a significant portion of the capital is assumed to be invested in assets with low or null risk: such assets are "safe" from a capital regulation point of view (so no capital has to be put aside against it) but yield little or no return at all. To avoid double-counting the impact of excess capital, the ROE should be adjusted accordingly:

$$Adjusted\ ROE = \frac{Net\ Income - [EXC \times r_f \times (1 - t_r)]}{Equity\ Book\ Value - EXC} \quad (5.16)$$

where *EXC* is the excess capital, r_f is the risk free rate (whose proxy can be the return of bills issued by a triple-A sovereign), and t_r is the corporate marginal tax rate.

As a closing remark, the three Discounted Return Models should yield the same valuation result as long as the assumptions are consistent and the formulas are used coherently. The peculiarities of the bank to be valued, the granularity of the data available about the bank and its comparables, and the modeling effort made by the valuator are all elements playing a role in the choice.

To sum up, DDM works well with financial institutions whose "dividend policy" is not biased by conservative (or aggressive) management policies or by other elements such as tax considerations. If the payout appears consistent with the profitability of the bank, then actual and expected dividends can be used as proper ingredients of the valuation process. The equity cash flow valuation is, on the contrary, based on a sort of "reverse engineering" of the dividends by working on the gross net income diminished by the investment in regulatory equity capital to be set aside: the resulting cash flow is the measure of the potential maximum dividend deliverable to shareholders. As such the FCFE is most precise measure of how much the bank equity capital is worth. Finally, excess return models allow us to distinguish between the value already in place at the bank and the value that is going to be created in future.

5.3   RELATIVE VALUATION

The basic principle the relative valuation techniques are based on is that similar assets should have similar prices on the market. Along this line, when valuing a financial company if there are institutions (comparable to the one to be valued) whose shares are traded in an efficient market, then their price can provide a reliable value estimate for the company under analysis. Moving from theory to practice, the apparent simplicity of the principle conceals a wealth of assumptions and analyses that have to be made in order to perform an accurate relative valuation. The three main sensitivities of relative valuations are the following:

Comparables. There is no such a thing as two identical companies. The identification of comparables is a highly subjective process where the inclusion or exclusion of any company is left to the judgment and experience of the valuator. As far as possible, it is therefore paramount to work on a reasonable set of criteria for the choice: among them, the key ones are the size, the business model, and the geographical scope (e.g., a large US investment bank is, for example, unlikely to be a good comparable for a small French commercial bank). The business model criteria should be considered at the most granular level possible: if the pool of comparables is large enough the selection criteria should not be limited to commercial versus investment

banking model but consider also other aspects such as the portfolio of ser-
vices/products offered (e.g., loans vs. mortgages, trading vs. advisory), the
client served (e.g., commercial vs. personal), and the financing structure
(e.g., deposits vs. securities). The selection criteria may also include the
performance/profitability (e.g., ROE), the growth potential, or the account-
ing/reporting principles. There is clearly a trade-off between the number of
comparables included in the panel (the more the comparables, the lower the
room for statistic bias), and the strictness of the criteria used (the stricter the
criteria, the more likely the valuation is accurate). The decision of relaxing
the selection criteria therefore comes at a cost, and only a deep understanding
of the banks to potentially be included determines the ultimate quality of the
valuation.

Meaningful price. The share (or equity) prices of the comparables picked for
the relative valuation should not be biased. Possible sources of distortion may
be market illiquidity and inefficiency, especially when prices come from the
deal markets. We are going to specifically present the considerations to be
made when dealing with "deal multiples" originated in M&A transactions.
When dealing with "market multiples" the valuator should assess whether
there are liquidity or specific market/corporate features that might influence
the price, and select accordingly the most appropriate reference price (e.g.,
closing price at the very day the valuation is done, average the price over the
past week or past month).

Multiple(s) choice. To perform a relative valuation, observed prices have to be
standardized usually by converting them into multiples of earnings, book values, or operating income. The question is then which value driver or multiple
to use, and depending on such a decision the accuracy of the valuation, as we
are going to see, may be severely impacted.

In the next paragraph we will review the practical issues of relative valuations,
highlighting both the advantages and the potential pitfalls associated with their
application to banks and other financial institutions.

Which Mean to Use?

One of the most important (and most overlooked) methodological decisions to
make when valuing a company is how to synthesize the information conveyed
by peers. Empirically, this translates into the question of what sort of multiples'
mean to adopt. The two most popular choices are the *arithmetic mean* and the
median value, and it is always good practice to report the maximum and
minimum values to identify the range to be considered.

Scholars do have a preference for the harmonic mean, which consistently
appears to be the most accurate in large sample empirical analyses. Technically,
the harmonic mean is the reciprocal of the arithmetic mean of the multiples'

reciprocals. Let's assume, for example, that we have the P/E (based on the market capitalization over total earnings) of three comparables. Their values are respectively 20/2, 62/2, and 12/1: the arithmetic mean is 17.7. Instead, the harmonic mean is:

$$Harmonic\ mean = \frac{1}{\left(\frac{2}{20} + \frac{2}{62} + \frac{1}{12}\right)/3} = 13.9 \tag{5.17}$$

Harmonic mean allows us to smooth out the impact of extreme value (in this case the multiple of the second comparable).

Aggregate multiples are based on the ratio between the sum of comparables market capitalizations and the sum of the value drivers considered. For example, assuming the data from the example above, the aggregate multiple would be:

$$Aggregate \frac{P}{E} = \frac{20 + 62 + 12}{2 + 2 + 1} = 18.8 \tag{5.18}$$

With aggregate multiples larger companies tend to have a higher weight: in this case the second bank, which happens to have the highest capitalization, drives the multiple upwards. In practice, the valuator should assess whether significant variation in the market capitalizations' of the comparables makes the aggregate multiple biased and unreliable.

	P/E Current 2012A	P/E Forward 2013E	P/BV 2012A	P/TBV 2012A
JP Morgan Chase & Co.	9,2x	8,6x	0,93x	1,26x
Bank of America Corporation	47,9x	12,1x	0,59x	0,90x
Citigroup Inc	11,6x	9,6x	0,73x	0,87x
Wells Fargo & Company	10,9x	9,9x	1,3x	1,7x
Bank of New York Mellon Corporation	13,5x	12,0x	0,90x	2,55x
U.S. Bancorp	11,7x	10,9x	1,82x	2,59x
Capital One Financial Corporation	8,6x	8,3x	0,76x	1,23x
State Street Corporation	14,6x	12,9x	1,30x	2,23x
BB&T Corporation	11,1x	10,6x	1,11x	1,82x
SunTrust Banks, Inc.	7,8x	10,4x	0,74x	1,09x
Mean	14,7x	10,5x	1,0x	1,6x
Median	11,4x	10,5x	0,9x	1,5x
Minimum	7,8x	8,3x	0,6x	0,9x
Maximum	47,9x	12,9x	1,8x	2,6x
Harmonic mean	11,5x	10,3x	0,9x	1,4x
Aggregate multiple	16,6x	10,1x	1,0x	1,4x

> The arithmetic mean (more than the median or the harmonic mean) may suffer for the presence of outliers in the comparable panel. In the case above, Bank of America's current P/E appears significantly different from the other values and it would be appropriate to drop it from the sample. Without BofA's multiple, the arithmetic mean of the sample would move from 14.7 to 11, with huge implications in terms of valuation.

5.3.1 Market Multiples

The use of market multiples is widespread among finance practitioners for financial companies as it is for non-financial ones. Most M&A valuation, equity research reports, and investment decisions are made by comparing a bank to comparable banks via P/E and P/BV multiples. The two multiples are by far the most popular ones for the valuation of financial institutions, but other multiples can be used as well. Before introducing the various multiples, it is worth recalling some common definitions that will be used going forward.

Depending on the denominator, multiples can be *current*, *trailing*, or *forward* (aka *leading*). Working on, for example, the P/E ratio, while the numerator (the price) is always the observed current one, the denominator (the earnings) can refer to:

- the total earnings recorded on the last yearly period (E_0) for which an annual report or company statement is available, and in this case the multiple is *current*;
- the sum of the earnings recorded over the last four quarters (E_{LTM} where LTM stands for "Last Twelve Months") for which a quarterly report or company statement is available, and in this case the multiple is *trailing*;
- the expected earnings over the next (E_1) or subsequent years (usually, E_2 or E_3) based on company's estimates or analysts' consensus. Forward multiples tend to perform better, because they are based on future results and the value of assets is more the function of future results than the past ones.

We stressed that the valuation of financial companies should be equity-side. Coherently, also all the multiples used for banks are equity-side. In particular, the numerator of the ratio is, as usual, the current price (either per share or as total market capitalization). The denominator can refer to other financial statement items such as the Earnings or the Equity Book Value. In Table 5.5 the multiples currently used to value banks are defined.

For banks, the two most popular multiples are the P/E and the P/BV. The P/E, which appears to be investors' favorite even outside the financial sector, should be based on "normalized earnings" that are the earnings adjusted to remove unusual or one-time influences. The unusual elements may be the extraordinary items, the charges for discontinued operations, and all the other one-time charges that, reasonably, it's unlikely will materialize again in forthcoming years. The normalization of earnings is a subjective process mostly left to the judgment and

Table 5.5 The multiples for the valuation of banks

Multiple	Driver	Per share multiple = Equity multiple
Price/Earnings (P/E)	Earnings	$\dfrac{Price\ per\ share}{Earnings\ per\ share} = \dfrac{Market\ Capitalization}{Net\ Income}$
Price/Book Value (P/BV)	Book Value of the Equity	$\dfrac{Price\ per\ share}{BV\ per\ share} = \dfrac{Market\ Capitalization}{BV}$
Price/Tangible Book Value (P/TBV)	Tangible Book Value (= Book Value of the Equity – Intangible Assets)	$\dfrac{Price\ per\ share}{TBV\ per\ share} = \dfrac{Market\ Capitalization}{TBV}$
Price/Deposits	Deposits	$\dfrac{Price\ per\ share}{Deposits\ per\ share} = \dfrac{Market\ Capitalization}{Deposits}$
Price/Revenues	Revenues	$\dfrac{Price\ per\ share}{Revenues\ per\ share} = \dfrac{Market\ Capitalization}{Revenues}$
Price/Operating Income	Operating Income before Extraordinary Items and Taxes	$\dfrac{Price\ per\ share}{Operating\ Income\ per\ share} = \dfrac{Market\ Capitalization}{Operating\ Income}$
Price/Net Asset Value (P/NAV)	Net Asset Value	$\dfrac{Price\ per\ share}{NAV\ per\ share} = \dfrac{Market\ Capitalization}{NAV}$
Price/Pre-Provision-Profit (P/PPP)	Total net revenue less noninterest expense	$\dfrac{Price\ per\ share}{PreProvision\ Profit\ per\ share} = \dfrac{Market\ Capitalization}{Pre\ Provision\ Profit}$
Price/Assets Under Management (P/AUM)	Assets Under Management	$\dfrac{Price\ per\ share}{AUM\ per\ share} = \dfrac{Market\ Capitalization}{AUM}$
P/Branches	Number of branches	$\dfrac{Price\ per\ share}{Number\ of\ branches\ per\ share} = \dfrac{Market\ Capitalization}{Number\ of\ branches}$

experience of the valuator: so when third parties will use the valuation outcome, it's always advisable to provide an explicit justification for the adjustments made.

Coherently with the importance of the equity capital in the banking industry, P/BV is a key multiple for the valuation of banks.

Should Multiples be Adjusted for Excess Capital?

If a bank maintains substantial excess capital, its multiples may be biased because the presence of excess capital weakens the relationship between the share price and the value driver.

Excess capital is the capital the bank may dispose of freely because it is not set aside against risky assets on the balance sheet: therefore it may be assumed that such capital is invested in low-risk or even risk-free investments and arguably its "market price" is strictly close to the book value. As a consequence, for example, the P/BV ratio is pushed towards one, thus distorting the multiple.

In such a situation, it may be appropriate to adjust the multiple. As an example, let's assume that a certain comparable bank X has a Book Value of the Equity equal to $ 50B and a current market capitalization of $75B: the P/BV multiple would be equal to 1.5. If for the banks the optimal capital (from a regulatory and market perspective) is $ 32B, there appears to be an excess capital of $ 18B (= $50B − $32B). The multiple can be adjusted by deducting the excess capital value from both the numerator and denominator of the P/BV ratio:

$$Adjusted\frac{P}{BV} = \frac{75B - 18B}{50B - 18B} = 1.8 \qquad (5.19)$$

The adjusted multiple taking into account the effect of the excess capital is 20% higher than the original one.

A similar approach can be used for the P/E multiple. In this case, while the excess capital is deducted from the numerator, the earnings (net of taxes) associated with such excess capital are deducted from the denominator. In order to estimate the earnings net of the excess capital effects, it may be assumed that the excess capital is invested in risk-less securities such as short-term triple-A rated governments' bills. Therefore, the income (net of taxes) generated by assuming the excess capital is entirely invested in risk-less securities is deducted from the total earnings of the bank in the P/E multiple denominator.

The accuracy of valuation based solely on the P/Revenues or P/Deposits multiple is usually limited as these are "indirect" multiples that say little about the income generation ability of the bank. Nevertheless, in many instances they can provide useful valuation insights, especially when used along other multiples or valuation approaches. On the contrary, multiples based on a direct measure of a bank's profitability are the P/Operating Income or the P/Pre-Provision Profit.

The Net Asset Value (NAV), as we will see in the next paragraphs, is a measure of the equity value which is obtained by deducting the market value of a bank's debt and claims from the market value of its assets. If all the assets and liabilities are at market value, the P/NAV will be higher than one only if investors consider that the bank has growth opportunities which are not (yet) reflected in the assets in place value. On the opposite, if P/NAV is lower than one the market is likely to believe that the bank is destroying value, arguably because the management is doing a poor job. The multiple P/Asset Under Management cannot be used properly for the valuation of entire banks but only, within a Sum Of The Parts approach (see following paragraphs) for the valuation of the asset management operations of diversified financial institutions. Finally, the P/Number of branches is a "business" multiple rather than a "financial one" because it is not based on a financial statement item but on an operations quantity. The multiple is clearly indicated for financial companies – mainly commercial banks – whose distribution model is mostly based on a branch network.

An alternative to the P/BV is the P/TBV with the numerator netted of the value of the intangible assets. The tangible book value is a rough proxy of the Tier 1 capital and it follows the same logic of excluding assets whose values are less solid in the sense that may/would be very difficult to recover those in case of bankruptcy or financial distress.

5.3.2   Deal Multiples

The stock market is not the only market that provides information about the equity prices of companies. The market for corporate control – the market where qualified minority stakes, majority stakes, or even the entire equity of companies are bought and sold – does convey price information as well. Similar to what was discussed for market multiples, the actual comparability to the banks under valuation is the key element. If a bank involved in a transaction for which precise data is available (i.e., percentage of capital bought, date, price paid, nature of the deal), then a meaningful multiple to use for valuation purposes can be extracted. In particular, deal multiples can provide useful data for M&A valuations because implicitly they contain information about the control premium magnitude.

However, by their very nature, the deal valuations are impacted by elements which may distort significantly the price recorded for a certain transaction. The analyst should therefore identify and investigate such potential sources of bias and, when possible, adjust the price accordingly. The four main sources of bias in deal prices are the following:

Payment method. Depending on the agreed payment method "shares for shares" versus "cash for shares" (or a mix of the two), the transaction price may differ significantly, being usually "shares for shares" deals relatively more inflated (because relatively less costly for the buyer's shareholders). Moreover, peculiar payment arrangements may take place among the parties involved in the transactions (e.g., earn-out payments) and overlooking such elements may leave the valuator with severely biased multiples.

Control premium and synergies. Majority transaction prices usually incorporate a control premium which reflects the right of the buyer to exercise legal or *de facto* control on the bought entity. Because of this premium, all else being equal, the value of a marginal or minority stake might be significantly lower (usually by 10–30%) than the price associated with a majority stake: therefore, using a multiple obtained from a majority transaction to value a minority stake for example, it's likely to lead to an inflated estimate. The most important justification for the control premium is the synergies that the buyer is expected to realize following the acquisition.

Time horizon. M&A deals are rarer than share trades on a stock exchange, or to put it in financial terms, the market for corporate control tends to be relatively illiquid. As a consequence, in order to collect enough observations, it is some- times necessary to include transactions that happened months or even several years before the moment the valuation was carried-out. But peculiar past mar- ket, macroeconomic, and financial situations may have impacted the prices paid for control or minority stakes, thus leading to multiples arguably differ- ent from the current ones. Importantly, M&A transactions happen sometimes in "waves" that may be the outcome of structural disruptions (i.e., regula- tory changes) but also of a sort industry acquisitive "exuberance." Figure 5.9 shows how dramatically the average P/E from large international banking deals changed from 2007 (still a "pre-financial crisis" phase for banks) to

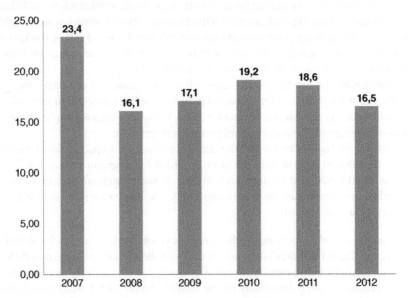

Figure 5.9   The implicit average P/E from banking M&A deals
Source: data from Zephyr.

the subsequent years. Deriving a multiple, which is in line with the 2007 average level, and applying it to a bank valued in 2012 may clearly result in an upward biased estimation.

Deal multiples can be useful input in the valuation process and in certain market situations or jurisdictions they may emerge as the most accurate valuation strategy, especially when the company to value is a party involved as a target or buyer in a M&A deal. But again the warning is that the level of complexity required by the use of such multiples is nevertheless higher than the one usually associated with market multiples, because they are likely to be affected by numerous transaction features that have to be identified and disentangled.

5.3.3 Multiples from Fundamentals

Technically speaking, these are not "relative valuations" because the value is not estimated in "relation" to comparable companies, but they are techniques that exploit the relative valuation tools, namely the multiples. In fact, this valuation technique relies on the decomposition of multiples by explicitly quantifying the relations between their fundamentals: once the equation that ties a multiple's fundamentals is defined, it is possible to estimate the multiple itself by just computing the value of fundamentals. Finally, once the multiple is obtained it can be applied to the company value driver, thus getting a "fair" estimate of the equity value. By construction, they are often also referred to as "fair multiples" or "justified multiples."

The starting point to decompose multiples is usually the stable growth DDM (our Gordon Growth Model) to estimate the current share price P_0:

$$P_0 = \frac{DPS_1}{k_e - g_s} \tag{5.20}$$

equivalent to:

$$P_0 = \frac{EPS_1 \times p_s}{k_e - g_s} \tag{5.21}$$

where the notations are the familiar ones and p_s is the payout ratio in stable growth. From formulas 5.20 and 5.21, it is possible to get both the current and the forward P/E:

$$\frac{P_0}{EPS_0} = \frac{(1 + g_s) \times p_s}{k_e - g_s} \tag{5.22}$$

$$\frac{P_0}{EPS_1} = \frac{p_s}{k_e - g_s} \tag{5.23}$$

The previous relations, in case of no growth, imply that:

$$\frac{P_0}{EPS_1} = \frac{P_0}{EPS_0} = \frac{p_s}{k_e} \qquad (5.24)$$

In case of positive growth, knowing that the payout ratio is a function of the expected growth rate and the return on equity (so that $p = 1 - g/ROE$), we can also write:

$$\frac{P_0}{EPS_1} = \frac{1 - \dfrac{g_s}{ROE_s}}{k_e - g_s} \qquad (5.25)$$

If the bank is already in stable growth, then formulas 5.20–5.25 can be used for computing a bank multiple just by replacing in the equation the observed or estimated fundamentals (ROE, growth, cost of equity, payout ratio). Once the multiple is estimated, it is straightforward to obtain the price per share.

What about the valuation of a bank that is not yet in stable growth? If an $n -$ years period of extraordinary growth (g_x) – with a payout ratio p_x – is expected for the bank and this will subsequently move to a stable growth phase, then we may start from a two-stages DDM written as such:

$$P_0 = \frac{EPS_0 \times p_x \times (1 + g_x) \times \left[1 - \dfrac{(1 + g_x)^n}{(1 + k_e)^n} \right]}{k_e - g_x}$$
$$+ \frac{\dfrac{EPS_0 \times (1 + g_x)^n \times p_s \times (1 + g_s)}{k_e - g_s}}{(1 + k_e)^n} \qquad (5.26)$$

This, in turn, thanks to some substitutions, delivers a decomposed current P/E multiple:

$$\frac{P_0}{EPS_0} = \frac{\left(1 - \dfrac{g_x}{ROE_x} \right) \times (1 + g_x) \times \left[1 - \dfrac{(1 + g_x)^n}{(1 + k_e)^n} \right]}{k_e - g_x}$$
$$+ \frac{\dfrac{\left(1 - \dfrac{g_s}{ROE_s} \right) \times (1 + g_x)^n \times (1 + g_s)}{k_e - g_s}}{(1 + k_e)^n} \qquad (5.27)$$

Again, by substituting the symbols in right-hand side of the equation with the estimated values, a fair multiple for a specific financial institution can be computed. Eventually, by applying the multiple to the bank current earnings, the equity valuation can be obtained.

In general, it is worth noting the role played by the fundamentals on the multiple: (1) the P/E ratio increases (for any given growth rate) as the payout ratios and returns on equity increase; (2) the P/E decreases as the riskiness as reflected in the cost of capital increases; and (3) the P/E increases as the growth rates increase (as long as ROE is higher than the cost of capital).

The same line of reasoning can be followed for the *P/BV* multiple and its determinants. Starting from the stable growth P/E_1 fundamentals presented earlier, and knowing that the expected earnings for next period are equal to the product $BV_0 \times ROE_1$, we obtain:

$$\frac{P_0}{BV_0 \times ROE_1} = \frac{p_s}{k_e - g_s} \tag{5.28}$$

from which, thanks to some substitutions, we eventually get:

$$\frac{P_0}{BV_0} = \frac{ROE_s - g_s}{k_e - g_s} \tag{5.29}$$

which leads us to:

$$P_0 = BV_0 \times \frac{ROE_s - g_s}{k_e - g_s} \tag{5.30}$$

The formula in 5.30 is also referred to as the *Warranted Equity Method* and is widely used in practice for the valuation of banks and insurance companies. The arrangement of the equation allows us also to appreciate the relevance of the "ROE − cost of capital" spread emerging from the last component of the formula $[(ROE - g)/(k - g)]$. If the spread is positive, then the bank is earning a return higher than the one expected by investors, therefore the bank is creating value and it is worth more than the current book value of its equity. The opposite is true when the spread is negative. Finally, in case the spread is equal to zero there is neither value creation nor value destruction, hence the bank is exactly worth its book value.

It's worth mentioning that the *P/TBV* multiple can be treated in the same way. Depending on the presence or not of the growth, the multiples are respectively:

$$\frac{P_0}{TBV_0} = \frac{ROTE_s - g_s}{k_e - g_s} \tag{5.31}$$

and

$$\frac{P_0}{TBV_0} = \frac{ROTE_s}{k_e} \tag{5.32}$$

where a consistent Return On Tangible Equity (*ROTE*) replaces the *ROE* (the *ROTE* being equal to the ratio between Earnings and the Tangible Book Value).

In case there is a growth pattern encompassing n-years high growth period first and a stable growth later, having defined the return on equity as $ROE = EPS_0/BV_0$ then, similar to what we have seen for the P/E two-stages decomposition, we get:

$$\frac{P_0}{BV_0} = ROE \times \frac{p_x \times (1 + g_x) \times \left[1 - \dfrac{(1 + g_x)^n}{(1 + k_e)^n} \right]}{k_e - g_x}$$
$$+ \frac{ROE \times \left[\dfrac{p_s \times (1 + g_x)^n \times (1 + g_s)}{k_e - g_s} \right]}{(1 + k_e)^n} \tag{5.33}$$

By substituting the estimated values in the right-hand section of the formula, it is possible to compute a *P/BV* multiple from fundamentals that, in turn, can be used to compute the equity value.

5.3.4   Value Maps and Other Regressions

Building on the analysis of multiples' fundamentals, to value financial institutions it is common practice to regress a multiple such as the *P/BV* against a measure of profitability like the ROE for a panel of comparable banks. Usually a simple linear regression is performed, and if the regression line fits reasonably well the set of data – the coefficient of determination (R^2) is assumed as an indicative measure of the fitting[11] – the regression line itself can become a valuation or investment selection tool. The basic intuition of this approach is that the profitability is the major driver of the banks' market valorization; therefore a certain level of profitability should affect (in a linear and/or non-linear manner) the multiple. The regression is usually presented through graphs called "Value Maps." Figure 5.10 shows, for example, a least-squares regression for 44 large European commercial banks. The first regression is linear and the second is quadratic. They both seem to have a good fit for the data: the R^2 is 0.48 for the linear model and 0.54 for the quadratic one. The coefficients indicate that the quadratic curve fits the data better than the linear one, so it's the regression of preference (we do not discuss here the theory and procedures for curve fitting, but most spreadsheet packages currently in circulation include functions and algorithms to perform regressions and best-fitting analyses).

From an investor's point of view, the value map can be a useful tool to make investment decisions. Banks below (and significantly distant from) the regression line (or curve) can be considered, all the rest being equal, as undervalued and

---

[11] For valuation purposes the R^2 coefficient could be sufficient as a rough indication of the regression or curve fitting. But for more accurate analyses, more advanced econometrics tools are required. A good starting reference is Studenmund, A.H. (2011), *Using Econometrics: A Practical Guide*, Pearson.

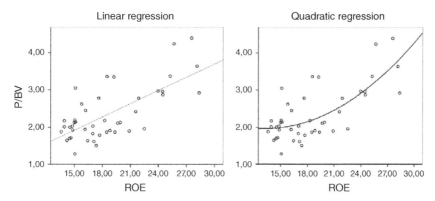

Figure 5.10 Value maps for a sample of European banks

therefore as investment opportunities. Specularly, banks above the regression line appear to be overvalued and are therefore potential divestment or shorting candidates. Finally, the banks positioned on the line or close to that, emerge as fairly valued by the market and they appear to deserve a "neutral" investment recommendation. Of course, value maps just offer a partial view of the value determinants and they overlook other potential factors impacting the multiple. In the example previously, the evidence is that ROE is an important element for multiples but definitely not the only one: statistically, half of the variance of the data remains unexplained or, to be more precise, could be explained by factors different from the ROE.

Apart from being a tool for portfolio decisions, value maps are straightforward to use as an equity valuation technique. For example, assuming that the 44 banks examined before are all adequately comparable to a bank we would like to evaluate. The regression equation expressing the quadratic curve for the banks is:

$$\frac{P_0}{BV_0} = 3.412 - 0.218ROE + 0.008ROE^2 \tag{5.34}$$

Knowing that the bank we are valuing has a ROE = 14.54%, by using such input in the equation we get a P/BV of 1.93. Considering then that the current Book Value of the equity for the bank is €3924M, we conclude that a fair valuation for the bank's equity would be €7587M.

When valuing a financial institution the regression of the P/BV multiple against ROE is a very popular choice, but other combinations of variables may perform equally or even better. In terms of multiples, the P/E ratio is usually an alternative good candidate, while in terms of profitability measures possible choices are: the Return On Average Equity (ROAE) that is the return over the mean of the current and expected equity book value, the Return On Tangible Equity (ROTE) that is a ROE computed on the Tangible Equity (Book Value of the Equity net of the intangible assets), the Return On Assets (ROA) that is the ratio between the operating income and the total assets, and the Return On Net Asset Value (RONAV) that is the ratio between net income and NAV (whose definition will be provided in the next paragraph).

Some warnings have to be cast about the preparation of value maps. The actual comparability of the banks included in the regression is key as usual. A trade-off between the number of comparables and the strictness of the comparability criteria does apply and has to be managed by the valuator. As shown in the previous example, a linear regression is not always the best approach: the goodness of fit of non-linear solutions should be explored in order to catch more precisely the nature of the relation between multiple and fundamentals. Finally, as for ROE and other profitability measures, the use of expected values rather than current ones is recommended. In fact, expected values do incorporate the growth element as well and so they add to the explanatory power of the regression. Actually, in case the industry analysis shows that the banks are expected to experience different growth patterns, the regression of the multiples may be run against the growth rate itself (g).

If the panel of comparable financial institutions is rather large, an alternative valuation strategy is to perform a regression of the multiples against more than one fundamental, thus overcoming the major limitation of value maps. For example, the regression may include the multiple as a dependent variable and several fundamentals – such as ROE, expected growth, beta (a proxy of bank's risk), or the level of capitalization – as independent variables. Other additional firm-level variables may be added to understand more granularly what elements do have an impact on the multiple. For example, we performed a regression using the data from the 136 largest listed US banks in 2012. The multiple (dependent variable) considered is the current *P/BV*, while the assumed multiple determinants (independent variables) are the long-term growth rate (g_s) forecasted by analysts, the Tier 1 Ratio (TR), the stock beta, and the return on the average book value of equity (ROAE). By running the regression, we obtain:

$$P/BV = 123.27 + 0.27 \text{ Growth} + 1.06 \text{ TR} - 54.00 \text{ Beta} + 2.94 \text{ ROAE}$$
$$[7.36] \quad\quad [0.74] \quad\quad [1.37] \quad\quad [-5.28] \quad\quad [6.84] \quad\quad\quad (5.35)$$

The R^2 of the regression is 49.60%, and the t-test statistics are shown under the independent variables. The signs of the determinants are coherent with predictions: growth, level of capitalization, and bank profitability contribute positively to the *P/BV* ratio, while the level of risk (reflected in the bank beta) has a negative impact. From a statistically point of view, the variables *Growth* and *TR* do not appear to be significant.[12] Actually, if we re-run the regression using only the last

---

[12] The evidence that the level of capitalization (Tier 1 Ratio) is not a statistically significant variable should not come as a surprise considering that, as we already mentioned, the level of leverage doesn't play an overwhelming role in defining the level of risk of banks.

two variables, we obtain a result with R^2 of 48.71% so not far from the previous result, but in this case we have a more parsimonious estimation model.

This sort of augmented regression can be used in two ways depending on the valuation purpose. On the one hand, it allows the identification of apparently undervalued or overvalued banks, thus suggesting possible investment (long or short) opportunities. On the other hand, the coefficient of the regression may be applied to a bank's fundamentals to compute the multiple and thus estimating the equity value.

5.4   ASSET/LIABILITY-BASED VALUATION

In asset/liability-based valuation, the existing asset value of a financial institution is first estimated and then the value of debt and other outstanding claims is deducted. The result is called the Net Asset Value (NAV) and it is a widely used measure of the equity value for banks and other financial companies and vehicles. This approach proves particularly useful for banks whose assets' market values appear to be significantly different from the book values. The reasons of such difference might be that the accounting criteria adopted allowed the bank to report items whose value is different from the fair market one (in case, for example, of historical cost accounting). Or it may be that, despite the adopted criteria is the marked-to-market, the market conditions have changed so dramatically since the moment the last financial statements were released, that the book values are in fact outdated. Once the possible areas of value divergence from the book numbers are identified, the valuator estimates what the market value of the assets and liabilities of the bank would be given the current market conditions. The technique simulates, therefore, what would happen in case the assets comprising the bank were sold (separately) on the market, and the same line of reasoning is followed for debt and liabilities. This perspective therefore simulates how much value would be left to shareholders in case the bank was to be liquidated. The asset/liability-based valuation approach therefore overlaps with the concept of "liquidation value."

For some assets, there might be a reliable market price to use as a reference: this is the case, for example, of merchant banks holding stakes in listed companies whose book value is prudentially reported using historical cost criteria (in jurisdictions where accounting principles allow to do so). The analyst in this case has just to assess how the asset-value of a bank would be affected if the current market price of the shareholdings was to be used. For most assets and liabilities reported in the financial statements of a bank, there is no market or the market appears illiquid and inefficient so the asset prices are not (fully) reliable. If the financial instruments pool of financial contracts cannot be valued on the basis of efficient market prices, their value should be estimated by discounting with an appropriate updated discount rate the expected future cash flows. Table 5.6 presents the main

Table 5.6 Formulas for the computation of market value of the main bank Balance Sheet items

Asset category	Market valuation model	Definition of variables
Interest-bearing time deposits	$MV = D\dfrac{(1+i_c)^n}{(1+i)^n}$	• D = deposit amount • i_c = contractual (coupon) rate • i = appropriate discount rate • N = fraction of the year remaining before maturity
Overnight funds	$MV = OF\dfrac{(1+i_c)^n}{(1+i)^n}$	• OF = amount of funds loaned
Treasury bills	$MV = M - M(i)\left(\dfrac{n}{360}\right)$	• M = maturity or face value • i = annual discount rate • N = number of days until maturity • $M(i)\left(\dfrac{n}{360}\right)$ = discount from face value
Treasury notes and bonds	$MV = \left[\displaystyle\sum_{t=1}^{n} \dfrac{\dfrac{(M)(CR)}{m}}{\left(1+\dfrac{i}{m}\right)^t}\right] + \left[\dfrac{M}{\left(1+\dfrac{i}{m}\right)^n}\right]$	• M = maturity or face value • CR = coupon rate • M = number of times per year interest is paid • $\dfrac{(M)(CR)}{m}$ = periodic (semi-annual) interest payment • N = number of (semi-annual) periods before maturity • i = annual discount rate • T = time period
Zero-coupon bonds	$MV = \dfrac{M}{\left(1+\dfrac{i}{m}\right)^n}$	• M = maturity value • N = number of years until maturity

Repos

$$MV = \sum_{t=1}^{n} \left[\frac{CP_t}{\left(1 + \frac{i}{m}\right)^t} \right] + \frac{SP}{\left(1 + \frac{i}{m}\right)^n}$$

- CP = coupon payment that the bank receives before resale $= CR\frac{(M)}{m}$
- CR = coupon rate of securities purchased
- M = maturity value of securities purchased
- SP = selling price specified in resale agreement
- N = number of periods before resale
- i = appropriate discount rate

Consumer instalment loans

$$MV = \left(\frac{L}{PVIFA_{\frac{i_L}{m},n}} \right) \left(PVIFA_{\frac{i}{m},n} \right)$$

- $\dfrac{L}{PVIFA_{\frac{i_L}{m},n}}$ = implied periodic payment based on the loan amount (L) and the contractual rate (i_L)
- i = discount rate
- i_L = instalment loan nominal rate
- N = number of monthly payments until maturity
- M = number of months per period

Commercial loans – bullet

$$MV = \frac{L\left(1 + \frac{i_L}{m}\right)^n}{\left(1 + \frac{i}{m}\right)^n}$$

- L = loan amount
- i_L = loan rate
- i = discount rate
- N = number of periods before the loan matures
- M = number of times per year interest is compounded

Commercial loans – working capital

$$MV = \frac{\left[A\left(1 + i_{LC}\right)^n + (MX - A)\left(\left(1 + i_{CF}\right)^n - 1\right)\right]}{(1 + i)^n}$$

- A = actual borrowings to date
- MX = maximum credit available
- i_{LC} = interest rate on borrowings
- i = discount rate
- i_{CF} = commitment fee
- n = average maturity of lines of credit or average time before they are paid off

(continued)

Table 5.6 (*Continued*)

Asset category	Market valuation model	Definition of variables
Commercial loans – term instalment	$$MV = \left(\dfrac{L}{PVIFA_{\frac{i_L}{m},n}} \right) \left(PVIFA_{\frac{i}{m},n} \right)$$	• $\dfrac{L}{PVIFA_{\frac{i_L}{m},n}}$ = periodic loan payments • i_L = contractual loan rate • i = discount rate • M = number of times per year that payments are made • N = number of monthly payments until maturity
Commercial loans – term interest only	$$MV = \left[L\left(\dfrac{i_L}{m} \right) \left(PVIFA_{\frac{i}{m},n} \right) \right] + \left[\dfrac{L}{\left(1 + \dfrac{i}{m} \right)^n} \right]$$	• $L\left(\dfrac{i_L}{m} \right)$ = periodic interest payment • i_L = contractual loan rate • i = discount rate • m = number of times per year that payments are made • n = number of monthly payments until maturity
Lease financing	$$MV = \left(\dfrac{L}{PVIFA_{\frac{i_L}{m},n}} \right) \left(PVIFA_{\frac{i}{m},n} \right) + R \left[\dfrac{1}{\left(1 + \dfrac{i}{m} \right)^n} \right]$$	• $\dfrac{L}{PVIFA_{\frac{i_L}{m},n}}$ = periodic lease payments • R = residual value • i_L = contractual lease rate • i = discount rate • m = number of times per year that payments are made • n = number of periods to lease terms
Real estate loans – fixed rate mortgages	$$MV = \left(\dfrac{L}{PVIFA_{\frac{i_L}{m},n}} \right) \left(PVIFA_{\frac{i}{m},n} \right)$$	• $\dfrac{L}{PVIFA_{\frac{i_L}{m},n}}$ = implied periodic payment based on the loan amount (L) and the contractual mortgage rate • i = discount rate • N = number of monthly payments until maturity • m = number of months per period

Real estate loans – balloon mortgages (interest only)	$$MV = \left[\dfrac{L\left(\dfrac{i_m}{m}\right)}{\left(PVIFA_{\frac{i}{m},n}\right)}\right] + L\left[\dfrac{1}{\left(1+\dfrac{i}{m}\right)^t}\right]$$	• $L = loan\ amount$ • $m = payments\ per\ year$ • $n\ or\ t = number\ of\ years\ (periods)$ • $L\left(\dfrac{i_m}{m}\right) = periodic\ interest\ payment$
Real estate loans – balloon mortgages (amortizing)	$$MV = \left(\dfrac{L}{PVIFA_{\frac{i}{m},n}}\right)\left[PVIFA_{\frac{i}{m},b} + B\left(\dfrac{1}{\left(1+\dfrac{i}{m}\right)^b}\right)\right]$$	• $B = Balloon\ (portion\ not\ amortized\ over\ the\ term\ of\ the\ loan)$
Non-accrual loans	$$MV = \sum_{t=1}^{n}\left[\dfrac{CF_t}{(1+i)^t}\right]$$	• $CF = adjusted\ anticipated\ cash\ flow\ in\ year\ t$ • $i = normal\ discount\ rate\ plus\ an\ additional\ risk\ premium$ • $N = number\ of\ periods$

Liability Category	Market valuation model	
Time deposits	$$MV = D\left(1+\dfrac{i_D}{m}\right)^n \dfrac{1}{\left(1+\dfrac{i}{m}\right)^n}$$	• $D = deposit\ amount$ • $i = market\ discount\ rate$ • $i_D = deposit\ rate$ • $m = number\ of\ times\ per\ year\ that\ interest\ is\ paid\ or\ compounded$ • $n = number\ of\ periods\ to\ deposit\ maturity$

(continued)

Table 5.6 (*Continued*)

Liability category	Market valuation model	Definition of variables
Short-term borrowings – repos	$$MV = \sum_{t=1}^{n} \left[\frac{CP_t}{\left(1 + \frac{i}{m}\right)^t} \right] + \frac{SP}{\left(1 + \frac{i}{m}\right)^n}$$	*For the definition of the variables involved in the computation please refer to the formula of repos appeared among assets*
Short-term borrowings – commercial papers	$$MV = M - M\,(i)\left(\frac{n}{360}\right)$$	• $M = $ *maturity or face value* • $i = $ *annual discount rate* • $N = $ *number of days until maturity* • $M\,(i)\left(\frac{n}{360}\right) = $ *discount from face value*
Long-term borrowings	$$MV = \left[\sum_{t=1}^{n} \frac{\frac{(M)(CR)}{m}}{\left(1 + \frac{i}{m}\right)^t} \right] + \left[\frac{M}{\left(1 + \frac{i}{m}\right)^n} \right]$$	*For the definition of the variables involved in the computation please refer to the formula of treasury notes and bonds appeared among assets*

General definitions of variables:

- MV = market value
- PVIFA = present value of an annuity

Source: adapted from Grier W.A., *Valuing a Bank Under IFRS and Basel III*, 2010.

discounting formulas to estimate the fair market value of the main assets typically included in a bank's Balance Sheet.

For a practical example, let us consider, for instance, a portfolio of commercial loans (bullet) in the Balance Sheet of a bank. The loans' portfolio (L) amounts to €500M which is also the book value reported in the financial statements, the contractual loan rate (i_L) is 7.5% compounded quarterly, and the average maturity is of 5 years. The portfolio is un-hedged against interest risks, and the current interest rate is 9%. The fair market value of the portfolio is therefore €35M lower than the book value:

$$Market\ Value = \frac{€500M \left(1 + \dfrac{7.5\%}{4}\right)^5}{\left(1 + \dfrac{8.5\%}{4}\right)^5} = €465M \tag{5.36}$$

When dealing with financial institutions, the asset/liability-based valuation is not always straightforward or feasible because of the opaqueness of the financial contracts held or issued by the bank and to the interrelation among various assets and liabilities. But when sufficient data is available and there is a strong case of significant discrepancy between book and market value, this is a viable valuation approach. However, if the bank is expected to experience significant growth, this approach may underestimate the equity value of the bank as the assets are analyzed as they are and they do not reflect the opportunities for future expansion. On the contrary, this approach is suitable when valuing mature financial companies, or banks in liquidation.

5.5 THE SUM OF THE PARTS FRAMEWORK

Although they are not necessarily universal banks, most banks in the world today are at least "multi-business." Following the deregulation of the industry that started in the 1980s in many countries, banks have progressively diversified their operations via external or internal growth. As a consequence, pure "mono-business" financial institutions are rather rare, and even the traditional commercial banks show a certain degree of diversification. The presence of unrelated businesses at the same company may have implications in terms of valuation approaches. In practice, if detailed data is available about the performance and value drivers of each business, the analyst may decide to value separately each business and then to get the entire equity value of the bank as the sum of all the businesses. Namely, this approach is the Sum Of The Parts (SOTP) and it allows analysts ample flexibility in picking the most effective valuation approach for each analyzed business.

As an example, Table 5.7 shows the valuation of a financial institution operating in commercial banking, investment banking, and asset management. The valuation approaches adopted for the three divisions – on the basis of the segment reporting information – are the Discounted Equity Cash Flow, the Price/Earnings, and the

Table 5.7   Structure of a SOTP valuation

Business division	Valuation approach	Equity Value ($ mln)
Commercial banking	DCF	1265
Investment banking	P/E	324
Asset Management	P/AUM	190
Corporate Center Costs	P/Operating Income	−125
Excess Capital		270
Minorities		−72
Total		1852

Price/Assets Under Management respectively. Separately, there is a valuation of the so-called Corporate Center Costs, which are costs that are shared by the divisions and cannot be allocated specifically. Overlooking those costs may result in an overestimation of the equity value, because the bank will continue to bear them thus decreasing the overall cash flow available for shareholders.

Corporate Center Costs are therefore a negative component of the equity valuation and two approaches can be followed to estimate them. The first is to use a DCF analysis to forecast the yearly costs – along a growth pattern consistent with the one foreseen for the bank – with the bank's cost of capital as relevant discount rate. The second is to apply a multiple obtained from a panel of comparable financial companies: the recommendation would be to use preferably the P/Operating Income (operating income is the item more directly impacted by shared corporate costs), or, alternatively the P/E. Finally, in the numerical example of Table 5.7, the Excess Capital is added and the Minorities subtracted to get the total Equity Value estimate.

5.6   BANK VALUATION IN M&A

When dealing with valuations for M&A, the methods and approaches seen so far should be enriched with the estimation of the synergies and operating improvements expected and, as a consequence, of the adequate acquisition premium to buy certain targets, and the exchange ratio in case the payment is done partially or in full via shares.

Setting aside other regulatory, macroeconomic, and political considerations, an M&A transaction takes place because there seem to be synergies to be realized from the merger, because the target bank appears severely undervalued, or because the buyer believes that a control change may unlock value via a break up or by improving the way the bank is run. Often, more than one of those reasons are mentioned as deal rationales, but usually synergies (at revenues and/or operating costs level) are the main motivation.

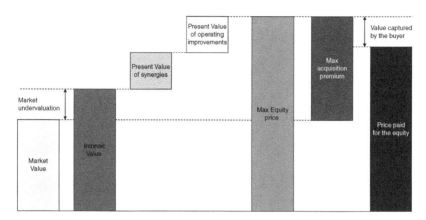

Figure 5.11   The strands of value in acquisitions

Figure 5.11 shows the conceptual stratification of the elements leading to definition of the maximum price to pay for a given target bank. The first aspect to assess is whether the market price of the target is fully reflective of the bank "intrinsic" value. If there appears to be a relevant market undervaluation, this might be an element in favor of the acquisition, provided that the intrinsic valuation has been carried out correctly and the execution of the deal does not spoil the opportunity. Synergies should be quantified by discounting the future expected differential revenues and differential costs the merger will generate. Analogously, the operating improvements associated with a better management of the bank and/or a restructuring of its businesses should be quantified by discounting the future expected differential post-merger revenues and costs.

A failure in forecasting the synergies and/or the operating improvements, or a poor execution of the deal may lead to a paid equity price, which nullifies the potential value captured by the buyer (and its shareholders), or even results in a value loss. Not differently from other industries, the financial services sector seems to give rise to poorly conceived/executed M&A transactions. In fact, the empirical analyses show that on average there is no statistically significant gain in value or performance from merger activity in this industry. On average, acquired firm shareholders gain at the expense of the acquiring firm. This is documented over the course of many studies covering different time periods and different countries (and it is true whether one looks at accounting data or the market value of equity).[13] Interestingly, bank mergers seem to deliver in terms of cost synergies but the improvements in cost efficiency appear to be transferred to bank clients, thus resulting overall in deteriorating ROE and cash flows. In order to define a sustainable acquisition premium, the correct valuation of the intrinsic value of

---

[13] B.D.D. Sergio and S.A.C.L. Gutiérrez (2009) Are M&A Premiums Too High? Analysis of a Quadratic Relationship between Premiums and Returns, *Quarterly Journal of Finance and Accounting*, 48 (3).

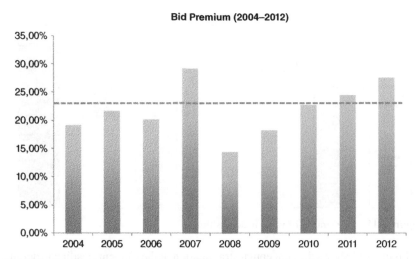

Figure 5.12   Acquisition premiums in the banking industry
Source: data from Zephyr. 609 deals involving listed target banks have been considered. The
bid premium is the difference between the price per share actually paid in the transaction
and the share price on the trading day before the first rumor about the deal spread.

the target bank, of the future expected synergies, and operating improvements is
therefore paramount.[14] In practice, deal multiples are often used to estimate the
reasonable price to pay for a control stake or for a total bid within an acquisition negotiation. Since there might be, as mentioned, deal features (such as the
payment method) that actually do have a sensible impact on the offered price,
such an approach would not be recommended. Also, the evidence that on average bank mergers have not created value for bidders would weigh negatively on
the practice of adding straightforwardly average historic premiums to the intrinsic value of the target. Actual premiums, as shown in Figure 5.12, change over
time and, again, they are likely affected by the deal characteristics and execution modes. The recommended approach remains to estimate the future expected
synergies/improvements via DCF.

The intrinsic value of the bank and expected post-deal synergies is not just a
concern for the buying company but for the target bank (and its shareholders) as
well. In particular, when the deal is agreed by both parties, an *exchange ratio* has to
be fixed. In a share-for-share deal, the exchange ratio is the number of buyer shares
offered per target shares. In a cash-for-share transaction, it is money exchanged per
target share. Assuming that the magnitude of the potential post-merger synergies
is known *ex-ante* by both parties, it is possible to define the "deal boundaries" for
the exchange ratio values (Table 5.8). For the buyer, there is maximum exchange

---

[14] E. Beccalli and P. Frantz (2013) The Determinants of Mergers and Acquisitions in Banking, *Journal of Financial
Services Research*, 43 (3), 265–291.

Table 5.8 Deal Boundaries

	Buyer's maximum acceptable exchange ratio	Target's minimum acceptable exchange ratio
Shares for shares (P/E boundaries)	$ER_B = \dfrac{S_B}{S_T} + \dfrac{E_B + E_T + E_{Synergies}}{P_B S_T} PE_{BT}$ (a)	$ER_T = \dfrac{P_T S_B}{PE_{BT}(E_B + E_T + E_{Synergies}) - P_T S_T}$ (b)
Shares for shares (DCF boundaries)	$ER_B = \dfrac{DCF_{BT} - P_B S_B}{P_B S_T}$ (c)	$ER_T = \dfrac{P_T S_B}{DCF_{BT} - P_T S_T}$ (d)
Cash for shares (P/E boundaries)	$ER_B = \dfrac{Cash}{S_T} = \dfrac{PE_{BT}\left(E_B + E_T + E_{Synergies}\right) - P_B S_B}{S_T}$ (e)	$ER_T = \dfrac{Cash}{S_T} = P_T$ (f)
Cash for shares (DCF boundaries)	$ER_B = \dfrac{Cash}{S_T} = \dfrac{DCF_{BT} - P_B S_B}{S_T}$ (g)	$ER_T = \dfrac{Cash}{S_T} = P_T$ (h)

Source: adapted from Bruner (2004).

ER_B = Maximum acceptable exchange ratio (buyer shares per target share) from the buyer's viewpoint.
ER_T = Minimum acceptable exchange ratio (buyer shares per target share) from the target's viewpoint.
P_B = Price per share of buyer today, before the transaction.
P_T = Price per share of target today.
S_B = Number of buyer shares outstanding today, before the transaction.
S_T = Number of target shares outstanding today.
E_B = Net Income of the buyer, next year,[15] stand-alone basis.
E_T = Net Income of the target, next year, stand-alone basis.
$E_{Synergies}$ = The change in net income of the combined firm arising from synergies.
DCF_{BT} = Discounted cash flow value of the equity of the combined firm.
PE_{BT} = Price/earnings ratio of the combined firm, based on leading estimates of earnings.

[15] Ball, M. (1996), Equity tailored to suit the strategy, *Corporate Finance*, October, 18–20.

ratio below which the transaction is convenient. At the same time, for the target, there is a minimum exchange ratio above which the deal makes sense. Out of the negotiating abilities of the two parties, the deal should be consummated in the range between target's minimum and buyer's maximum exchange rates.

5.7   THE VALUATION OF WELLS BANK

Having introduced the main methodologies available to estimate the value of a bank, it is worthwhile looking at a case study to get a better grasp on how such methodologies are applied in practice. The case study can be read in two steps:

- In Step 1, we move from the historical financial statements of Wells Bank, a standard commercial bank, and provide an insight on how to build financial projections. The goal is to show the main logic underlying the operating model of a bank.
- In Step 2, we apply a range of methodologies to estimate the value of Wells Bank. The output of this process is the so called "valuation football field", that is, a summary of the results of the valuation process that can be used to establish and visualize the estimated valuation range for the company.

Step 1

Financial projections are built according to the techniques described in Chapter 4, that is, by starting from the evolution of volumes and risk taken (Balance Sheet) and then forecasting earnings (P&L) by making assumptions on margins. At last, we are able to estimate retained earnings and the expected capital evolution of the bank.

Forecasts are presented in two stages. In the first stage, called "explicit forecasts", volume growth rates and margins are determined by the expected evolution of the macroeconomic and competitive landscape. In the second stage, called "normalization years", we assume that bank's performance grows in line with the expected long-term growth rate. The time span for the two stages is very short for simplicity. However, in practice, it is advisable to carry out explicit forecasts for at least 5 years and have growth rates gradually reverting to long-term levels.

In order to account for volatility in future performance, three scenarios have been prepared. In our example, these are based solely on different paths for GDP, interest rate, and cost of risk evolution. However, one could think of including other elements such as market share and mark-up/mark-down on base rate. Each scenario has been assigned a probability (in our example 50% to Base, 30% to Upside and 20% to Downside). This is required in order to compute, in Step 2, a weighted average valuation by valuing each scenario separately and then blending the results.

Step 2

Wells Bank has been valued by applying a mix of "relative valuation" techniques and "discounted return" models. The use of different methodologies is required to cross check results and obtain higher comfort on the reliability of the estimated valuation range.

As far as relative valuation is concerned, we applied the following techniques:

- Market multiples: 1 and 2-year forward P/E and 1-year forward P/BV.
- Value maps: 1-year forward P/TBV regressed over 2-year forward ROTBV.
- Multiples from fundamentals: Warranted Equity Method (WEM).

It is important to highlight that for both the value map and the WEM excess capital has been stripped out from book value and added to the valuation carried out on the adjusted basis.

Table 5.9   The valuation of Wells Bank – key assumptions

Key Assumptions

Selected scenario: Base

				Explicit Forecasts			Normalisation Years	
		2011A	2012A	2013E	2014E	2015E	2016E	2017E
Macroeconomic Assumptions								
$Bn								
GDP Evolution								
U.S. Nominal GDP		15.076	15.653	16.198	16.913	17.768		
Nominal GDPGrowth		4,0%	3,8%	3,5%	4,4%	5,1%		
Base case				3,5%	4,4%	5,1%		
Upside case	1,0%			4,5%	5,4%	6,1%		
Downside case	(1,0)%			2,5%	3,4%	4,1%		
Aggregated Loans Evolution								
Total loans / GDP		57,3%	57,3%	57,3%	57,3%	57,3%		
Total loans		8.645	8.976	9.288	9.698	10.189		
Total loans growth			3,8%	3,5%	4,4%	5,1%		
Retail loans / GDP		38,4%	37,7%	38,0%	38,0%	38,0%		
Retail loans		5.789	5.901	6.163	6.435	6.760		
Retail loans growth			1,9%	4,4%	4,4%	5,1%		
Corporate loans / GDP		18,9%	19,6%	19,3%	19,3%	19,3%		
Corporate loans		2.856	3.075	3.125	3.263	3.428		
Corporate loans growth			7,7%	1,6%	4,4%	5,1%		
Interest Rate Evolution								
Libor		0,50%	0,56%	0,58%	0,81%	1,06%	1,06%	1,06%
Base case				0,58%	0,81%	1,06%	1,06%	1,06%
Upside case	0,20%			0,78%	1,01%	1,26%	1,26%	1,26%
Downside case	(0,20)%			0,38%	0,61%	0,86%	0,86%	0,86%

(continued)

Table 5.9   (*Continued*)

Company Assumptions: Balance Sheet

Loans Market Share Evolution

Total loans	8,5%	8,4%	8,4%	8,4%	8,4%		
Retail loans	7,2%	6,9%	7,1%	7,1%	7,1%		
Corporate loans	11,0%	11,2%	11,1%	11,1%	11,1%		
Implied total loans growth	*(3,2)%*	*2,2%*	*4,3%*	*4,4%*	*5,1%*	*2,0%*	*2,6%*

Other Assets Evolution

Grow in line with loans	(3,2)%	2,2%	4,3%	4,4%	5,1%	2,0%	2,0%

Deposits Evolution

Loans to deposits	92,0%	86,0%	89,0%	89,0%	89,0%	89,0%	89,0%
Demand as % of total deposits	24,0%	28,0%	26,0%	26,0%	26,0%	26,0%	26,0%
Term as % of total deposits	76,0%	72,0%	74,0%	74,0%	74,0%	74,0%	74,0%

Other Liabilities Evolution

Grow in line with deposits		9,3%	0,8%	4,4%	5,1%	2,0%	2,0%

Company Assumptions: Income Statement

Yields

Due from financial institutions mark-up on Libor	0,01%	0,01%	-	-	-	-	-
Due from financial institutions yield	*0,5%*	*0,6%*	*0,6%*	*0,8%*	*1,1%*	*1,1%*	*1,1%*
Retail loans mark-up on Libor	6,32%	5,08%	5,70%	5,70%	5,70%	5,70%	5,70%
Retail loans yield	*6,8%*	*5,6%*	*6,3%*	*6,5%*	*6,8%*	*6,8%*	*6,8%*
Corporate loans mark-up on Libor	3,34%	3,69%	3,52%	3,52%	3,52%	3,52%	3,52%
Corporate loans yield	*3,8%*	*4,3%*	*4,1%*	*4,3%*	*4,6%*	*4,6%*	*4,6%*
Financial assets yield	5,16%	3,75%	4,45%	4,45%	4,45%	4,45%	4,45%
Due to financial institutions mark-up on Libor	0,01%	0,01%	-	-	-	-	-
Due to financial institutions yield	*0,5%*	*0,6%*	*0,6%*	*0,8%*	*1,1%*	*1,1%*	*1,1%*
Term deposits mark-down on Libor	(0,03)%	(0,19)%	(0,11)%	(0,11)%	(0,11)%	(0,11)%	(0,11)%
Term deposits yield	*0,5%*	*0,4%*	*0,5%*	*0,7%*	*0,9%*	*0,9%*	*0,9%*
Borrowings yield	2,19%	2,10%	2,14%	2,14%	2,14%	2,14%	2,14%

Other P&L Assumptions

Net commission fees on loans		1,9%	1,6%	1,7%	1,7%	1,7%	1,7%	1,7%
Service charges on deposits		0,6%	0,5%	0,6%	0,6%	0,6%	0,6%	0,6%
Net average fee on AuM		1,6%	1,7%	1,7%	1,7%	1,7%	1,7%	1,7%
Cost income ratio		60,6%	59,4%	60,0%	60,0%	60,0%	60,0%	60,0%
Cost of risk		1,4%	1,1%	1,3%	1,3%	1,3%	1,3%	1,3%
Base case				1,3%	1,3%	1,3%	1,3%	1,3%
Upside case	(0,2)%			1,1%	1,1%	1,1%	1,1%	1,1%
Downside case	0,2%			1,5%	1,5%	1,5%	1,5%	1,5%
Effective tax rate		28,7%	28,8%	28,8%	28,8%	28,8%	28,8%	28,8%

Other Company Assumptions

AuM growth (in line with nominal GDP growth)	4,0%	3,8%	3,5%	4,4%	5,1%	2,0%	2,0%
RWAs as % of total assets	75,5%	74,6%	74,6%	74,6%	74,6%	74,6%	74,6%
Payout ratio	50,0%	50,0%	50,0%	50,0%	50,0%	50,0%	50,0%

Table 5.10 The valuation of Wells Bank – financial statements

Financial Statements

Selected scenario: Base

			Explicit Forecasts			Normalisation Years	
	2011A	2012A	2013E	2014E	2015E	2016E	2017E

Balance Sheet
$Bn

Assets	2011A	2012A	2013E	2014E	2015E	2016E	2017E
Cash and cash equivalents	16	19	20	21	22	23	23
Due from financial institutions	81	44	46	48	51	52	53
Due from customers (net)	734	750	782	817	858	876	893
Retail	419	406	435	454	477	487	497
Corporate	315	345	347	363	381	389	396
Financial Assets	277	350	365	381	401	409	417
Intangible assets	41	39	39	39	39	39	39
Fixed assets	10	10	10	10	11	11	11
Other Assets	100	101	105	110	116	118	120
Total Assets	1.258	1.314	1.369	1.427	1.498	1.527	1.556
Liabilities							
Due to financial institutions	50	47	78	87	97	91	88
Due to customers	798	873	879	919	965	984	1.004
Demand	191	244	228	238	250	255	261
Term	607	629	651	680	714	729	743
Borrowings	212	174	174	174	174	174	174
Other liabilities	70	78	85	86	89	94	96
Total Liabilities	1.130	1.172	1.217	1.266	1.325	1.343	1.362
Capital & Reserves	128	142	142	151	162	172	184
Retained earnings for the year	-	-	10	10	11	11	11
Shareholders' funds	128	142	151	162	172	184	195
Total Liabilities and Equity	1.258	1.314	1.369	1.427	1.498	1.527	1.556
Check	-	-	-	-	-	-	-

Income Statement
$Bn

	2011A	2012A	2013E	2014E	2015E	2016E	2017E
Interests and other income	52,9	49,4	56,8	61,3	66,5	68,8	70,2
Due from financial institutions	0,3	0,4	0,3	0,4	0,5	0,5	0,6
Due from customers	39,8	37,3	40,6	44,3	48,5	50,2	51,2
Retail	25,5	23,3	26,4	29,0	31,5	32,6	33,3
Corporate	14,3	14,0	14,2	15,4	17,0	17,6	18,0
Other interest Income	12,8	11,8	15,9	16,6	17,4	18,0	18,4
Interests and other expenses	(8,1)	(6,6)	(7,0)	(9,0)	(11,3)	(11,6)	(11,7)
Due to financial institutions	(0,2)	(0,3)	(0,3)	(0,6)	(0,9)	(1,0)	(1,0)
Due to customers	(2,8)	(2,3)	(3,0)	(4,7)	(6,6)	(6,8)	(7,0)
Demand	-	-	-	-	-	-	-
Term	(2,8)	(2,3)	(3,0)	(4,7)	(6,6)	(6,8)	(7,0)
Borrowings	(5,0)	(4,1)	(3,7)	(3,7)	(3,7)	(3,7)	(3,7)
Net interest income	44,8	42,8	49,8	52,3	55,2	57,2	58,5
Net fee and commission income	38,4	40,3	42,6	44,3	46,4	48,0	49,0
Total income	83,3	83,1	92,4	96,6	101,6	105,2	107,5
Operating expenses	(50,5)	(49,4)	(55,4)	(58,0)	(61,0)	(63,1)	(64,5)
Operating income	32,8	33,8	37,0	38,7	40,6	42,1	43,0
Net write downs on loans	(10,8)	(7,9)	(9,6)	(10,0)	(10,5)	(10,9)	(11,1)
Profit before tax	22,1	25,9	27,4	28,6	30,2	31,2	31,9
Taxes	(6,3)	(7,4)	(7,9)	(8,2)	(8,7)	(9,0)	(9,2)
Net profit	15,7	18,4	19,5	20,4	21,5	22,3	22,7

Other items
$Bn

	2011A	2012A	2013E	2014E	2015E	2016E	2017E
AuM	1.404	1.457	1.508	1.575	1.654	1.688	1.721
RWAs	950	980	1.021	1.065	1.117	1.139	1.161
Dividends	8	9	10	10	11	11	11
Tangible book value	87	103	112	123	133	144	156
Tier 1	85	99	109	119	130	141	152

Key Ratios

	2011A	2012A	2013E	2014E	2015E	2016E	2017E
NIM (Loans)	6,0%	5,8%	6,5%	6,5%	6,6%	6,6%	6,6%
NIM (Loans+Deposits)	3,9%	2,7%	3,0%	3,1%	3,1%	3,1%	3,1%
Net fee and commission margin (Loans+Deposits+AuM)	1,5%	1,3%	1,4%	1,4%	1,4%	1,4%	1,4%
Cost to Income Ratio	60,6%	59,4%	60,0%	60,0%	60,0%	60,0%	60,0%
Cost of risk	1,4%	1,1%	1,3%	1,3%	1,3%	1,3%	1,3%
Effective Tax Rate	28,7%	28,8%	28,8%	28,8%	28,8%	28,8%	28,8%
Loans to Deposits	92,0%	86,0%	89,0%	89,0%	89,0%	89,0%	89,0%
Customer Loans Growth	(3,2%)	2,2%	4,3%	4,4%	5,1%	2,0%	2,0%
Tier 1 ratio	8,9%	10,1%	10,7%	11,2%	11,6%	12,4%	13,1%
RoAE	13,0%	13,7%	13,3%	13,0%	12,9%	12,5%	12,0%
RoTBV	18,0%	19,4%	18,1%	17,4%	16,8%	16,0%	15,2%
RoAA	1,3%	1,4%	1,5%	1,5%	1,5%	1,5%	1,5%

Table 5.11   The valuation of Wells Bank – dividend discount model

Cost of Equity

Beta calculation

$Bn

	Mkt Cap	Beta	Adjusted Beta
JP Morgan Chase & Co.	187	1,48	1,32
Bank of America Corporation	133	1,93	1,62
Citigroup Inc	136	2,03	1,69
Bank of New York Mellon Corporation	33	1,51	1,34
U.S. Bancorp	64	1,05	1,03
Average		1,60	1,40
Weigthed Average		1,68	1,45

Cost of Equity

Risk-free rate	1,75%
Beta	1,40
Equity risk premium	6,14%
Cost of Equity	10,4%

Table 5.11 *(Continued)*

Dividend Discount Model

Selected scenario | Base

				Explicit Forecasts			Normalisation Years	
	2010A	2011A	2012A	2013E	2014E	2015E	2016E	2017E
Excess Capital Method								
$Bn								
Dividend Calculation								
Tier 1 BoP				99	102	106	112	114
Net Income				19	20	21	22	23
Tier 1 Capital EoP - Pre-Dividend				118	122	128	134	137
RWA				1.021	1.065	1.117	1.139	1.161
Tier 1 Ratio Pre-Dividend				11,6%	11,5%	11,5%	11,8%	11,8%
Tier 1 Ratio Target				10,0%	10,0%	10,0%	10,0%	10,0%
Dividend				16	16	16	20	21
Tier 1 Capital EoP - Post-Dividend			99	102	106	112	114	116
Adjusted RoE Calculation								
Equity BoP				142	145	149	154	157
Net Income				19	20	21	22	23
(-) Dividends				(16)	(16)	(16)	(20)	(21)
Equity EoP			142	145	149	154	157	159
Tangible equity EoP			103	106	110	115	117	120
Adj RoE (excl. excess capital)				13,6%	13,9%	14,2%	14,3%	14,4%
Adj RoTBV (excl. excess capital)				18,7%	18,9%	19,1%	19,1%	19,2%
Discounting and Terminal Value								
Time				30-giu-13	30-giu-14	30-giu-15	30-giu-16	30-giu-17
Period				0.50	1.49	2.49	3.50	4.50
Discount Factor		10%		0,95	0,86	0,78	0,71	0,64
Dividends				16	16	16	20	21
Terminal Value								250
Present value				16	14	13	14	174
Value		230						

Sensitivity on Terminal Value
$Bn

Key Inputs	
Cost of Equity	10,4%
Long Term Growth Rate	2,0%
P/BV WM	1,49x
P/E 1yr fwd	11,2x

Terminal Value Calculation	
Perpetual Dividend Growth	161
WarrantedM Book Exit Multiple	152
P/ E1yr fwd Exit Multiple	164

Valuation	
Perpetual Dividend Growth	230
WarrantedM Book Exit Multiple	221
P/ E1yr fwd Exit Multiple	233

Table 5.12 The valuation of Wells Bank – warranted equity method

Warranted Equity Method

Selected scenario : Base

WEM
$Bn

Equity 2012A	142
Excess capital	16
Equity 2012A net of excess capital	125
CoE	10,4%
Long Term Growth Rate	2,0%
Long Term RoE - Adj.	14,4%
WEM P/ BV	1,49x
Value	203

		Long Term Growth Rate		
		1,5%	2,0%	2,5%
CoE	10%	207	211	216
	11%	187	189	192
	12%	171	172	174

Table 5.13 The valuation of Wells Bank – trading comps and regression based valuation

Trading Comps and Regression Based Valuation

Selected scenario Base

Selected Peer Statistics

	P/EPS Multiple			P/BV Multiples		P/TBV Multiples		RoAE			RoTBV		
	2012A	2013E	2014E	2012A	2013E	2012A	2013E	2012A	2013E	2014E	2012A	2013E	2014E
JP Morgan Chase & Co.	9,4x	9,0x	8,5x	0,96x	0,89x	1,29x	1,16x	11,1%	10,4%	10,3%	13,7%	12,9%	12,4%
Bank of America Corporation	48,7x	12,4x	9,5x	0,60x	0,58x	0,92x	0,86x	1,8%	5,0%	6,2%	1,9%	6,9%	8,3%
Citigroup Inc	11,6x	9,7x	8,4x	0,71x	0,68x	0,86x	0,80x	4,1%	7,2%	7,8%	7,4%	8,2%	8,7%
Bank of New York Mellon Corporation	14,0x	12,5x	11,1x	0,94x	0,89x	2,65x	2,12x	7,1%	7,0%	7,9%	18,9%	16,9%	17,6%
U.S. Bancorp	12,0x	11,2x	10,5x	1,86x	1,70x	2,65x	2,34x	14,2%	16,0%	15,5%	22,0%	21,0%	20,0%
Average		11,0x	9,6x		0,95x		1,46x			9,5%			13,4%
Median		11,2x	9,5x		0,89x		1,16x			7,9%			12,4%

Valuation
$Bn

Selected multiple	11,2x	9,5x	0,89x	1,16x	
Company metric	19	20	151	112	
Value	218	139	134	131	

Regression Based Valuation
$Bn

Company Metric	
TBV 2013E (net of excess capital)	106
Excess capital	16
RoTBV 2014E (excl. excess capital)	18,9%
Regression (RoTBV 2014E vs. P/TBV 2013E)	
Constant	(0)
Slope	14
R2	98%
Implied Multiple	2,21x
Implied Valuation	250

Table 5.14 The valuation of Wells Bank – valuation summary

Valuation Summary

Selected scenario ⌐ Base ⌐

	Valuation			
	Min	Value	Max	Gap
Football Field				
$Bn				
Trading Valuation				
P/E 2013E	197	218	240	44
P/E 2014E	174	193	213	39
P/ BV2013E	121	134	148	27
Reg. P/ TBV 2013E vs. RoTBV 2014E	225	250	275	50
WEM				
Long term growth 1.5%	168	187	206	37
Long term growth 2.0%	170	189	208	38
Long term growth 2.5%	173	192	211	38
DDM				
Via Gordon	207	230	253	46
Via P/ BV Warranted Exit Multiple	199	221	243	44
Via P/ E 1yr fwd Exit Multilpe	210	233	256	47
Average	184	205	225	41

Base Case

$Bn

	Min	Value	Max	Gap
Trading Valuation				
P/E 2013E	197	218	240	44
P/E 2014E	174	193	213	39
P/ BV2013E	121	134	148	27
Reg. P/ TBV 2013E vs. RoTBV 2014E	225	250	275	50
WEM				
Long term growth 1.5%	168	187	206	37
Long term growth 2.0%	170	189	208	38
Long term growth 2.5%	173	192	211	38
DDM				
Via Gordon	207	230	253	46
Via P/ BV Warranted Exit Multiple	199	221	243	44
Via P/ E 1yr fwd Exit Multilpe	210	233	256	47
Average	184	205	225	41

(continued)

Table 5.14 *(Continued)*

Upside Case

$Bn

Trading Valuation				
P/E 2013E	196	218	239	44
P/E 2014E	199	221	243	44
P/ BV2013E	215	239	263	48
Reg. P/ TBV 2013E vs. RoTBV 2014E	239	265	292	53
WEM				
Long term growth 1.5%	180	199	219	40
Long term growth 2.0%	182	203	223	41
Long term growth 2.5%	186	206	227	41
DDM				
Via Gordon	209	232	255	46
Via P/ BV Warranted Exit Multiple	201	223	246	45
Via P/ E1yr fwd Exit Multilpe	211	235	258	47
Average	202	224	247	45

Downside Case

$Bn

Trading Valuation				
P/E 2013E	172	191	210	38
P/E 2014E	171	191	210	38
P/ BV2013E	214	237	261	47
Reg. P/ TBV 2013E vs. RoTBV 2014E	177	196	216	39
WEM				
Long term growth 1.5%	157	174	192	35
Long term growth 2.0%	158	176	194	35
Long term growth 2.5%	160	178	196	36
DDM				
Via Gordon	177	197	217	39
Via P/ BV Warranted Exit Multiple	170	189	208	38
Via P/ E1yr fwd Exit Multilpe	181	201	221	40
Average	174	193	212	39

Weighted Average

$Bn

Trading Valuation				
P/E 2013E	191	213	234	43
P/E 2014E	181	201	221	40
P/ BV2013E	168	186	205	37
Reg. P/ TBV 2013E vs. RoTBV 2014E	219	244	268	49
WEM				
Long term growth 1.5%	169	188	207	38
Long term growth 2.0%	172	191	210	38
Long term growth 2.5%	174	194	213	39
DDM				
Via Gordon	202	224	247	45
Via P/ BV Warranted Exit Multiple	194	215	237	43
Via P/ E1yr fwd Exit Multilpe	204	227	250	45
Average	187	208	229	42

Table 5.15   The valuation of Wells Bank – valuation summary

Valuation Summary

Weighted Average

$Bn

| | | Implied Multiples | | Valuation Mid-point | | | |
		P/E 2014E	P/BV 2013E	Base	Upside	Downside	Weighted Average
Trading Valuation							
P/E 2013E	191 ■·■ 234	10,3x	1,40x	218	218	191	213
P/E 2014E	181 ■·■ 221	9,8x	1,33x	193	221	191	201
P/BV 2013E	168 ■·■ 205	9,1x	1,23x	134	239	237	186
Reg. P/TBV 2013E vs. RoTBV 2014E	219 ■·■ 268	11,9x	1,61x	250	265	196	244
WEM							
Long term growth 1.5%	169 ■·■ 207	9,1x	1,24x	187	199	174	188
Long term growth 2.0%	172 ■·■ 210	9,3x	1,26x	189	203	176	191
Long term growth 2.5%	174 ■·■ 213	9,4x	1,28x	192	206	178	194
DDM							
Terminal value via Gordon	202 ·○· 247	10,9x	1,48x	230	232	197	224
Terminal value via WEM P/BV Exit Multiple	194 ·○· 237	10,5x	1,42x	221	223	189	215
Terminal value via 1yr fwd P/E Exit Multilpe	204 ·○· 250	11,0x	1,50x	233	235	201	227
Average	187 ·○· 229	10,1x	1,37x	205	224	193	208

100   200   300   400

As for the discounted return models, we focused on the Discounted Cash Flow to Equity Model, which is currently the most used in this category of valuation techniques. Such a methodology is extremely sensitive to terminal value calculation. As a result, we present three alternative ways to estimate such value:

• Gordon growth formula: based on assumed cost of capital and long-term growth rate.
• WEM exit multiple: based on assumed cost of capital, long-term growth rate and ROE.
• 1-year forward P/E: based on current trading multiples for selected peers.

The final valuation range has been computed in two steps. As a first step, each methodology has been applied to financial projections in the three scenarios considered, resulting in a probability weighted average valuation. Secondly, we have computed the average point for the list of results deriving from the application of the different valuation techniques. The valuation range was established by allowing for a customary +/− 10% interval around this value.

See Tables 5.9–5.15 for the full valuation of Wells Bank.

6

Insurance Business Models and Financial Statements

Insurance companies provide their clients with economic protection for clearly identified risks that will take place within a certain (predetermined) time period. Unlike in other industries, in the insurance sector costs for the granted service are usually unknown before the actual occurrence (if any) of the insured event, while the stream of premium from policyholders (revenue) is determined or determinable at the set of the contract. We will organize the discussion about insurance business models by pointing out the main business lines and the most relevant distribution strategies for insurance companies. Although insurance companies often offer also services that involve little or no insurance protection (e.g., investment management and other fee-based financial services), our focus will be on the core insurance business of granting economic protection against risks.

6.1 THE BUSINESS MODEL OF INSURANCE COMPANIES

Insurance companies can be seen as facilitators of risk transfer, and especially the largest ones are among the few skilled financial actors able to design and place most risk-related financial instruments. As such, insurers play a prominent role in financial markets by packaging (risk pooling) and diversifying them (risk spreading). Technically, the underlying idea is as simple as it seems: since the correlation among different contracts is not supposed to be perfect, there's some room for portfolio diversification. The uncertainty concerning future results of a portfolio of similar uncorrelated event-assets is less than the one related to a single contract (Allen and Santomero, 1998).

Other two features should be mentioned before entering into the details of the insurance business. First, regardless of the specific segment in which insurance companies compete, generally speaking, all the insurance companies carry out the following activities: underwriting insurance policies (e.g., assessing the acceptability of risks, the contractual terms of coverage, and the premium to receive), billing and collecting premiums, and investigating and settling claims.

Second, premiums from policyholders are paid up-front while the possible disbursements, which follow the actual occurrence of an insured event, take place after a certain time period. That time gap is not simply due to the fact that events get reimbursed after being insured, and usually after the premiums (at least some

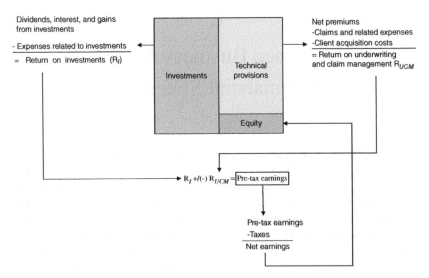

Figure 6.1   The two "jobs" of insurers

of them) get paid, but other elements typically extend the period between the event occurrence and the payment. Such circumstances are: (1) sometimes insured losses are *discovered* many years after the event occurrence; (2) litigations may delay the settlement and payment; and (3) for some insurance products, reimbursements are not paid in a single settlement (e.g., pension plans). These three further sources of "*float*" are recognized in the Balance Sheet and Income Statement under the names reserves for losses and loss adjustment expenses. The inverted cash conversion cycle defines the business model of insurers that involves two distinct but interrelated activities: one focused on the management of premiums and claims, and the other related to the investment of the collected premiums themselves. As a consequence, the source of profitability and of remuneration for insurance companies' shareholders is twofold: it is the return from investments on the one side, and the return from the core "technical insurance" operations on the other side (see Figure 6.1). Interestingly, a value creating insurance company should not necessarily excel or even have a positive performance on both sides of the business: as long as a good performance of one of the two can more than offset the poor performance of the other, the company may overall achieve above-average profitability.

6.2   SEGMENTATION BY PRODUCTS

6.2.1   Life and Health

Life policies refer primarily to death benefits or to life-contingent annuities, therefore the risks are generally associated with either death or longevity. Health contracts provide economic protection against reduction of income due to disability or medical expenses.

Life insurance may be in the form of a term insurance or it may cover the whole life. Term insurance covers a period usually ranging from 1–15 years, a whole life insurance grants the payment of the entire face value agreed in the contract once the insured person dies, regardless of when the event occurs. Obviously, as risk of death increases with age of the insured person, a whole life insurance policy (with constant premiums) involves higher payments for the insurer in the earlier years of the contract than the ones paid in case of a term insurance for the same years, and it also involves lower payments as time goes by.

Life-contingent annuities or similar investment contracts can earn either a variable or fixed return. In particular, "qualified" annuities are those resulting from employer-sponsored plans (e.g., retirement benefits), are tax deductible (for employers) and taxed once received by the employee. "Unqualified" annuities, on the other hand, are just purchased with after-tax income.

6.2.2   Property and Casualty

Property insurance is technically an insurance protecting against property (car, house, business) losses. Casualty insurance protects against liabilities for losses brought about by injury to other people or damage to their property. Both commercial and personal items that are likely to be covered by two such kinds of policies are hard to identify in an exhaustive list. In fact, they may vary from automobiles, ships and cargos, to the coverage of work-related injuries or death, to professional liability. The case of car is of particular relevance in many countries. When automobile car is insured (and insurance is mandatory in most jurisdictions), coverage gets usually granted for personal injury, property damage (caused by unknowns), car damage caused by the insured person (collision, comprehensive, un-/under-insured motorist property damage), and the related legal liability.

6.2.3   Reinsurance

A third specific segment of the insurance business is reinsurance which can be considered as a niche in the industry as it comprises just a limited number of companies in the world. Reinsurance contracts involve two insurance entities and the following scheme: the first insurance company, after having agreed policies with its customers, decides to indemnify its operations from the insurance risks related to the entire policy portfolio insured or some portion of that. In some countries, reinsurance is mandatory in order to get a better diversification of risks throughout the whole system. In essence, reinsurance is the insurance of insurance risks. While reinsurance usually involves the coverage of prospective insured events, what sometimes happens is referred to as retroactive coverage:

reinsurer, in fact, may also agree to cover future liabilities incurred as a result of past events.

6.3   DISTRIBUTION CHANNELS

The two principal distribution channels used by insurance companies worldwide are basically direct and indirect writing. By direct writing we refer to those companies selling their policies through their own sales force, by telephone or on the Internet. On the other hand, indirect writing refers to the practice of selling policies through brokers or agents who may propose different policies issued by *different* companies to their *own* clients. The most important difference between these two strategies lies in the ownership of the client list: while in the previous case, it's the insurance company the owner of that list (and, in a way, of the relation with the client): in the latter it belongs to the independent agent. As a result, in case of independent writing, although the upfront initial investment and fixed costs (so, operating leverage) are definitely lower, running variable costs are much higher. Finally, the development of bank-led distribution channels (bank-assurance) – with banks selling insurance products via their branches – is crucially related to the presence of skills to thoroughly assist customers in choosing the specific insurance products. That's exactly one of the main reasons why the distribution of Property and Casualty insurance products in particular does not rely widely on banks. The distribution channels adopted by an insurer affect the Balance Sheet structure and are an important element in the assessment and preparation of business plans.

6.4   INSURANCE BALANCE SHEET UNDER US GAAP

Most accounting principles presented in Chapter 2 do apply to the items in insurers' financial statements. Here, we will therefore just briefly focus on a few aspects which are peculiar to the accounting for insurance companies.

6.4.1   Reserves and Separate Accounts

On the liability side, the most relevant category is by far represented by *insurance reserves*, which comprise *liability for future policy benefits* (Life and Health insurance companies), *claim reserves* (both Property and Casualty and Life and Health), and reinsurance reserves.

6.4.1.1   Liability for Future Policy Benefits

The liability for future policy benefits is computed by summing the *present value* of future benefits that will be paid to policyholders to any additional expense related to those claims and subtracting the present value of future *net premiums*.

Collected premiums must necessarily cover the cost of claims (e.g., the mortality costs). However, if the premiums were exactly equal to the estimated amount, the insurance business would probably not survive. First, the mortality costs have to be reduced by an amount equal to the investment income the insurer expects to earn during the time of the contract. Second, premiums are increased to cover the company marketing and administrative expenses. Third, taxes considerations should be taken into account. Fourth, insurance companies usually increase the required premiums to be able to sustain the insurer's risk related to not correctly predicting future losses. Finally, profits should be delivered to shareholders. All these premium elements summed together result in the gross premium charge.

Net premiums, instead, are gross premiums net of the *embedded underwriting profit*, and so they represent the portion of premium that is strictly devoted to the coverage of the future benefits and expenses. The net investment yield expected at the origination of the contract is reflected in the discount rate.

The expected return rate is estimated taking into consideration the current level of interest rates as well as the projected levels, the portfolio diversification effects, and the contractual maturity.

A *provision for the risk of adverse deviation* must also be incorporated in the liability for future policy benefits. In other words, there is a risk arising from unexpected adverse departures from the computational assumptions with regard to investment yields, mortality rates, and all the other assumptions that have been made for the estimates.

Looking at the computations, the value of net premiums (discounted) at the moment the contract is originated, should be exactly equal to the value of future claims and expenses (also discounted) considering also the risk of adverse deviations from computational assumptions. For example, expected gross premiums are reduced for the risk of a higher than expected mortality rate, and the discount rate (net investment yield) is reduced to consider unexpectedly low investment returns. Finally, net premiums are equal to the lowered value of gross premiums found by matching the new present value to those premiums.

Since expected net premiums are generally higher than predicted claims and expenses in the first years of life insurance policies, the liability (whose initial value is zero) augments over time. Unless the excess of claims and expenses over net premiums is higher than the time-related component (the rate "charge" due to the passage of time in the present value calculation of net payments), the reserve augments over time. Nevertheless, after a certain level, that difference becomes larger than the interest cost and the liability gets reduced (Nissim, 2010).

For subsequent periods, US GAAP has established a rule, which is referred to as the *lock-in concept*, requiring that initial assumptions must be maintained as long as a premium deficiency is not present. A *premium deficiency* is simply a possible loss over a group of contracts grouped together in a coherent way (i.e., considering their marketing, servicing, and required computations). A loss of that kind may for instance occur when assumptions regarding mortality rates or yields get reviewed.

A premium deficiency is, in fact, measured as the difference between the new liability estimated using "corrected" assumptions and the previously recognized liability less deferred policy acquisition costs. From the computational point of view, it should be mentioned that the revised liability is obtained by discounting gross premiums instead of net and excludes any provision for the risk of adverse deviation (Nissim, 2010). A premium deficiency is expensed in the same period in which it is recognized, accompanied by a reduction in DAC or an increase in the liability for future policy benefits. Moreover, once premium deficiency has been identified, any subsequent evaluation of the liability must be carried out following the revised assumptions. In the computation of premium deficiency, subjectivity arises from two sources: apart from the usual discretion embedded in both the original and revised assumptions, subjectivity also comes from a second source, that is, the applied criteria according to which to group contracts.

6.4.1.2 Claim Reserves

Claim reserves are computed as the sum of estimated future disbursements (related to the settlement of claims) for any insured events that have already taken place before the Balance Sheet date. Aside from expected claim payments, claim reserves also comprehend estimates of additional expenses related to those claims, such as litigation costs.

Although we have already stated that claim reserves are found in both a PC and LH insurer Balance Sheet, the term used to refer to that item is typically different. In fact, while a PC insurer will call it "*the loss reserve*," an LH insurer will designate the claim reserves as "*the liability for policy and contract claims*."

The loss reserve measures the estimated obligation for all claims incurred, whether reported or unreported to the insurer, which have not been settled yet. The unreported portion is the result of an estimation process taking into account knowledge of past events as well as actuarial assumptions on the then-current situation. In accordance with US GAAP, changes in the loss reserve account are reflected in the profit and loss immediately as they occur.

On the other hand, the liability for policy and contract claims represents the estimated disbursement for claim settlement of any incurred death or disability, whether reported or unreported to the insurer, which has not been settled yet. Actuarial estimates, as usual, are crucial for the computation of those reserves. It's worth noting that, in accordance with US GAAP, changes in the reserve are reflected in the profit and loss (policyholder benefits and claims expenses) immediately as they occur.

From what was just said, it's clear that a significant level of discretion is involved while estimating claim reserves: some insurers, in fact, exploit that discretion to carry out earning-management or even capital-management strategies. Some major incentives for exploiting accounting techniques by insurance companies are to obtain "unfavorable" numbers with regard to tax effects and to be in compliance with regulatory metrics. The considerable uncertainty and the subjectivity inherent in the estimation process make the number observed in the Balance Sheet vague and easy to manipulate. Insurance companies generally tend to minimize their reserves: the principal reason, which will probably be clearer after reading the chapter about insurance capital regulation, is that by increasing policyholder surplus, namely the insurer's net worth, management is indirectly augmenting the insurer underwriting capacity. Nevertheless, on the contrary, the overstatement of claim reserves also constitutes a likely scenario. There is one main reason why that could be the case in the context of loss reserve: due to the consideration that property and casualty insurance policies are short-term contracts, lack of discounting should result in an increase in the loss reserves proportional to the time span between the incidence of a loss and the settlement of the claim. However, Nelson (2000) discovered that what occurs in reality is a higher understatement of loss reserves with respect to the length of the settlement period.

6.4.1.3   Policyholder Account Balances and Separate Accounts

For our purposes, it is worth considering two more items on the liability side to be able to provide the reader with an almost complete overview of a Balance Sheet for an insurance company: policyholder account balances and separate accounts.

- *Policyholder account balances* are simply account deposits into which positive interest is added and any withdrawal and additional related expense subtracted. The policyholder account may also comprehend dividends due and unpaid or undrawn by policyholder. Policyholder accounts technically are a reserve.
- *Separate accounts* are distinguished because of a unique feature: the return on investment assets, net of fees, directly accrues to contract holders. They are mainly used in contracts where the insurance company is not obliged to furnish a specific amount to the contract holder, such as in case of variable universal life contracts. On the asset side of the Balance Sheet, they are matched by separate account assets consisting of a number of diversified portfolios of assets managed by the insurance company, thus making them more similar to mutual funds. Contract holders construct their own portfolio by selecting among these funds, with the separate accounts liability representing their claim. Both separate account assets and liabilities are measured at fair value, given that all "risks and rewards" of those investments are credited directly to contract holders. Moreover, separate accounts are not incorporated in the determination of regulatory capital, as the insurer is not exposed to fluctuations in portfolio values, aside from potential fees related to performance.

Net investment income from separate accounts is excluded for profit and loss, because under those particular contracts, the insurer provides only a service to the contract holders; that is, managing assets practically owned by contract holders. Therefore, it is appropriate to include only investment management fees, policy administration fees, and other similar items. Nonetheless, performance in those investments is beneficial for the company and constitutes a useful factor for an analyst for both forecasting performance-related management fees and assessing the ability of the insurance company to expand its client base: both factors, in fact, augment total management fees.

6.4.1.4   Revenue Recognition and Major Expense Categories Related to Reserves

US GAAP – and specifically SFAS 60 – have established different ways of recognizing revenue that must be followed depending on the specific duration of the traditional insurance products whose related revenue we are interested in reporting. Property and casualty as well as health and disability contracts represent some of the examples of short-duration traditional insurance policies. In the case of short-duration contracts, premiums are reported as revenues to the extent that they provide an insurance protection.

On the contrary traditional life policies and life-contingent annuities fall in the category of long-term traditional insurance policies. In this latter case, premiums are simply recognized as revenues once due from policyholders. Nevertheless, if premiums span a *significantly* shorter period than the one over which benefits are granted, insurers have to defer profits accordingly.

Finally, as far as investment contracts and universal life policies are concerned, the received amounts of money are regarded as deposits and are, therefore, excluded from the company's revenue. Evidently, the collected amounts must be reported in the proper account (the distinction between policyholders' account balances and separate accounts must be always kept in mind). On the contrary, fee income and other general charges (e.g., surrender charges and administration fees) are reported as revenue according to the revenue principle.

As a final point, some of the major revenue-related Balance Sheet items are made of premium receivables (which represent the amount of premiums due from policyholders) and unearned fee revenue.

As far as the major expense categories in an insurance company are concerned, *policyholders' benefits expenses* represent the expense related to liability for future policy benefits. They are equal to benefit disbursements plus any change in that reserve. As previously discussed, provided that the liability for future policy benefits is equal to the discounted value of future payments, policyholders' benefits expenses will also comprehend an interest expense computed on amount of the liability as of at the start of the year.

Finally, the Income Statement item related to claim reserves is "*losses and loss expenses*", which is obtained by summing all estimated costs for claim settlement during the year and estimate changes to settle prior year claims and then subtracting corresponding "reimbursements" from reinsurance contracts.

6.4.2   Deferred Policy Acquisition Costs

Deferred Acquisition Costs (DACs) are those costs directly related to the acquisition or renewal of insurance policies, not including fixed costs. Some examples may be provided by agent's commissions or examination costs. Accrual accounting requires that these initial costs be allocated over the life of the insurance contract, resulting in a matching between premium earned and the related expenses (Nissim, 2010). In synthesis, DAC constitute a significant asset category in insurance company balance sheets (reaching 6% as a mean value for LH insurers from 1999–2009) to be amortized over the life of the insurance contract. Since LH insurance policies are generally longer than PC contracts, we could expect (and is actually confirmed by data) that LH insurers have a higher proportion of DAC to total assets. An important additional rule refers to the situation in which the terms and conditions of an already existing policy get *significantly* modified: in that case, we should immediately expense the related DAC and capitalize a new amount of DAC, if any, related to the new policy.

Under Phase I of IFRS 4, it is worth noting that capitalization of DAC is neither forbidden nor mandatory and that, in addition, it is not established whether to capitalize DAC as an asset or as a contra-liability account. Therefore, we can deduce that US GAAP prescriptions, as far as DAC is concerned, are permitted by IFRS as well (Nissim, 2010).

As a final point of the current paragraph, VOBA (Value Of Business Acquired) also has to be mentioned. VOBA is simply the fair value (present value of future profits) related to contracts acquired in a life insurance acquisition transaction. Hence, VOBA, broadly speaking, represents the money paid in an acquisition for those future benefits embedded in the already existing acquired contracts.

6.5   INSURANCE CONTRACTS UNDER IAS/IFRS

In this section, we will briefly present IFRS 4, which addresses accounting methods specific to insurers, while it leaves aside the aspects related to policyholders (however, it seems likely that in the second phase of the framework, currently under discussion, the two accounting issues will probably be addressed conjointly). Before introducing the main features concerning insurance contracts accounting, it is worth mentioning a key specific characteristic of IFRS 4: it does not forbid the application of the previously used (country-specific) accounting methods that either satisfy minimum requirements or that just need some limited adjustments.

6.5.1 Recognition of Insurance Contracts

An insurance contract is an agreement between two parties, through which the insurer accepts a significant insurance risk by compensating policyholders (the insured party), once the specified uncertain event adversely affecting the policyholder or other beneficiary occurs.

Key to this definition is the concept of insurance risk. For our purposes, insurance risk is any risk transferred other than financial risk (see Chapter 7 for a discussion about insurance risk determinants). Furthermore, IFRS 4 has redefined financial risk to include all those non-financial variables not specific to at least one party of the contract: for instance, mortality rates in a certain region, weather, and catastrophe indices are now included as variables for financial risk purposes. On the other hand, the health of the policyholder or another beneficiary, the change in value of an asset actually held by the policyholder and even survival risk (that reflect uncertainties about the future cost of living) all qualify as possible sources of insurance risk. However, policies that do not transfer significant insurance risk, such as pension plans, are considered financial instruments treated under IAS 39.

To avoid providing companies with a subjectively chosen threshold that may arbitrarily divide significant from insignificant insurance risks, IFRS 4 does not offer details on the meaning of "significant" in the context of insurance risk. To be considered significant, the insurance risk of an insured event should be able to result in the insurer paying significant additional benefits in any scenario, except those without commercial substance. It is suggested, however, that significance must be evaluated taking into account two factors: the probability that the event actually occurs and the magnitude of the consequential effects. Nevertheless, the probability of the event may be assessed according to a logic of commercial substance. In fact, unlikely events pass the probability test, as long as they represent a threat to an entity's economic position and that entity is willing to buy insurance against that risk. In the same way, the magnitude of the effect must be assessed comparing cash flows, once the event occurred, with the minimum benefits payable in a scenario of commercial substance. For instance, presence of significant insurance risk is suggested when benefits to be paid are significantly higher compared to those upon maturity. Finally, the significance of the insurance risk is not evaluated at the portfolio level, but for a single contract. Nonetheless, if a portfolio of homogeneous contracts is known to be subject to a significant insurance risk, each individual contract can be treated as if it satisfies the requirement.

As for the definition of insurance risk, some further points to highlight the requirement of dealing with an *insurable interest* if present in the contract. Even though the insurer is not forced to evaluate the presence of such an interest, IASB opted for the inclusion of that requirement in order to make it easier to distinguish between insurance contracts and other financial (hedging) contracts. This is why weather or catastrophe bonds not requiring an insurable interest as a precondition for receiving payments fall generally outside the perimeter of IFRS 4.

As a final remark, it is worth mentioning that, unlike most of the categories of financial contracts, the uncertainty in insurance contracts comes from three sources:

- The occurrence of the event itself (think about a term life insurance);
- The timing of the occurrence (while, unfortunately, you are completely aware that in a whole life insurance contract the occurrence of the event is certain, timing may be not); and
- The magnitude of the effect.

6.5.2   Adequacy of Insurance Liabilities

At each reporting date, as required by IFRS 4, insurers must evaluate the adequacy of their recognized insurance liabilities. The test to carry out considers then-current estimates of all future contractual cash flows and ancillary expenses (e.g., handling costs). If the carrying amount of insurance liabilities is found insufficient, considering the estimated future cash flows, the full amount of such deficiency must be recognized in the current profit or loss statement. If the accounting policies of the insurance company do not contemplate an adequacy test meeting the two features described previously, the entity is required to:

- Compute the carrying amount of the related insurance liabilities, subtracting (1) any related deferred acquisition costs; and (2) any related intangible assets;
- Evaluate whether the carrying amount of the net insurance liabilities is lower than the carrying amount demanded if the relevant insurance liabilities were within the scope of IAS 37.

Since the level computed through the test based on IAS 37 is regarded as the minimum requirement, the entire negative difference must be immediately recognized in the profit or loss and either decrease the carrying amount of deferred acquisition or intangible assets or increase the carrying amount of liabilities.

Having a closer look at the test contemplated by IAS 37, it is carried out by comparing insurance liabilities net of the related assets to the amount determined under IAS 37. As IAS 37 requires market-related margin (which reflects both the value of money and the risks embedded), the best-estimate under IFRS 4 is significantly more prudent than IAS 37.

Finally, impairment under IAS 36 is applied to all the assets other than financial assets (which is accounted for under IAS 39). For instance, if a 10-year insurance contract with quarterly payments is priced profitably, the value of that contract represents an asset. In case of insurance assets, initial cost is usually the net selling price, while the value-in-use is computed using market-related discount rates.

Concluding, as far as the recognition of premium deficiency under the US GAAP is concerned, the application is also consistent with IFRS 4. For short-term contracts, US GAAP requires the comparison between total expected claims and unearned premiums. On the contrary, for long-term contracts, the comparison is between the present value of benefits and related settlement costs and the existing liability for future policy benefits.

6.5.3 Unbundling

IFRS 4 sets specific requirements for the unbundling of elements of insurance contracts and the separation of embedded derivatives. Unbundling simply means a separate accounting for the components of a contract. Some insurance contracts in fact consist of two parts: the *insurance* and the *deposit* component. Unbundling is mandatory if both of the following conditions are met:

1. the deposit component shall be separately measured; and
2. insurer accounting policies do not require recognizing all obligations and rights arising from the deposit component.

On the contrary, unbundling is permitted, but not required, if only the first of the two previous conditions is met. Finally, in case the insurer cannot measure the deposit component separately, unbundling is prohibited.

Once unbundled, the two elements of the contract must be separately recognized and measured. The financial assets or liabilities related to the deposit component are accounted for under IAS 39. Therefore, the classification reflects several rules already treated in the chapter about IAS 39. On the contrary, the insurance component (assets and liabilities) is treated according to IFRS 4. Receipts and disbursements relating to the deposit component are recognized as assets and liabilities, while those relating to the insurance components are, broadly speaking, recorded in the Income Statement.

As far as the separation of embedded derivatives is concerned, the salient aspects have been already covered in Chapter 2 in relation to the banking Balance Sheet. Here we will just add some further points that are specifically relevant to insurance companies.

One of the requirements of the embedded derivatives to be separated is that its economic characteristics and risks are not closely related to those of the host contracts. As to derivatives embedded in insurance contracts, they are regarded as closely related to the host contract if interdependent and so strong that the derivative cannot be separately measured. A surrender option gives the policyholder the possibility to terminate the insurance contract before maturity and receive a surrender value. Driving factors can be, for instance, the improvement of policyholders' health or favorable market conditions. Several surrender options, such as the ones where the surrender value is specified in a schedule, not indexed, or based on a principal amount and a fixed or variable interest rate, are exempt from the application of IAS 39. Nonetheless, if the surrender value responds to changes in financial variables, the insuring entity is required to separate the embedded derivatives.

Some other interesting examples may be given by embedded derivatives containing insurance risk. These derivatives, in fact, are not required to be separated, and measured at fair value, but such a separation is not prohibited. Some examples are a death benefit linked to equity prices and an option to take a life-contingent annuity at a guaranteed rate. Finally, a typical case of terms and conditions in an insurance contract that may represent embedded derivatives requiring separation is given by equity or commodity indexed benefit not contingent on an insured event.

6.5.4 Reinsurance

IFRS 4 explicitly forbids any offsetting of reinsurance assets against related insurance liabilities as well as income or expenses related to them. It is very common that, thanks to some reinsurance contracts, an insurer shall recognize some gains in the income statement. Although not prohibiting such a practice, IFRS 4 tries to regulate it. Disclosing information about gains and losses immediately recognized or gains and losses that have been deferred and amortized (as well as the amortization period and the unamortized amount) is necessary because sometimes reinsurance is a way for the ceding party to finance its operations.

Finally, when the following conditions are conjointly met it is suggested that reinsurance impairment should take place:

1. there is an objective evidence that the ceding party may not receive all the amounts due under the reinsurance contract; and
2. the impact of the event can be reliably measured.

6.5.5 Discretionary Participation Features

The presence of discretionary participation features (DPF) depends on the fact that, in some long-term insurance contracts, the effect of deviations in some assumptions (such as those relating to financial or mortality risk) is transferred to the policyholders in the form of performance-linkage clauses or retroactive modifications of the insurance premium. Economic reasons (e.g., competition and market pressure) or regulatory requirements could motivate insurers to refund a part of the excess premium to policyholders. The insurer performance may play an important role in the determination of the participation features: this is certainly one of the main sources of the high level of discretion involved. All the details about the right to participate and the related amount of timing and benefits are usually set in the contract.

There are some other elements, apart from the contractual requirements, which can affect the participation features. Rules or regulator judgment as well as management judgment could determine policyholders' expectation to receive additional benefits.

As established by IASB, the presentation of the amounts related to the DPF cannot be reported in an intermediate Balance Sheet as equity or liabilities and the policyholders' rights recognized as equity have to be disclosed. Moreover, if in a financial instrument the amount relating to a DPF is reported as equity, the related liability shall not be less than the amount resulting from the application of IAS 39 to the guaranteed element. In presence of DPF in the insurance contract, an adequacy test is required for liabilities.

From IFRS 4, it can be easily inferred that the difference between guaranteed elements and DPF. Guaranteed elements are payments or benefits that give the policyholder or the investor unconditional rights not subject to the discretion of the issuer. As they are not determined unilaterally, they are based on conditions independent from the control of the insurer.

The DPF, as explained previously, is the policyholders' contractual right to receive some additional benefits, which have to represent a significant part of the total contractual benefits and are related to the performance of the entity (e.g., the profits and losses of the entity and the realized/unrealized investment returns on a specific pool of assets held by the insurer) and whose timing and amount are contractually subject to insurer discretion. The discretion may have a different extent: it can be inherent only in the timing or the amount, but to qualify as DPF returns must be related to a share of the entity's (the issuer of the contract) profit or loss or return of a pool of assets. Other voluntary payments (i.e., those without a contractual or a legal basis) must be distinguished both from the DPF and from the guaranteed elements: they cannot be reported as liabilities if an appropriate decision of allocation is not made and disclosed.

The same rules for insurance contracts under IFRS 4 also govern insurance contracts with discretionary participation features. However, here are some relevant specific rules:

- The guaranteed element, regardless of its accounting methodology (if it is accounted for separately or with the DPF), must be recognized as a liability;
- If the DPF is not separated from the guaranteed portion of the contract, that contract in its entirety must be recognized as a liability;
- A separate DPF may be accounted for either as equity or as liability, according to a consistent logic;
- Any portion of the DPF recognized as equity should be separately reported. Any net income that belongs to that DPF portion should be reported as an allocation of profit or loss, instead of an integral part of income or expenses.

6.6 CASE STUDY

MetLife is the largest insurance company in US and the fourth largest worldwide (by asset size). It offers both LH and PC products meeting with over 90 million clients in more than 60 countries.

Next, we present the company's Income Statement and Balance Sheet.

Revenues	2011	2010
Premiums	36 361	27 071
Universal life and investment-type product policy fees	7806	6028
Net investment income	19 606	17 511
Other revenues	2532	2328
Net investment plus net derivative gains (losses)	3957	−673
Total revenues	70 262	52 265
Expenses		
Policyholder benefits and claims	36 903	30 670
Interest credited to policyholder account balances	5603	4919
Capitalization of DAC	−6858	−3299
Amortization of DAC and VOBA	5391	2843
Amortization of negative VOBA	−697	−64
Interest expense on debt	1629	1550
Other expenses	18 265	11 734
Total expenses	60 236	48 353
Income (loss) from continuing operations before provision for income tax	10 026	3912
Provision for income tax expense	−3075	−1165
Income (loss) from continuing operations, net of income tax	6951	2747
Income (loss) from discontinued operations, net of income tax	20	39
Net income (loss)	6971	2786

Expectedly, premiums represent the largest portion of revenues followed by net investment income. On the other hand, the largest expenses are related to policyholder benefits and claims. Three aspects are worth mentioning at this stage. First, fees from universal life and investment-type products represent just the fee income for universal life-type contracts, while the amounts collected from policyholders are added to policyholders' account balances and separate account investments. Second, the distinction between net investment income and net investment gains (losses) is due to the fact that, while the previous item includes interest, dividends, and other earnings arising from the invested assets (less all the associated expenses), it excludes capital gains or losses (both realized and unrealized ones). Third, an almost new relevant item is amortization of negative VOBA. Negative VOBA is determined by computing the excess of the fair value of the policyholder liabilities using market participants' assumptions over the corresponding fair value as measured using GAAP assumptions (therefore its amortization is a positive number).

Assets

Consolidated Balance Sheets December 31, 2011 and 2010 (In millions)	2011	2010
Investments: Fixed maturity securities	350 271	324 797
Equity securities available-for-sale	3023	3602
Trading and other securities	18 268	18 589
Mortgage loans	72 093	62 297
Policy loans	11 892	11 761
Real estate and real estate joint ventures	8563	8030
Other limited partnership interests	6378	6416
Short-term investments	17 310	9384
Other invested assets	23 628	15 430
Total investments	511 426	460 306
Cash and cash equivalents	10 461	12 957
Accrued investment income	4344	4328
Premiums, reinsurance and other receivables	22 481	19 799
Deferred policy acquisition costs and value of business acquired	27 971	27 092
Goodwill	11 935	11 781
Other assets	7984	8174
Assets of subsidiaries held-for-sale	0	3331
Separate account assets	203 023	183 138
Total assets	799 625	730 906

Liabilities

Future policy benefits	184 252	170 912
Policyholder account balances	217 700	210 757
Other policy-related balances	15 599	15 750
Policyholder dividends payable	774	830
Policyholder dividend obligation	2919	876
Payables for collateral under securities loaned and other transactions	33 716	27 272
Bank deposits	10 507	10 316
Short-term debt	686	306
Long-term debt	23 692	27 586
Collateral financing arrangements	4647	5297
Junior subordinated debt securities	3192	3191
Current income tax payable	193	297
Deferred income tax liability	7535	1856
Other liabilities	30 914	20 366
Liabilities of subsidiaries held-for-sale	0	3043
Separate account liabilities	203 023	183 138
Total liabilities	739 349	681 793
Contingencies, Commitments and Guarantees		
Redeemable non-controlling interests in partially owned consolidated subsidiaries	105	117
Equity	60 171	48 996

We will analyze briefly MetLife's Balance Sheet in order to give substance to the considerations just made.

The first aspect to stress is that investments represent the largest item in the balance sheet, constituting almost 64 and 63% of the total assets in 2011 and 2010 respectively. The second major item is the separate account assets: along with investments they account up to almost 90% of the total assets. It's worth noting that separate account assets and separate account liabilities have the same value, because, contract-holders own those assets and are entitled to the related income. DAC and VOBA, goodwill, premium and reinsurance receivables, and accrued investment income are the key remaining assets.

Accrued investment income, in particular, encompasses the income earned but not yet received, and it is mostly associated to interest-bearing investments and equity investments.

As for the liability side, we recall that MetLife is primarily a life insurer; therefore the presence of significant liabilities for future policy benefits doesn't come as a surprise. However, MetLife also operates in the auto and home insurance business (PC), future policy benefits include also "liabilities for unpaid claims and claim expenses for property and casualty insurance and represent the amount estimated for claims that have been reported but not settled and claims incurred but not reported."

Then, in relation to universal life insurance and investment-type contracts, we notice policyholder account balances, which are deposit accounts whose value is usually not different from the accounting value. Policyholders' account balances include the credited accrued interest.

The third most relevant liability item is given by separate account liabilities, which have already been mentioned previously.

As a new item, we have other policy-related balances. They generally include policyholder dividends left on deposit and policyholder dividends due and unpaid related primarily to traditional life and health contracts and premiums received in advance.

On the contrary, while policyholder dividend payables represent simply the amount of dividends to be due in the following calendar year, policyholder dividend obligation is a very interesting item and is worth a deeper discussion. Policyholder dividend obligation is closely related to the demutualization process in which Metropolitan Life Insurance Company ("MLIC") was involved to turn into a stock life insurance company and become a wholly-owned subsidiary of MetLife, Inc. Policyholders of a mutual life insurance company possess contractual rights to receive dividends that represent a share of the surplus earnings of the company and, hence, their rights must be untouched. However, conflicting interests arise from the demutualization process: stockholders benefit of any earnings not distributed to policyholders. Therefore, we can deal with a situation in which dividends to policyholders are reduced on purpose. "To provide assurance that the policyholders' reasonable dividend expectations will be met,"[1] the concept of *closed block* arose. By setting aside specific assets that can be sufficient to support obligations and liabilities relating to those policies, a closed block of assets will provide benefits only to the holders of the policies in the closed block. If cash flows from the closed block assets and claims related to the closed block turn out to be more favorable than what was originally estimated, total dividends paid to closed block policyholders in the future may be greater than the total dividends that would have been paid to these same policyholders. Any excess cash flows will be distributed to closed block policyholders and not to stockholders. If, on the other hand, the closed block funds are not sufficient, payments will be made from assets outside of the closed block. The closed block assets will be exhausted once the last closed block policy terminates. In our case, the expected life of the closed block is over 100 years and this is not unusual as the expected life is generally over 75 years in all situations. As mentioned earlier, the Company will pay out "the excess of the actual cumulative earnings of the closed block over the expected cumulative earnings to closed block policyholders as additional policyholder dividends", and (eventually, here we are) the excess will be reported as a *policyholder dividend obligation.*

Finally, *payables for collateral under securities loaned and other transactions* are primarily related to some security lending transactions into which MetLife entered in the past.

---

[1] Report prepared by the *Task Force on Mutual Life Insurance Company Conversion* (www.metlife.com).

7

Regulatory Capital for Insurance Companies

Marco Grotteria

As it happens for banks, capital requirements play a key role in business and financial planning of insurance companies, and in their valuation. Contrary to the banking system, there is not such a thing as a global regulatory framework in the industry, but – although a certain progressive convergence can be observed internationally – the regulation remains mostly national and in some jurisdictions even sub-national. We will therefore briefly sketch out the main features of the regulatory schemes in US and Europe.

7.1 INSURANCE INDUSTRY REGULATION IN THE US

Different from the other financial service industries, the US insurance sector is not regulated at federal but at state level. All that said, it's worth noting that the entire US history was marked by continuous tensions between federal institutions and states, and by some temporary attempts of deeper intervention made by the Federal Authority. Nevertheless, the content of the several state regulations clearly shows a high level of harmonization, thanks to the work of the NAIC, as will be explained next.

The most important event in the history of US insurance regulatory system is undoubtedly the Supreme Court decision in *Paul versus Virginia* (1868). Samuel Paul was an agent in Virginia for some insurance companies based in New York and not licensed in Virginia. After being denied the license to sell insurance policies and having sold them anyway, he was declared guilty of violating the state statute. That Supreme Court decision resulted in a reinforcement of the unquestioned state authority on the insurance industry.

Three years later, 50 insurance commissioners, aware of the necessity of uniformity in the insurance regulatory system, but committed to preserving state authority in the regulation field, formed the NAIC (National Association of Insurance Commissioners). The NAIC was established as a voluntary association with a private nature, and progressively in order to enhance state level regulation, the "NAIC has increasingly assumed a national role, centralizing many basic regulatory functions and operating as a quasi-federal agency by attempting to enforce national standards."[1]

A further relevant event in the insurance regulation-making process happened in response to congressional criticism after several bankruptcies of insurance companies in the 1980s: the NAIC initiated what was called the *accreditation program*. According to NAIC's definition, accreditation is "a certification given to a state insurance department once it has demonstrated it has met and continues to meet a wide range of legal, financial, functional and organizational standards as determined by a committee of its peers."

Nowadays, US regulation of insurance companies covers all the aspects of that business from the process of fair pricing of insurance policies to the settlement of minimum capital requirements (in order to avoid insurers' insolvency), and to the prevention of unfair competitive behavior.

The organization of regulators works as follows: within each State, an *ad hoc* department in the executive branch regulates insurance. The head of that department, the insurance commissioner, the director, or the superintendent, either elected directly by citizens or appointed by governors, is in charge for determining which insurance companies may conduct business in his state and the rules to follow.

7.2   CURRENT US SYSTEM

Being aware of the principal computational methods as regards regulatory Risk-Based Capital measurement is crucial for any analyst approaching the valuation of insurance companies. Nevertheless, for simplicity reasons, we will discuss just the final formulas to apply to compute the RBC and we'll skip the computations necessary to reach those involved elements.

The calculation of the minimum capital level for insurers depends on their specific business features, namely the precise kind of business in which insurance companies competes, the asset categories they invests in, and other risks related to both assets and the liabilities.

7.2.1   Risk-Based Capital

In US a rule-based valuation of insurance reserves is carried out. With pre-scribed assumptions regarding the elements necessary for computation of life insurance reserves, such as interest and mortality rates, the adopted rule-based approach is sometimes criticized as not being kept up-to-date, given that the tables are seldom reviewed. Therefore, a principle-based reserving was proposed,

---

[1] Randall, S. (1999), *Insurance Regulation in the United States: Regulatory Federalism and The National Association Of Insurance Commissioners.*

which found application (at least initially) only on regulation of Property and Casualty.

Computing the value of assets may be burdensome and complex as it will follow specific rules prescribed in each state.

Before deriving the Total Adjusted Capital (TAC), NAIC requires the application of two more items to life, accident, and health insurers, which have not been analyzed yet in previous chapters: *Asset Valuation Reserve* and *Interest Maintenance Reserve*. While the former is an explicit liability reserve aimed at providing a cushion against potential equity or credit losses (e.g., in case of stocks, bonds, or real estates), the purpose of the latter is to report accumulated realized gains and losses related to interest rate movements and to amortize them over the life of the sold assets (the amortization impacts the net investment income).

The RBC ratio is finally measured dividing Total Adjusted Capital over Authorized Control Level Risk-Based Capital. Depending on what specific business is involved (life, health, or PC), a different model for the computation of risk-based capital is employed. The idea behind risk-based capital computation is to individually analyze every risk category and determine the capital amount insurers would need to maintain to reach an acceptable probability that the company would have enough capital to survive that specific risk. This is usually the probability of ruin of less than 5% due to that specific risk over an unspecified period of time, unspecified by general rules, in the future. Then each piece enters a summation and the RBC level is measured.

For life insurance, the formula of the Authorized Control Level, also referred to as the 100% RBC level, is the following:

$$RBC = C_0 + C_{4a} + \sqrt{(C_{1o} + C_{3a})^2 + (C_{1cs} + C_{3c})^2 + (C_2)^2 + (C_{3b})^2 + (C_{4b})^2}$$

$$(7.1)$$

where:

- C_0, out from C_1, is the Asset Risk of Affiliates;
- C_1 is the Asset Risk related to common stock (C_{1cs}) and other Asset risk (C_{1o});
- C_2 represents the Insurance Risk;
- C_3 represents the Interest Rate Risk (C_{3a}), Health Credit Risk (C_{3a}), and Market Risk(C_{3c});
- C_4 relates to the Guaranty Fund Assessment Risk (C_{4a}) and the Health administrative expense risk (C_{4b}).

The asset risk of affiliates refers to their risk of default: in case of a percentage of ownership lower than 100%, that measure must be corrected proportionally (prorated). The asset risk – other than that referring to affiliates – is related to fluctuations in value of assets, such as fixed income and stock investments. What we define here as insurance risk for life companies is the same as the underwriting risk that will be presented in case of property/casualty and health companies. In case of life insurers, the risk of excess claims, due to fluctuations or reserving errors, is the insurance risk. Interest rate risk, which is specific to life insurance companies, refers to the risk of losses caused by changes in interest rate levels. Finally, as reported by the NAIC, business risk, which is an item only present in the formulas applied to life and health insurers, *is based on premium income, annuity considerations, and separate account liabilities.* Litigation issues must be also considered in the computation of business risk exposures, as well as ASO and ASC expenses (especially for health insurers).

As far as health insurance is concerned, the formula is the following:

$$RBC = H_0 + \sqrt{(H_1)^2 + (H_2)^2 + (H_3)^2 + (H_4)^2} \qquad (7.2)$$

where:

- H_0 is the Asset Risk of Affiliates;
- H_1 is what is defined as the other Asset Risk;
- H_2 represents the Underwriting Risk;
- H_3 represents the Credit Risk;
- H_4 is the Business Risk.

While all the other elements have already been treated in a sufficient detail, business risk for Health insurers can due to the following sub-categories of risk: *Administrative Expense Risk (variability of operating expenses), Non-Underwritten and Limited Risk (collectability of payments for administering third party programs), Guaranty Fund Assessment Risk and Excessive Growth* (NAIC, 2009).

Finally, for property and casualty insurance companies, the risk categories to consider are six, referred to as R_0 through R_5:

- R_0 covers off-Balance Sheet risks and risk related to investments in insurance affiliated companies;
- R_1 refers to the risk (principally credit default risk) on fixed income securities;
- R_2 represents the market risk in equity or real estates;
- R_3 corresponds to credit risk on reinsurance receivables (in which case ceded reinsurance credit risk is generally speaking divided between R_3 and R_4) or other receivables;
- Finally, R_4 is the reserving risk (e.g., basic reserving risk or loss concentration risk) and R_5 refers to written premium risk and growth risk (broadly speaking, what we have previously referred to as Underwriting Risk).

The relevant formula is as follows:

$$\text{Total RBC After Covariance} = R_0 + \sqrt{(R_1)^2 + (R_2)^2 + (R_3)^2 + (R_4)^2 + (R_5)^2}$$
$$(7.3)$$

The Authorized Control Level RBC (ACL RBC) for PC insurers is finally computed as 0.5 × RBC After Covariance.

To conclude this paragraph, it's worth stressing, although we believe it should be already very clear, that the right categorization of risks is crucial for a correct analysis of the Regulatory-Based Capital. Nevertheless, it's also important to note that the exclusion of some risk categories from the square root rule and the imposition of a correlation, between different risk categories, either equal to 0 or 1 (the assumption of total independence may undervalue combined risk and that of perfect correlation may exaggerate it) are certainly some primary issues as regards NAIC risk measurement system which have been often raised by analysts.

7.2.1.1   Action Levels

The five possible actions, as set by the NAIC, resulting from the calculation of the RBC ratio are the following:

1. Whenever Total Adjusted Capital is equal to or higher than 200% of the Authorized Control level, "*no action*" has to be carried out.
2. If Total Adjusted Capital is between 150 and 200% of Authorized Control Level (so it falls in the *Company Action Level*), the insurance company is asked to report to the relevant regulator through a financial plan explaining the causes that have led to that financial situation. That plan shall include financial projections both with and without any new corrective measurements (proposed by the insurer). Failing to prepare the plan, the company will be subject to the Regulatory Action Level.
3. In case Total Adjusted Capital ranges between 100 and 150% of Authorized Control Level, the insurance company will be subject to the *Regulatory Action Level*. In this case, insurance companies are also required to prepare a responsive action plan while commissioner is expected to carry out deeper investigations on the insurers' business.
4. When Total Adjusted Capital is between 70 and 100% an *Authorized Control Level* is activated. Among all the levels seen earlier, this is the first one in which a commissioner is permitted to take the insurance company under control. It's worth noting that although the company may still be in a situation of technical solvency, control is automatically permitted by the current legislation.
5. A RBC ratio less than 70% sparks a series of actions established for *Mandatory Control Level*. Regulators must put the insurer under control even though the insurance company is still profitable or has a positive level of capital.

7.3   SOLVENCY II – EUROPEAN-BASED REGULATION

With the term *Solvency II*, we refer to the European insurance regulatory directive issued in 2009 and whose implementation will probably start in 2015.

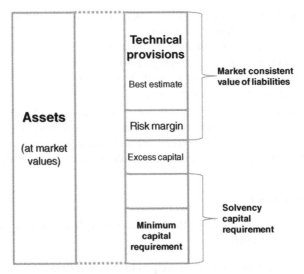

Figure 7.1   Outline of the Solvency II structure

Similar to Basel II, Solvency II is organized around three main pillars which actually appear to be modeled using Basel II as a paradigm. The three pillars are the following:

The first pillar is mainly dedicated to valuation criteria for assets and liabilities, identification and measures for admissible capital items, computational methodologies to obtain SCR (Solvency Capital Requirement) and MCR (the minimum capital requirement).

The second pillar concerns qualitative requirements and supervisory activity imposed to insurance companies. Especially as regards the former (concerning governance, risk management, and internal control), it's worth mentioning the principle of "Own Risk and Solvency Assessment" (ORSA), according to which the insurer has to regularly assess its risk and solvency position.

Mirroring Basel II, the third pillar regulates market transparency and market discipline in insurance companies.

Given its preeminent valuation implications, only the first pillar will be subject to further discussion in this chapter. Figure 7.1 shows the issues at stake as regards the first pillar.

7.3.1 Valuation of Assets and Liabilities

As a general principle, article 75 of the Directive establishes that the valuation rules for asset and liabilities in insurance companies must be *market consistent*. Fair value evaluation recall the idea of a *price that would be received to sell an asset or paid to transfer a liability in an orderly transaction between knowledgeable market participants at arm's length at the measurement date*: this is the same idea already discussed in Chapter 2 about the Balance Sheet for banks. In particular, when liabilities are evaluated, no adjustment related to the insurance company creditworthiness or reinsurance is carried out.

As the reader may have already imagined, the basic idea (which is explicitly expressed in the directive) is to comply with IAS/IFRS, unless valuation carried out following international accounting standards doesn't result in *economic values*.

QIS 5 also establishes that, to measure the economic value of assets and liabilities, insurers must prefer a mark to market approach, relying on available prices in orderly transactions.

Whenever the market consistent approach just treated cannot be applied, for instance due to a lack of ordinary transactions on active markets, insurance companies can apply mark-to-model techniques relying on benchmarks and computations based as much as possible on observable market inputs (trying to avoid the non-observable ones). A further requirement is the following: before using those inputs, insurance companies have to assess the accuracy and the practical use of the specific inputs. Moreover, insurance companies must comply with guidance issued by IASB and already treated in Chapter 2 about banking Balance Sheets as regards all the aspects of the previous definition of fair value.

Nevertheless, as it has been already affirmed, insurance companies can opt not to apply IAS/IFRS in case the hypothetic accounting value doesn't reflect the economic value of the item. However, a motivated justification must be provided in such a case and insurance companies must show the difference in the two values (computed according to IAS/IFRS and following the new applied methodology) as well as a more or less detailed description of the chosen technique.

As regards technical provisions, they must be evaluated at economic values. Unfortunately, for reserves it's a bit harder (probably impossible) to find an active insurance policy market. Therefore, European legislator, in article 76, established as follows:

1. The value of technical provisions shall correspond to the current amount insurance and reinsurance undertakings would have to pay if they were to transfer their insurance and reinsurance obligations immediately to another insurance or reinsurance undertaking.
2. The calculation of technical provisions shall make use of and be consistent with information provided by the financial markets and generally available data on underwriting risks (market consistency).
3. Technical provisions shall be calculated in a prudent, reliable and objective manner.

Moreover, in the next article it is stated that the value of technical provisions must be equal to the sum of the *best estimate* and the *risk margin*.

We will not enter into the details on how to identify and use the inputs to compute reserves, but as for the realistic hypothesis suggested by EIOPA, we notice that the approach is slightly different for life and health compared to property and casualty, and that technical provisions are classified according to lines of business.

7.3.2 Best Estimate and Risk Margin

The definition of *best estimate* and *risk margin*, have a key role in the new European framework. Before analyzing those two concepts, it is worth underlining that, when computing their technical provisions, insurers must segment their obligations into homogeneous risk groups (substance must prevail over form, that is, if a contract includes aspects of diverse nature, such as features about life and casualty, unbundling is demanded) and at least by line of business.

In article 77, the European directive defines two central concepts of best estimates and risk margin as follows:

> The best estimate shall correspond to the probability-weighted average of future cash-flows, taking account of the time value of money (expected present value of future cash-flows), using the relevant risk-free interest rate term structure;

> The risk margin shall be such as to ensure that the value of the technical provisions is equivalent to the amount that insurance and reinsurance undertakings would be expected to require, in order to take over and meet the insurance and reinsurance obligations.

The idea to weight future cash-flows by their probability simply means that uncertainty in future cash-flows must be considered while computing best estimates. Therefore, possible changes in timing, frequency, and severity of insured events, uncertainty on the claim amount or interdependency among more than one cause, as well as in the liquidation timing, must be taken into account. This should indicate how relevant the commitment of insurance companies is in terms of both technological resources and methodological capabilities.

Risk margin must be intended as the cautionary margin applied in order to remunerate for the uncertainty embedded in the evaluation of technical provisions. To be more precise, it is computed by defining the cost of providing eligible own funds to the SCR necessary to support insurance claims. The rate applied while determining that cost is referred to as the Cost-of-Capital rate.

7.3.3 Own Funds

Own funds comprise basic own funds and ancillary own funds. Inspired by Basel II, own funds are classified into three tiers. Moreover, the Directive recognizes different categories (whether basic or ancillary) based on the specific characteristics of own funds:

- permanent availability (to absorb losses on a going-concern basis);
- seniority;
- original maturity;
- absence of incentives to redeem;
- other peculiar features.

To be more specific, the principal Tier 1 funds, conditional upon satisfaction of the classification criteria for Tier 1 basic instruments as defined next, comprise the following items:

Paid-up equity capital less treasury shares;
Share premium account;
Other reserves, such as retained earnings or reserves arisen due to changes of accounting measures;
Other paid in capital instruments, that is, preferred shares, subordinated liabilities or other subordinated instruments.

Some adjustments, such as reducing the Tier 1 funds as stated previously by any participation the insurance company holds in financial and credit institutions, have to be carried out.

However, some of the major requirements that funds have to comply with in order to be admitted in the Tier 1, as given by QIS5, are the following:

- The item should be the most subordinated claim during the liquidation of the insurer.
- The item should not give rise to or speed up the insolvency of the insurer. The holder of the instrument must have no right to ask for such an insolvency. The instrument should not even be considered while determining whether or not the institution is actually insolvent. Moreover, the insurance company must be in the position to cancel coupon/dividend payments without risking being subject to default or legal insolvency.
- The item must guarantee temporary cessation of repayments or redemption if the insurance company does not comply with its Solvency Capital Requirement or would do so, had the instrument been repaid or redeemed.
- The item is immediately capable of absorbing losses.
- The item has no fixed maturity or its original maturity is at least equal to 10 years.
- No incentive to redeem or step-ups should be embedded and redemption is only allowed conditional upon national supervisor's approval.
- The item is entitled to discretionary coupon/dividend payments.

Moreover, other paid-in capital instruments must include one of the following principal loss absorbency characteristics related to a trigger event, which represents a significant breach of the Solvency Capital Requirement:

(a) Automatic conversion either into ordinary share capital or into the initial fund is determined.
(b) The principal amount is reduced together with retained earnings, by the amount of the breach of the Solvency Capital Requirement. That item can brought to its previous value only by future profits once the insurer is compliant with the Solvency Capital Requirement.
(c) A principal loss absorbency mechanism resulting in a measure equivalent to those mechanisms set out in the previous points is established.

The list of Tier 2 funds is shorter than the previous one. In fact, Tier 2 funds, conditional upon satisfaction of the classification criteria for Tier 2 basic Instruments as defined next, comprise the following items:

1. Called up ordinary share capital;
2. Own funds exceeding amounts used to support related risks in case of restricted reserves and other called up capital instruments that either absorb losses first or rank pari passu, in going concern, with capital instruments that absorb losses first;
3. Other paid-in capital instruments (including preference shares, subordinated mutual members accounts and subordinated liabilities that do not have the features required for Tier 1 but that meet the criteria below).[2]

On the other hand, basic Tier 2 funds must meet the following requirements:

- The item should be junior to all policyholders and beneficiaries and non-subordinated creditors.
- If the instrument has been called up but not paid up, it should meet the criteria for Tier 1;
- The item should not give rise to or speed up the insolvency of the insurer. The holder of the instrument must have no right to ask for such an insolvency;
- The item has no fixed maturity or its original maturity is at least equal to 5 years;
- The item is repayable or redeemable at the option of the insurer only conditional upon national supervisor's approval;
- The item must guarantee the temporary cessation of repayments or redemption if the insurance company does not comply with its Solvency Capital Requirement or would do it, had the instrument been repaid or redeemed.

Finally, Tier 3 instruments are net deferred tax assets and other capital instruments (see previously) not meeting previous requirements. In fact, any basic own

---

[2] QIS5 Technical Specifications, July 5, 2010, European Commission.

fund, which doesn't meet requirements as shown previously as regards basic Tier 1 and Tier 2 funds, may be included in the Tier 3 category in case the following criteria are met:

- The item should be junior to all policyholders and beneficiaries and non-subordinated creditors.
- The item should not give rise to or speed up the insolvency of the insurer;
- The item has no fixed maturity or its original maturity is at least equal to 3 years.
- The item must guarantee the temporary cessation of repayments or redemption if the insurance company does not comply with its Solvency Capital Requirement or would do it, had the instrument been repaid or redeemed.
- Coupon or dividends related to the instrument must be deferred if the insurance company does not meet the Minimum Capital Requirement or if, completing the payment, it will breach it.

Finally, we have Tier 2 and Tier 3 ancillary funds, namely all remaining capital instruments that can be called up to cover losses. In particular, in case the following instruments are not included in the basic own funds category, in the Tier 2 ancillary funds we will find unpaid share capital or initial fund that has not been called up, letters of credit or guarantees, and other legally binding commitments received by insurers. The last issue related to the definition of funds regards Tier 3 ancillary funds. They comprise in-force arrangements qualified for meeting solvency requirements that would constitute ancillary own funds under the directive principles, but that would not be allowed to be included in Tier 2 ancillary own funds as they would not be classified in Tier 1 if they were called up and paid in.

In the *QIS5 Technical Specifications* issued by the European commission and to which we refer in this entire paragraph, it has been also affirmed that Tier 1 own funds must represent at minimum 50% of SCR and Tier 3 funds at maximum 15% of the same SCR. Moreover, to satisfy the MCR, eligible items are only the Tier 1 elements and basic Tier 2 items (not exceeding the 20% of the MCR).

7.3.4   SCR and MCR

The SCR should equal the Value-at-Risk of the basic own funds of an insurance company over a one-year period subject to a confidence level of 99.5%.

The SCR is determined as follows: $SCR = BSCR + Adj + SCROp$, where $BSCR$ is the Basic SCR, Adj is the adjustment necessary to consider the risk absorbing effect of technical provisions and deferred taxes and SCR_{Op} is the SCR for the operational risk. In particular the BSCR is the capital requirement before any adjustments, considering the capital requirements of six classes of risk:

- Market Risk;
- Counterparty default risk;

- Life underwriting risk;
- Non-life underwriting risk;
- Health underwriting risk;
- Intangible assets risk.

Moreover, it's determined as follows:

$$BSCR = \sqrt{\sum_{ij} Corr_{ij} \times SCR_i \times SCR_j} + SCR_{Intangibles} \qquad (7.4)$$

where SCR_i and SCR_j are the capital requirements for the individual SCR risks. As it may easily be imagined, the term correlation in the formula, unlike US RBC formula, is not imposed to be either 0 or 1.

On the opposite side, the MCR represents a further solvency measure, standing for the minimum level of eligible basic funds below which risk becomes unacceptable for policyholders. The European directive affirms that it shall be computed *in a clear and simple manner, and in such a way as to ensure that the calculation can be audited*. Although the exact formula is not provided by the directive itself, but (as usual) by the Technical Specifications related to the directive, that statement is crucial to understand the basic idea underlying that "number". The European regulators seemed to choose to leave more room of freedom in the computation of SCR, while maintaining a deeper control of the MCR.

The directive establishes that the linear function used to calculate MCR "shall be calibrated to the Value-at-Risk of the basic own funds of an insurance or insurance undertaking subject to a confidence level of 85% over a one-year period." Given that in this paragraph, to keep it simple, we will not consider composite undertakings, the linear function is simply the result of the sum of two elements:

The linear formula component for non-life insurance or reinsurance obligations.
The linear formula component for life insurance or reinsurance obligations.

Starting to analyze non-life insurance obligations, the following two inputs are necessary:

TPj = technical provisions (not including the risk margin) computed for each specific business line, net of reinsurance, subject to a minimum of zero;
Pj = premiums for each line of business written over the last 12-month period, net of reinsurance, subject to a minimum of zero.

The MCR_{NL} (non-life) is simply computed according to the following formula:

$$MCR_{NL} = \sum_j \max \left(\alpha_j \times TP_j; \beta_j \times P_j \right) \qquad (7.5)$$

Table 7.1 α and β coefficients for MCR_{NL} by line of business

j	Line of business	αj (%)	βj (%)
A.1	Motor vehicle liability and proportional reinsurance	12	13
A.2	Motor, other classes insurance and proportional reinsurance	13	9
A.3	Marine, aviation, transport insurance, and proportional reinsurance	18	22
A.4	Fire and other property damage insurance and proportional reinsurance	14	13
A.5	General liability insurance and proportional reinsurance	14	20
A.6	Credit and suretyship insurance, and proportional reinsurance	25	28
A.7	Legal expenses insurance and proportional reinsurance	12	9
A.8	Assistance and proportional reinsurance	14	7
A.9	Miscellaneous financial loss insurance and proportional reinsurance	20	17
A.10	NP reinsurance – property	26	23
A.11	NP reinsurance – casualty	26	22
A.12	NP reinsurance – MAT	26	21
A.13	Medical expense	13	5
A.14	Income protection	18	11
A.15	Workers compensation	14	7
A.16	NP reinsurance – health	26	22

Just to provide a deeper insight, calibration of the formula for coefficients α and β is provided by the following segmentation by lines of business (see Table 7.1).

On the other hand, as the formula for the MCR_L follows the same logic as the previous one (a sum of weighted elements segmented by lines of business), although it's not identical, we will not analyze it deeper. Nevertheless, we need to mention that while *TP,* technical provisions, are still one of the two components of the formula for MCR_L, a new element, represented by Capital at Risk for all contracts (CAR) (weighted by 0.1%), appear in the formula. As defined in QIS5, CAR is

"the sum of financial strains for each policy on certain and immediate death or disability". The latter is the amount currently payable on death or disability of the insured and the present value of annuities payable on death or disability of the insured less the net technical provisions (not including the risk margin) and the increase in refundable reinsurance which is directly caused by death or disability of the insured".

In principle, that assessment should be performed on a policy-by-policy approach.

Then, after obtaining the MCR_{linear} as the sum of those two elements (MCR_{NL} + MCR_L), we may easily compute the $MCR_{combined}$. A last detail to notice, which is extremely important for the computation of the $MCR_{combined}$ is that the MCR linear function is subject to a floor of 25% and a cap of 45% with respect to the SCR.

In fact, $MCR_{combined} = \{min\ [max(MCR_{linear};\ 0.25 \times (SCR));\ 0.45 \times (SCR)]\}$. Finally, in order to reach the MCR, a last comparison must be carried out: $MCR = max\{MCR_{combined};\ AMCR\}$ where AMCR is the Absolute Floor for the MCR, which is equal to €2.2M for non-life insurance and €3.2M for the life.

7.4 MAIN DIFFERENCES BETWEEN SOLVENCY II AND US REGULATION

The aim of this paragraph is to identify the major points of difference between US regulation (for simplicity we will carry out our analysis just referring to NAIC RBC for life insurers) and Solvency II. Such differences are of paramount importance when dealing with the relative valuation of companies across the two jurisdictions.

Solvency II SCR should be equal to the *Value-at-Risk* of the basic own funds of an insurance company over a *one-year* period subject to a confidence level of 99.5%. On the contrary, we can affirm that *several risk metrics* have found application under NAIC rules. Recently new methods, such as conditional tail expectation (CTE) approach, namely the method of measuring the expected value of losses exceeding VaR, are finding application. Although results are harder to interpret,[3] the application of CTE allows us to overcome two VaR shortfalls, namely violation of sub-additivity and non-consideration of the size of losses in excess of VaR.

As regards aggregation of risks, NAIC formulas impose a *correlation* coefficient among different risk categories either equal to 0 or to 1, while Solvency II prescribes less extreme solutions to follow.

Even as regards the appropriate *time horizon* to develop the analysis of risk-based capital, US regulation and Solvency II have made different choices. In US there is no strictly prescribed time horizon as it's recognized that different risks may gradually appear and develop over different time periods. On the opposite side, Solvency II SCR establishes a time horizon of one year for all the risks.

The role covered by time horizon choice in the determination process of risk-capital measure is crucial. Quoting Painter and Isaac:[4]

> Risk can look very different over time. A risk that can dominate the risk landscape over a short time horizon can be more benign over a longer time horizon. [...] Therefore, a single economic capital metric is a current-point-in-time measure that does not consider how risks interact over many different

---

[3] Campbell, M.P. (2012), *A Tale of Two Formulas: Solvency II SCR and RBC*, Society of Actuaries.

[4] Painter, R.A. and Isaac, D. (2007), *A Multi-Stakeholder Approach to Capital Adequacy*, www.conningresearch.com.

time horizons. They view risk over a single time horizon. It is important to understand how these risks interact and aggregate over different time horizons to understand the appropriate level of capital to hold.

As far as *internal models* are concerned, in the US a "healthy skepticism", which allows some insurance companies to apply their own internal models so long as a standard scenario with predetermined factors is used as well for comparison, is dominant. On the opposite side, it seems that Solvency II shows a high level of reliance on the sophisticated methods developed in the industry and on the advanced capabilities of insurers, so as to foster a technological competition among insurers by "awarding" the best risk measurement practices.

8

Assessing the Business Plan for an Insurance Company

Amedeo Giammattei

This chapter offers a framework for analyzing the business plan of an insurance company from a valuation perspective. The goal of the analysis and the underlying method are not different from what we presented for banks in Chapter 4: assessing the sustainability of forecasts and highlighting areas of potential inconsistency by applying three broad categories of checks on the business plan:

- *Status quo analysis*: determine if potential adjustments should be applied to key Balance Sheet items. Areas which are particularly critical for insurers include asset valuation, reserve adequacy, and solvency,
- *Internal consistency*: assessment of the business plan projections to verify internal coherence, that is, consistency between historical performance and projected performance, the expected evolution of P&L items and that of Balance Sheet items, asset side and liability side, financial forecasts, and operating forecasts.
- *External consistency*: assessment of those elements that are not directly controlled by company management but, especially in the case of insurance companies, have a significant impact on expected performance; that is, macroeconomic trends and competitive dynamics. Benchmarking business plan targets against market consensus, whenever available, provides an additional and important external reference.

8.1 *STATUS QUO* ANALYSIS

A credible business plan should move from a reliable representation of the current financial and operating position of the company. Therefore, it is important for the analyst to start from a thorough investigation of the historical financial statements to evaluate whether adjustments are required to better reflect the current situation and expected evolution of the business. Such adjustments might include:

- Additional write-downs on specific investments to better reflect their value (*asset valuation*);

- Reserve additions in case the company appears to be under-reserved (*reserve adequacy*);
- The need to improve the solvency ratio by increasing the available solvency margin or shrinking the required solvency margin, given higher projected capital requirements imposed by market expectations or regulators (*solvency*).

As already mentioned for banks, the valuation of each of these items is intrinsically related to expectations and forecasts. For this reason, any consideration has to be performed in connection with the examination of the business plan as a whole.

8.1.1 Asset Valuation

Asset valuation is of critical importance for insurance companies given its relevant impact on the investment result, which is a large component of an insurer's overall performance. Insurers carry almost all of their assets at market value, which leads to significant investment income volatility when markets end up in extreme situations.

There are two important aspects that need to be stressed in this respect:

- For illiquid assets a functioning market no longer exists. Therefore, it is difficult to estimate their value accurately. In this case, it is useful to check the ratio between cumulative write-downs and total gross exposure and compare it to peer levels. Thus, the analyst can establish whether the ratio is sufficiently conservative or is an element to be flagged and further investigated.
- During the recent financial crisis, companies were allowed to reclassify, both under US GAAP and IAS, financial instruments in fair value categories to historical cost categories. In other words, companies could effectively avoid the fair value charge on these instruments and, in turn, report higher capital ratios for solvency purposes.

Overall in the current framework there are elements of discretion in the classification and valuation of financial instruments, which can have a significant impact on the value of financial instruments and consequently on financial statements. Hence, it is important for the analyst to be comfortable with the different classification and valuation choices made by the company with respect to its investment portfolio.

8.1.2 Reserve Adequacy

Assessing reserve adequacy is of paramount importance when analyzing the financial strength of an insurance company. At the same time, the level of technical expertise required to express a judgment on this matter is extremely high. There-fore, this task is performed directly by actuaries who certify that the stated level of reserves is adequate given business prospects.

8.1.3   Solvency

Not dissimilar from banks, the concept of adequate level of capitalization for insurers has been evolving rapidly. Regulators have been refining the set of rules defining capital requirements (e.g., Solvency I, Solvency II) and, simultaneously, the number of subjects involved in this process has increased (national supervisors, European Union, EIOPA, and rating agencies). Investors also play a significant role in the definition of adequate solvency ratios. Moreover, market expectations might vary according to the stage of the economic cycle: lower ratios will be required in case of economic expansion, allowing insurers to generate earnings by employing capital to grow the business. Vice versa, in time of economic crisis, a higher capital buffer would be expected to absorb the impact of unforeseen events.

In this environment, it becomes more and more challenging to establish univo-cally whether the solvency position of an insurance company is sufficiently robust. Therefore, it is important to cross-check the results derived by the application of different methodologies. In addition, this exercise has to be performed not only on the company as it is but also after potential adjustments deriving from analysis on the two areas discussed before (asset valuation and reserve adequacy).

From a practical standpoint, the solvency position of the company can be assessed according to different evaluation frameworks:

- Current regulatory framework (e.g., Solvency I);
- Expected regulatory framework (e.g., Solvency II);
- Rating agencies framework given target company rating (e.g., S&P risk based capital model);
- Market expectations and peer benchmarking.

Any issues with solvency not effectively addressed in the business plan should lead to anticipate the need of a rights issue or the implementation of a deleveraging program. In both cases, it is important to estimate what the impact would be on the final valuation.

8.2   INTERNAL CONSISTENCY

Once the analysis of the *status quo* has been carried out, the focus should move to business plan forecasts, and in particular, on the assessment of their internal consistency. It is important to concentrate the attention on connections between different elements of the plan to verify if they are easily understandable and justifiable in terms of "what drives what and why". Those which are not should be questioned and investigated further.

The set of checks that can be performed to assess internal consistency can be broken down into four main categories:

- Consistency between forecasts and historical data;
- Consistency between P&L items and Balance Sheet items;
- Consistency between the asset and liability sides of the Balance Sheet;
- Consistency between financial and operating forecasts.

Internal consistency can be best assessed by being familiar with the key dynamics of insurance companies' business models, the structure of their financial statements, and the basic concepts behind their forecasting model. While the first two elements were discussed in Chapter 6, a review of the key notions underlying forecasting will be presented at the end of this chapter.

8.2.1   Historical versus Projected Performance

A first area of investigation related to internal consistency concerns the relationship between historical data and future projections. The goal is to identify short-term and long-term trends in operating performance, in order to assess the quality and sustainability of forecasted earnings. In the following paragraphs, two different and complementary methodologies of assessment are presented.

8.2.1.1   Express P&L and Balance Sheet in Percentage Terms

A common way to analyze the evolution of historical and projected financials is to express both the P&L and the Balance Sheet in percentage terms and question any significant variation. As for the P&L, each item should be expressed as a percentage of premiums, while for the Balance Sheet total assets are used as denominator. Usual areas of investigation in the P&L are revenue and cost composition. In the Balance Sheet, one should focus on asset and liability mix.

8.2.1.2   Key Drivers' Evolution

A second way to assess potential inconsistencies in the projections compared to historical data is to look at the evolution of the key P&L and Balance Sheet drivers to spot any abrupt jumps or inconsistent trends. Typical drivers to be examined include:

- Premium growth: represent the evolution of business volumes and pricing;
- Retention ratio: measures the extent of reinsurance;
- Combined ratio: sum of claim and expense ratios, signals how profitably the company is underwriting;
- Investment return: represent profitability of the investment portfolio;
- Reserve ratio: estimate of reserve strength;

- Solvency ratio: capital requirement coverage;
- Payout ratio: percentage of earnings distributed as dividends;
- ROE: key profitability measure and valuation driver.

In particular, for life insurance, one should also look at:

- New business value margin: profitability margin on new business written in the last year;
- Return on embedded value (ROEV): a key profitability measure and valuation driver for life insurance.

If an explanation for abnormal variations cannot be found, either in the set of management actions announced with the business plan or in the expected evolution of the macroeconomic and competitive landscape, the matter should be an object of further investigation.

8.2.2 P&L versus Balance Sheet

The P&L and Balance Sheet evolve according to some fundamental patterns underlying the business model of an insurance company. Such patterns can be summarized into three main stages:

- When the insurer sells insurance contracts, the company collects premiums and incurs some acquisition and administrative costs (P&L). Premiums are immediately invested in assets and reserves are created to cover future claims (balance sheet).
- Investments generate investment income while some ongoing administrative costs are also incurred (P&L). Reserves are strengthened or released, reflecting updated estimates of future claims (Balance Sheet). Reserve additions or releases are also reflected in the P&L.
- The insurer pays actual claims on the insurance contracts. The difference between estimated and actual claims flows through P&L. Claims-handling costs are also incurred (P&L). Reserves are adjusted according to actual claims while part of the investments is used to pay claims (Balance Sheet).

As a result, when checking for consistency between the evolution of P&L and Balance Sheet items, there are two main relationships that should be monitored: the development of reserves given the evolution of premiums and claims, and the amount of investment income given the asset allocation in the investment portfolio.

8.2.2.1 *Reserves Evolution*

Reserves are created by the insurer when premiums are received based on initial estimates of future claims. Afterwards, their value evolves in relation to updated estimates of future claims, and eventually to actual claims. Moreover, while in certain countries reserves represent the nominal value of future claims, in other countries reserves are discounted to reflect present value. All these elements make it very difficult to establish potential inconsistencies between P&L items and reserves evolution. However, a good proxy for reserve strength is provided by the ratio of net technical reserves over net written premiums. In addition, it is also possible to check if the percentage of reinsurance assets over gross technical reserves is consistent with the retention ratio reported on premiums.

8.2.2.2 Investment Income versus Asset Allocation

Unlike industrial companies, insurers heavily rely on investment performance to generate earnings. Therefore, two key elements to be analyzed in the business plan are investment income and the underlying investment portfolio: the projected level of investment return should be consistent with the assumed asset mix. In other words, it is important to verify that the expected investment return matches the risk/return profile of the investment portfolio. Moreover, for life insurance, part of the investment return is credited to policyholders as a result of different profit-sharing mechanisms attached to different products. Hence, for life insurance, product mix has a direct impact on the investment income generated by the insurer for its shareholders.

8.2.3 Asset Side versus Liability Side

A third area of investigation related to the business plan internal consistency concerns the relationship between the asset side and the liability side of the Balance Sheet. The goal is to assess whether the projected evolution of assets and liabilities can be sustainable for the company.

An element that is particularly critical for insurers is asset-liability management. As a matter of fact, it is important that cash inflows from investments approximately match cash outflows required to pay claims when these are settled. In other words, investments and reserves should have roughly the same duration.

Overall, a life insurer will generally have an investment portfolio that is less liquid and with a longer time horizon compared to that of a non-life insurer. However, even inside non-life insurance significant differences might arise among different insurers according to their mix of short-tail (short time interval between loss event and claim settlement) and long-tail business (long time interval between loss event and claim settlement). Insurers facing long-tail liabilities should invest with a longer time horizon. It is important that such investments cover inflation, as well. For this reasons, assets that provide an inflation hedge, such as equities and real estate, are popular among insurers with long-tail business. On the other hand, investments for short-tail business would include liquid assets like cash and government securities.

8.2.4   Financial versus Operating Forecasts

A final set of considerations around the business plan internal consistency refers to the relationship between financial and operating forecasts. In particular, there are two elements which should be carefully monitored for insurance companies: distribution mix and product mix.

8.2.4.1   Distribution Mix

There are different channels through which insurance products can be distributed. Each channel presents specific advantages and disadvantages for the insurer in terms of cost structure, capillarity, range of products offered, and quality of advisory to customer. Moreover, the distribution structure of a given market can have a significant impact on the level of competition. The main distribution channels are listed next:

- *Insurance company sales force*: company employees who only distribute products of their employer.
- *Agents*: there are two main categories of agent. Tied agents distribute products of a single insurer, while multi-tie agents work for several insurers and act independently.
- *Brokers*: offer a variety of product from a broad range of insurers working on the side of insurance buyers and trying to find the best policy on their behalf.
- *Bank assurance*: agreements with banks for distribution of insurance products. Similarly, products can also be distributed by other institutions such as post offices and supermarkets.
- *Direct sales*: customers buy directly from insurers, either on their web site or on price-comparison platforms.

When evaluating the business plan, it is important to analyze the distribution mix evolution and check that its impact on acquisition costs is properly reflected. An increase of the direct sales component, for instance, should have a positive impact on acquisition costs given the absence of commission for intermediaries. In contrast, a rise of the broker or multi-tie agent sales component should cause an increase in acquisition costs. In fact, given competition with other insurance providers in these channels, fees paid as incentives to sell own products are particularly high.

8.2.4.2   Product Mix

The evolution of the product portfolio and the relative weights of premiums of different product categories have a crucial impact on the expected performance of an insurance company. Product mix can influence directly and indirectly both underwriting and investment performance in a significant way. Before presenting some of the most relevant connections between product mix and performance to be analyzed when evaluating a business plan, we describe next a brief classification of insurance products.

As far as life insurance is concerned, products can be classified according to the following criteria:

- By type of premium: single, recurring or regular premium, depending on whether there are, respectively, a one-off payment at the beginning of the contract, payments at discretion of the policyholder, or at regular intervals;
- By type of return: investment return can be guaranteed or not, and policyholders can participate or not in excess profits or losses;
- By type of objective: protection, savings, or mixed.

As far as non-life insurance is concerned, there are two main criteria of classifications:

- By type of customer: personal or commercial lines, respectively for individuals and corporate clients;
- By type of risk covered: motor, property, health and accident, marine, aviation, transport, general liabilities (e.g., professional indemnity), legal expenses, and so on.

We have already seen before how different products generate liabilities with different durations, and how this can impact the investment decisions of a company both in terms of duration and liquidity of the assets in the investment portfolio. Hence, the analysis of the product mix should, first of all, focus on this critical aspect. In particular, it is important to concentrate the attention on the distinction between life and non-life products, and between short-tail (such as motor and property lines) and long-tail products (such as asbestos related health insurance).

A second important point to be addressed in the analysis of the product mix is the presence of life insurance contracts with a guaranteed return to policyholders. Many insurers have recently faced difficulties in matching the guaranteed return given the current low interest rate environment compared to when contracts were sold, reporting significant losses in this segment. Therefore, it is essential to try and estimate the impact that this component of the product portfolio could have on future performance and understand if such effect is properly reflected in the business plan.

8.3   EXTERNAL CONSISTENCY

After checking that business plan forecasts move from a solid and reliable basis (*status quo* analysis) and that the set of projections is internally consistent, it is possible to extend the analysis to external consistency. The idea is to verify that future macroeconomic trends and expected developments in the competitive landscape are properly reflected in the plan. Another important point is to establish whether the targets set in the business plan are above or below market expectations. This can be verified by comparing such targets with market consensus, whenever the latter is available.

8.3.1 Macroeconomic Outlook

The insurance business is strongly impacted by macroeconomic trends and capital markets movements. However, there are significant differences between life and non-life insurance. The main elements to be considered in the analysis of the business plan are summarized next.

8.3.1.1 Life Insurance

The life insurance market is highly correlated with the economic cycle. As a matter of fact, life insurance is a non-compulsory product, that is, it is paid by customers with discretionary income. Therefore, expenditure for life insurance products is likely to increase in periods of economic expansion and decline during downturns.

Volumes are also driven by the movement in asset values. When the value of assets composing the investment portfolio of insurers (e.g., bonds, equities, real estate) rises, the performance of saving-type products improves and, consequently, such products are more attractive to customers. Vice versa, volumes are negatively affected in period of market turmoil.

A final important element that can have a significant impact on life insurance volumes is country-specific regulation. Governments might decide, for instance, to encourage people to buy particular insurance products (e.g., death protection) through fiscal incentives. In other cases, some products can even be made compulsory as in the case of pension products.

8.3.1.2 Non-Life Insurance

Contrary to what happens for life insurance, non-life insurance volumes have limited correlation with the economic cycle. This is especially true for personal rather than commercial lines, as individuals have less flexibility in reducing their expenses for car or house insurance. On the other hand, in downturns, companies are used to cutting expenses including insurance fees.

As far as pricing is concerned, there is a positive correlation with inflation. The main reason for that is the increase in claim severity determined by inflation. As a result, insurers account for this effect in their pricing models. However, as we will see later, competitive dynamics are the main drivers behind pricing. Therefore, in some cases, competitive pressure can prevent insurers from adjusting prices according to expected inflation trends.

The impact of the economic cycle on claims is mixed. On one side, economic slowdown or recession generally determines a decline in claim frequency (e.g., cars are not used as much; companies do not operate at full capacity). However, on the other side, fraud can spread in time of crisis. Finally, as previously stated, inflation might increase claim severity and, if the insurer is not able to pass the higher cost to final customers, the loss ratio can be negatively affected.

Similar to what we said for banks, a potential way to model the uncertainty embedded in macroeconomic forecasts is to build a set of scenarios that reflect different evolutions of the macro picture and assign to each scenario a probability. When the company being valued provides a business plan based on different scenarios, it is important to verify that each scenario is correctly reflected in financial forecasts and that the probabilities assigned to each scenario are sufficiently conservative.

8.3.2   Competitive Dynamics

Competitive landscape evolution is one of the main elements shaping business plan projections for insurance companies. As a matter of fact, especially for non-life insurance, competitive dynamics are considered the single most relevant factor predicting pricing and underwriting performance. Before presenting what is commonly referred to as the "pricing cycle", it is important to underline that the analysis of competitive forces should move in any case from the following three fundamental elements:

- The strategic positioning of the company and its main strengths and weaknesses in relation to peers;
- The evolution of competitive pressure as a result of expected changes in the industry (e.g., new regulation, consolidation);
- The expected performance of peers to be used as a reference to check the reliability of business plan assumptions.

8.3.2.1   Pricing Cycle

Competitive pressure significantly influences the evolution of underwriting performance. The industry, especially on the non-life side, is characterized by the succession of phases of underwriting profitability, greater capacity, and declining rates – soft market – and moments of underwriting losses, lower capacity, and increasing rates – hard market. This pattern is referred to as the *pricing cycle*:

- When the industry combined ratio is below 100%, insurers deploy more capital in non-life underwriting. Prices decline as a result of insurers trying to gain market share.
- Competition for market share puts underwriting profitability under pressure, although investment returns allow insurers to remain profitable despite lower underwriting returns.

- Eventually falling prices generate underwriting losses that erode insurers' capital. Insurance companies shift their focus from market share to profitability and underwriting discipline. As a result, prices start to increase.
- Less capital deployed brings the level of competitive pressure down and prices can grow further. Underwriting profitability is restored and the cycle restarts.

In the analysis of the business plan it is important to verify that cyclicality is properly reflected. If projections move, for instance, from a phase of strong underwriting profitability, it is reasonable to expect an upward trend in combined ratio. Vice versa, if the starting point is a hard market, a downward trend in combined ratio is to be expected. Another important check to be made is on market share and underwriting profitability evolution. From what we said before, it is clear that a growing market share while improving combined ratio can be very hard to achieve. Therefore, a similar trend in forecasts should be flagged and carefully investigated.

8.3.2.2   Payout Ratio

As we mentioned before, the payout ratio determines the portion of earnings distributed out as dividends. This ratio has a crucial impact on valuation methodologies which apply multiples on expected values of equity or tangible equity. As a matter of fact, a lower payout ratio will increase the base of the valuation (i.e., the expected book value or tangible book value). Therefore, it is essential to check that the dividend policy assumed by the company in the business plan is consistent with industry levels; that is, it is not significantly below peers and in line with what is demanded by investors.

8.3.3   Business Plan versus Market Consensus

Comparing business plan targets with market consensus, that is, with expectations on the company future performance published regularly by research analysts, is an additional and important reference in the examination of the business plan.

As we said for banks, discrepancies between business plan targets and market expectations can be attributed to two different sets of motivations. On the one hand, market consensus cannot anticipate the impact of future actions that the company is going to implement but has not disclosed yet. On the other hand, what the market expects in terms of macroeconomic outlook or competitive dynamics can differ from what has been assumed in the plan. In this second case, and especially if the plan proves to be less conservative in relation to market expectations, it is essential to evaluate the impact on the final valuation of shifting to market assumptions.

8.4   THE FORECASTING MODEL

There are five main areas that need to be addressed when modeling an insurance business: underwriting and investment performance on the P&L side; investments, reserves, and solvency on the Balance Sheet side. In order to build a solid forecasting model, it is essential to start from premiums. Based on premiums it is possible to model reserves and future claims. Underwriting results can be computed by deducting expenses and claims from premiums. Investment results can be derived by applying an investment return on total investments (equal to the sum of reserves and shareholders' funds). Finally, the model can be completed by computing retained earnings and equity. A thorough examination of the resulting projections and main value drivers is of paramount importance to conclude the forecasting process.

8.4.1   Non-Life Business

As for any other business, non-life insurance can be modeled based on three fundamental value drivers: volumes, margins, and risk. Each of these elements is influenced by both external factors such as macro trends and pricing cycle, and internal factors such as cost discipline and investment strategy. What we present next is a simplified framework to connect the three fundamental value drivers in a robust forecasting model.

8.4.1.1   Premiums

Premium projections are the starting point of the forecasting model. Gross written premiums (GWP) are the result of volumes and pricing. Using a top down approach, it is possible to first estimate the aggregated amount of premiums in the market and second, compute premiums for the company according to its market share expected evolution.

As far as aggregated premiums are concerned, these are a function of GDP growth, inflation, and penetration of insurance products in the market. Mature markets tend to show higher penetration rates compared to developing economies, which generally also present higher GDP growth and inflation rates. As a result, a large part of growth potential will come from exposure to developing economies.

As for market share evolution, this is mainly related to the pricing policy of the company. An aggressive pricing policy is likely to lead to a market share increase. Vice versa, if the company is focused on profitability and underwriting discipline and intends to achieve this by increasing prices, market share will most likely decrease. In the first case, GWP growth rate will be above average market growth. In the second case, GWP growth rate will be below average market growth.

Once GWP have been forecasted, it is possible to compute net written premiums (NWP) by estimating the evolution of the retention ratio, that is, the portion of the business that is not reinsured. The reinsurance policy of the company is influenced by a number of elements including:

- Willingness to smooth earnings: as a result of risk diversification benefits and ability to mitigate large losses;
- Capital management: reinsurance is effectively an alternative source of capital as it brings a certain capital relief at a given cost.

From NWP it is possible to estimate net earned premiums (NEP). A simple way to do it is to apply a constant ratio of NEP to NWP. Alternatively, it is possible to model in detail the unearned premium reserve, based on written premiums and earn-out patterns.

8.4.1.2   Underwriting Result

In order to compute the underwriting result, it is necessary to estimate net claims and net expenses incurred. As far as claims are concerned, their amount is driven by expected claim frequency and severity. In addition, in order to estimate the amount of claims incurred, it is necessary to forecast for each year the amount of claims that have been incurred but not reported (IBNR). A simplified approach is to project the claim ratio based on the pricing cycle evolution and apply it on NEP.

As for expenses, there are three main components that should be considered:

- Acquisition expenses: commissions paid to the distribution network.
- Administration expenses: mainly cost of personnel and IT platform.
- Claims handling expenses: costs connected with the process of settling claims.

Each component should be modeled separately based on expected management actions. In particular, as we have discussed before, the distribution mix evolution can significantly move the ratio of acquisition expenses on NEP. A simplified approach is to model the expenses at an aggregated level by projecting the expense ratio and applying it on NEP.

No matter how analytical the modeling of claim and expense ratio is, the resulting combined ratio should move consistently with the pricing cycle. In particular, the evolution of combined ratio or "underwriting cycle" lags pricing cycle. The main reasons for that is the time delay between the moment in which premiums are received and that of claims settlement. In soft markets, when prices start to fall, insurance companies may underwrite lower quality policies to improve market share. As a result, claims are likely to increase but only at a later stage. In contrast, in hard markets when prices start to rise the bad risks previously taken will keep affecting the combined ratio for some time before underwriting performance recovers.

8.4.1.3 Reserves

There are two main ways to model the evolution of non-life insurance reserves:

- Simplified forecasts based on reserve ratio: reserves are computed as a given percentage of NWP or GWP. In the first case, net reserves are grossed up for reinsurance to compute gross reserves and reinsured reserves that show up as assets. In the second case, net reserves are computed by applying the retention ratio on gross reserves.
- Analytical forecasts: unearned premium reserve and claim reserve are modeled separately. The former is forecasted by assuming a certain earn-out pattern on written premiums. The latter is projected on the basis of claims pay-out patterns, the so called "loss triangles".

Overall, the company should appear always adequately reserved. In particular, forecasts should be consistent with the evolution of business mix, especially with reference to different weights of long tail and short tail products.

8.4.1.4 Investment Result

Once reserves have been modeled it is possible to estimate the investment result. Total investments should equal the sum of net reserves and shareholders' funds. It is possible to use both the opening balance and the average balance (introducing circularity in the model). Asset allocation can be kept constant or moved according to the investment strategy set by the company. The key constraint is portfolio duration which needs move in line with that of liabilities. Investment result can be computed by applying normalized investment returns on the different asset classes in the portfolio.

8.4.1.5 Retained Earnings and Equity

The model can now be completed with the usual steps required to get to retained earnings. Tax rate should be modeled carefully to account for tax loss carried forward. Pay-out ratio should take into account the historical dividend policy of the company but also the target solvency ratio. Finally, retained earnings are used to compute the equity closing balance.

8.4.2 Life

Life insurance is a long-term business, with some degrees of differentiation compared to non-life. However, similar to non-life companies, life insurers make both underwriting profit and investment profit. The former derives from pricing policies above actual cost of claims and expenses. The latter depends not only on asset allocation but also on the structure of profit sharing mechanisms and guarantees. In the next paragraphs, we will present how to address those aspects of insurance modeling specific to life insurance.

8.4.2.1 Premiums

There are two important elements to be considered when forecasting life insurance premiums:

- Different to non-life, life premiums can be either *single* (lump sum) or *regular* (e.g., monthly or annual). Therefore, it is common to look at more consistent measures of total premiums:
  - Annual premium equivalent (APE) where single premiums are converted into regular premiums and then added to regular premiums;
  - Present value of future premiums.
- Premium can decline as a result of surrender rates and mortality rates. Both these factors need to be accounted for when estimating the appropriate growth rate for life premiums.

8.4.2.2 Fees and Commissions

Fee and commission income is relevant for life insurers, especially on savings-type products. In particular, on these products there are two broad categories of fees to be considered:

- Commissions and management fees: these are usually higher for unit-linked policies, where the full investment yield is paid back to the policyholder, compared to traditional products. They are applied as a percentage of the amount insured.
- Performance fees: based on the performance generated for the policyholder.

8.4.2.3 Claims

In life insurance, claim frequency is generally driven by mortality rates. Therefore it is modeled on the basis of adjusted public mortality tables. The amount to be paid to policyholders is determined either as an absolute or as the value of premiums paid plus a guaranteed return.

Another relevant aspect when forecasting life claim evolution is the impact of surrenders. In most policies, surrenders determine penalties for policyholders. However, some products come with guaranteed withdrawal benefit; that is, a fixed payout to be received by the policyholder is set in case of surrender.

8.4.2.4 Reserves

Mathematical reserves are generally calculated directly from actuaries as the present value of future claims. However, it is possible to provide here an intuition about what drives the change in life insurance liabilities: reserves increase as a result of premiums and return credited to policyholders and decline as a result of claims and surrenders.

8.4.2.5 Investment Result

The investment result of a life insurer depends not only on total investment balance, asset allocation, and investment return, but also on profit sharing mechanisms and level of guarantees agreed with the policyholder. Moreover, in the case of unit-linked or index-linked products the entire investment risk is born by the policyholder. Therefore, for life insurance it is necessary to model both total investment return and the portion of investment return credited to policyholders.

8.4.2.6 Embedded Value

Rolling forward the embedded value can be useful for valuation purposes. The general rule is that embedded value increases by the amount of embedded value profits and decreases by the amount of dividends. Embedded value profits are the sum of the following components:

- Value of new business: present value of future cash flows related to contracts sold during the year.
- Profits generated on existing business (unwind of in-force value): portion of profits on contracts sold in previous years which unwinds and is realized.
- Investment return on retained surplus capital.

8.4.3 Checking Forecasts

When the forecasting process is completed, it is critical to check that the resulting projections are sensible, achievable and sustainable from a business and financial perspective. Checks to be performed are not different from those already described in Sections 8.1–8.4.

Forecasting is an iterative process and checking forecasts provides input for a fine-tuning of the assumptions of the model. The number of iterations required to achieve a satisfactory result is generally high.

An additional element of sophistication of the model is the production of multiple scenarios embedding different sets of macroeconomic and competitive assumptions. Different scenarios can be blended by assigning a probability to each of them. In addition, the availability of multiple scenarios is an effective way to express the potential volatility of company results going forward.

9

Insurance Companies Valuation

The valuation of insurance companies does not differ substantially from the valuation of banks. The considerations we made about the reasons that set bank valuation apart from the valuation of non-financial corporations hold for insurance companies as well. In fact, insurers transform liabilities in investments, and the liabilities (and associated risks) are not, strictly speaking, a source of financing for insurers but rather a raw material to be transformed in financial assets. Therefore, similarly to what we have seen for banks, the valuation of insurance companies is equity-side, and the cost of capital for insurers can be estimated using the CAPM without requiring any adjustments for the leverage.

The DDM, DCF, and Excess Return Models as well as most of the multiples presented in Chapter 5 can be applied to insurance companies in the same way they are to banks. We will therefore focus here on what is peculiar to insurance companies' valuation, and redirect the reader to the presentation of bank valuation approaches in Chapter 5. Naturally, while the structure and logic of valuation is the same, the definition of regulatory capital is industry-specific and country-specific as discussed in Chapter 7. We will present at the end of the chapter a detailed case of an insurance company valuation using the Discounted Result Models.

We will discuss the specific insurance business multiples, but our focus will be first on a valuation approach *ad hoc* for insurance companies – namely the *Appraisal Value* approach – which will be presented in the next paragraph. Figure 9.1 shows the tree of choices to be made when dealing with insurance companies' valuation.

9.1 APPRAISAL VALUE

The appraisal valuation is based on a value measurement rooted in the actuarial techniques, hence it is also referred to as *actuarial appraisal valuation*. At the bare minimum, appraisal value can be defined as the sum of three components:

Appraisal Value = Value of In-Force Business + Adjusted Net Asset Value
+ Value of Future New Business.

Before introducing each of the three components, it is worth mentioning that the sum of the first two is usually referred to as *Embedded Value*, so the Appraisal Value is the sum of the Embedded Value and Value of Future Business. The Embedded Value is the key measure for the appraisal valuation approach as it is a metric that many insurance companies do estimate and disclose regularly

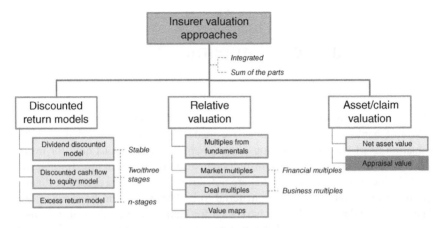

Figure 9.1   The valuation choices for insurance companies

to investors. As a general warning, it should be highlighted that, although the core principles of the appraisal and embedded value estimations are shared by companies and analysts, moving from theory to practice, the empirical application of this methodology is made following different fashions. Here we will focus just on the key concepts that an analyst should grasp to understand such measures and to value an insurance company.

9.1.1   The Value-In-Force

The Value-In-Force (VIF) is the present value of the profits that will emerge from a portfolio of life insurance policies over time. In particular, the VIF business is the present value of expected future earnings on "in-force" business less the present value cost of holding capital required to support the in-force business. The in-force portfolio is considered as "closed" in the sense that it includes all the existing contracts at the time of the valuation with the assumptions that in future no new policies will be added. Formally, at time t the *VIF* value is:

$$VIF_t = PVFP_t - COTS_t \tag{9.1}$$

In the equation, $PVFP_t$ is the acronym of the *Present Value of Future Profits*, which is the value of the future income profits (*IP*) expected from the contracts included in the existing portfolio, discounted using an appropriate cost of capital (usually, the cost of capital of the entire insurance company itself is used). Formally, the definition is therefore:

$$PVFP_t = \sum_{i=t+1}^{n} \frac{IP_i}{(1 + K_e)^i} \tag{9.2}$$

where n reflects the expiry date of the portfolio contract(s) with the longest maturity.

On the other hand, $COTS_t$ is the *Cost Of Target Solvency capital* and it represents the implicit financial costs borne by the insurance company in relation to the closed portfolio because a portion of the company's capital, for the known regulatory reasons, has to be invested in low risk activities that yield a return below the one expected by a company's shareholders. Practically, the *COTS* is measured as the present value of the implicit future losses emerging as the difference between the shareholders' expected return (K_e) and the return (i)[1] from the capital (M) allocated to the existing business portfolio to meet the solvency capital requirements:

$$COTS_t = \sum_{i=t+1}^{n} \frac{M_{i-1} \times (K_e - i)}{(1 + K_e)^i} \tag{9.3}$$

In order to quantify the future income profit for a portfolio, projections about the expected profitability for each insurance contract (or for each group of homogenous contracts) are prepared on the basis of assumptions and scenario analyses complying with the best estimate principle. Among the key input and assumptions to be made, there are: the mortality rate; the evolution of the operating expenses and tax expenses; the expected investment returns: the contract churn-out rate; and the impacts of reinsurance activities and DAC amortization policy.

Some of those elements are of a strict economic/financial nature, others of demographic or actuarial ones. For the latter, usually sophisticated actuarial expertise is needed, and such elements coupled with low visibility on the actual composition of the VIF business make usually difficult the proper estimation of the Embedded Value by external financial analysts.

By definition, the *VIF* will shrink over time as the existing contracts expire or are terminated by customers. Along the same pace, the VIF contraction will progressively free-up the associated allocated capital. In consideration of the strict link between the VIF and the allocated capital, some practitioners do actually use "Value-In-Force" as the expression to indicate the sum of the "pure" Value-In-Force Business and of the allocated capital (for sake of clarity, we will use the acronym VIF* to indicate the latter definition: see Figure 9.2).

Figure 9.3 summarizes the relationships between the various components of the Appraisal Value. It's worth highlighting that in insurers' jargon, allocated capital refers to the exact capital amount needed to meet the minimum capital/solvency requirements established by regulators. The surplus capital – the capital that is not allocated to the existing portfolio – is therefore different and, to be more precise, higher than the excess capital to be estimated for corporate valuation purposes. As we have seen for banks, the definition of excess capital should be based not only

---

[1] As mentioned, i is close or even below the risk-free rate because it is invested in safe low-risk assets such as cash or triple A government bonds.

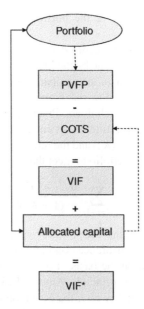

Figure 9.2 VIF and VIF* value

on the strict fulfillment of the industry regulations or authority recommendations but should typically also include an extra buffer that meets the expectations of investors.

Since the VIF calculation is articulated and complex viewed from outside, the valuator should usually rely on the estimates provided by the company itself. Despite the increased transparency of the Embedded Value reported by insurance companies, an adequate granularity of the main data is often still missing, thus making difficult both the critical assessment of the VIF accuracy and the comparability against similar insurers.

9.1.2 The ANAV

The Adjusted Net Asset Value (ANAV) or Adjusted Net Worth (ANW) is a measure of capital of insurance companies based on the concept of NAV as presented in Chapter 5. Technically, the starting point for the ANAV estimation is the book (IFRS or GAAP) shareholder equity, including the statutory capital and related surpluses, and the asset valuation reserves. Unrealized capital gains/(losses) on asset classes for which the Balance Sheet does not reflect current market values should then be added/(deducted). The value of all the intangible assets (e.g., goodwill, DAC) should be subtracted. Further specific adjustments include items associated with the differences between local regulatory and IFRS/GAAP values

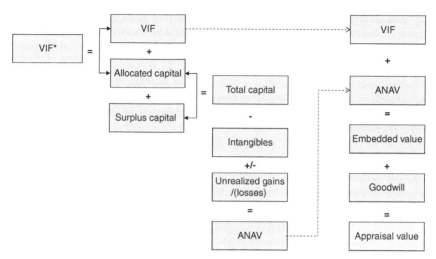

Figure 9.3   The Appraisal Value components

of assets and liabilities, and the subtraction of unrealized capital gains included in the projection of future cash-flows (VIF).

As mentioned, the embedded value, which is equal to the sum of ANAV and VIF, is a popular measure of value for life insurance companies especially in Europe and Asia. In practice, the concept of embedded value can be extended to other portfolios – even outside the insurance realm – when there is a set of financial contracts which by inertia will not be augmented in future but will continue to generate a visible stream of profits till its maturity.

9.1.3   The Business Goodwill

VIF and Embedded Value measure closed portfolios, but most insurance companies are "open" businesses in the sense that, apart from the existing policies, they will try to generate further new business (and growth) by selling new policies to new and existing clients. The value of these new future contracts is the business "goodwill" and is a key component of the appraisal value. While the Embedded Value estimate is usually provided by the insurance company itself, the business goodwill has to be estimated by the external valuator on the basis of specific and often subjective assumptions. The measure of the business goodwill should capture the insurer's ability to get new clients and/or to cross-sell new products to the existing ones: in this sense, the estimation process should rely on a solid quantitative and qualitative considerations about the market size and potential, the customer segmentation, the products design, the structure and management of the sales channels, and the commercial and marketing strategy. The behavior and strategy of exiting and potential competitors should be factored in as well.

In practice, the strategy to define the value of the business goodwill is based either on a DCF modeling or on a multiple. If the former approach is chosen, it is necessary to prepare a punctual year-by-year estimation of the new policies expected to be sold (net of the related commercial costs and of the capital requirements implications) in both the explicit forecast period and in the steady growth stage. If enough information about the market structure and about the commercial strategies of the company is available, the DCF approach tends to be the most precise for the Business Goodwill estimation.

Usually, the latter approach – namely, the use of an empirical multiple – is adopted. To estimate such multiple, the driver is typically the New Business Value (NBV), an item usually disclosed by insurance companies. Technically, NBV is the present value of the future profits (net of taxes and net of the costs due to the associated capital requirements and solvency ratios) from the new contracts sold in the current year (or in the last 12 months).

The Business Goodwill is therefore computed as the product of NBV and a multiple m, which represents the ability to replicate the current commercial results for a certain number of years:[2]

$$\text{Business Goodwill} = m \times \text{NBV} \qquad (9.4)$$

The coefficient m should be based on a qualitative and quantitative assessment of the length of the competitive advantage period (if any) for the insurance company – being lengths in the range of 3–7 years the most popular choices. The line of reasoning in this case is similar to the one implied by the Excess Return Models when ROE is assumed to converge on the cost of equity, thus making the value of the further business generated beyond the explicit forecast period equal to zero.

Alternatively, m can be estimated on the basis of the value implicitly reflected in the (market or deal) prices of comparable insurance companies. In fact, observing the market capitalization and the *Embedded Value* of C, a comparable insurance company, m can be computed on the basis of the following relationship:

$$m = \frac{GW_C}{NBV_C} = \frac{P_C - EV_C}{NBV_C} \qquad (9.5)$$

where GW, NBV, P, and EV are, respectively, C's Business Goodwill, New Business Value, Market Capitalization, and Embedded Value. When data and comparability allow so, it would be better to consider the average value obtained not just from a single one but from a panel of comparable companies. Having estimated m, and knowing the current NBV the computation of the Business Goodwill for an insurance company is obtained as the product of the two.

---

[2] Alternatively, the *Business Goodwill* is sometimes estimated by applying a coefficient to the *Embedded Value* (*Business Goodwill* = $m \times$ EV) with m obtained as a multiple by observing comparables' share prices.

To conclude, it is worth underlying that, if a DCF approach is used to estimate the Goodwill, both the VIF and the Business Goodwill are present values of future profits. As for the former, the profits come from existing contracts already held by the insurer, while, for the latter, they come from policies to be sold in future. This segmentation of the profits to be added to the current invested capital (in the form of ANAV) mimics the structure of the Excess Return Model which ends up being equivalent to the Appraisal Value Model.

9.2 RELATIVE VALUATION

Most of the considerations made about the relative valuation of banks apply to insurance companies as well. In particular, the P/E, P/BV, and P/TBV are the most popular market/deal multiples for insurance companies.[3]

There are, nevertheless, at least two industry-specific multiples worth mentioning: the P/Premiums and the P/Embedded Value defined in Table 9.1.

The P/Premiums can be justified on the basis of the DDM. Assuming there is no growth and that, as a consequence, there is no re-investment and the net income is entirely returned to shareholders, we can state that:

$$P = \frac{DIV}{k_e} = \frac{Net\ Income}{k_e} \tag{9.6}$$

Assuming for sake of simplicity that there is no taxation, we can restate the Net Income as *Net Income = Premiums – Claims – Operating Expenses + Income from Investments*, and a company's equity value can be written as:

$$P = \frac{Premiums - Claims - Operating\ Expenses + Income\ from\ Investments}{k_e} \tag{9.7}$$

Table 9.1 The industry-specific multiples for the valuation of insurance companies

Multiple	Driver	Per share multiple = Equity multiple
Price/Premiums	Premiums	$\dfrac{Price\ per\ share}{Premiums\ per\ share} = \dfrac{Market\ Capitalization}{Premiums}$
Price/Embedded Value (P/EV)	Embedded Value	$\dfrac{Price\ per\ share}{EV\ per\ share} = \dfrac{Market\ Capitalization}{Embedded\ Value}$

[3] See for example Nissim, D. (June 2013), Relative valuation of U.S. insurance companies, *Review of Accounting Studies*, 18 (2), 324–359.

By dividing both sides by Premiums, the equation can be rearranged in the following form:

$$\frac{P}{Premiums} = \frac{1}{k_e} \times \left(1 - \frac{Claims}{Premiums} - \frac{Operating\ Expenses}{Premiums} + \frac{Income\ from\ Investments}{Premiums}\right)$$

(9.8)

The sum of Claims/Premiums and Operating Expenses/Premiums is actually the Combined Ratio, and we can further consider that the Income from Investments is the product of the Investments and the investment return rate (r_{Inv}). Finally, if we introduce an Investment Leverage coefficient (IL) defined as the ratio Total Investments/Premiums, we obtain:

$$\frac{P}{Premiums} = \frac{1}{k_e} \times \left[\underbrace{(1 - Combined\ Ratio)}_{Insurance\ activities} + \underbrace{IL \times r_{Inv}}_{\substack{Investment \\ activities}}\right]$$

(9.9)

Equation 9.9 shows that the P/Premiums multiple is, as usual inversely related to the level of risk reflected in the cost of capital. The multiple is positively related to both the technical and the investment performance. The former depends on the "pure" insurer job (gathering of premiums, risk pooling and transformation, claims management), the latter on the investment decisions namely how much (investment leverage) and how much risk/return to take.

As for the P/Embedded Value multiple, its determinants are (similarly to the P/BV) the following:

$$\frac{P}{EV} = \frac{ROEV - g}{k_e - g}$$

(9.10)

Being the ROEV the Return On Embedded Value computed as Operating Earnings (after taxes)/Embedded Value.

To conclude, Value Maps as presented in Chapter 5 are frequently used for the valuation of insurance companies as well. In terms of business multiples, as long as the distribution channel is agent based and similar across comparables, the multiple P/number of agents can be used.

9.3   THE CASE OF "GENERAL INSURANCE"

Having introduced the main methodologies available to estimate the value of an insurance company, a case study can be helpful to get a better understanding of how such methodologies are applied in practice. The case study can be read in two steps:

- In Step 1, we move from the historical financial statements of General Insurance, a standard non-life insurer, and provide insight on how to build financial projections. The goal is to show the main logic underlying the operating model of the non-life insurance business.

In Step 2, we apply a range of methodologies to estimate the value of General Insurance. The output of this process is the so called "valuation football field", that is, a summary of the results of the valuation process that can be used to establish and visualize the estimated valuation range for the company.

9.3.1   Step 1

Financial projections are built according to the techniques described in Chapter 8, that is, by starting from the evolution of premiums and reserves, and then forecasting earnings by making assumptions on underwriting and investment performance. At last, we are able to estimate retained earnings and the expected solvency position of the company.

Forecasts are presented in two stages. In the first stage, called *explicit forecasts*, premium growth rate as well as underwriting and investment margins are determined by the expected evolution of the macroeconomic and competitive landscape. In the second stage, called *normalization years*, we assume that the insurer's performance moves in line with the expected long-term growth rate. The time span for the two stages is held very short for simplicity. However, in practice, it is advisable to carry out explicit forecasts for at least 5 years and have growth rates gradually reverting to long-term levels.

In order to account for volatility in future performance, three scenarios have been prepared. In our example, these are based just on different paths for GDP and claim ratio evolution. However, one could think of including other elements such as market share and investment yield. Each scenario has been assigned a probability (in our example 50% to Base, 30% to Upside and 20% to Downside). This is required in order to compute, in Step 2, a weighted average valuation by valuing each scenario separately and then blending the results.

9.3.2   Step 2

General Insurance has been valued by applying a mix of "relative valuation" techniques and "discounted return" models. The use of different methodologies is required to cross check results and obtain higher comfort on the reliability of the estimated valuation range.

As far as relative valuation is concerned, we applied the following techniques:

- Market multiples: 1- and 2-year forward P/E and 1-year forward P/BV.
- Value maps: 1-year forward P/TBV regressed over 2-year forward ROTBV.
- Multiples from fundamentals: Warranted Equity Method (WEM).

It is important to highlight that, for both the value map and the WEM, excess capital has been stripped out from book value and added to the valuation carried out on the adjusted basis.

As for the discounted return models, we focused on the Discounted Cash Flow to Equity Model, which is currently the most used in this category of valuation

Table 9.2   The valuation of General Insurance – Key assumptions

Key Assumptions

Selected scenario | Base

		2011A	2012A	Explicit Forecasts 2013E	Explicit Forecasts 2014E	Explicit Forecasts 2015E	Normalisation Years 2016E	Normalisation Years 2017E

Macroeconomic Assumptions

$Bn

		2011A	2012A	2013E	2014E	2015E	2016E	2017E
GDP Evolution								
U.S. Nominal GDP		15.076	15.653	16.198	16.913	17.768		
Nominal GDP Growth		4,0%	3,8%	3,5%	4,4%	5,1%		
Base case				3,5%	4,4%	5,1%		
Upside case	1,0%			4,5%	5,4%	6,1%		
Downside case	(1,0)%			2,5%	3,4%	4,1%		
Aggregated GWP Evolution								
Total GWP / GDP		50,0%	50,0%	50,0%	50,0%	50,0%		
Total GWP / GDP		7.538	7.827	8.099	8.456	8.884		
Total GWP growth			3,8%	3,5%	4,4%	5,1%		

Company Assumptions

		2011A	2012A	2013E	2014E	2015E	2016E	2017E
Premiums Evolution								
GWP market share		2,7%	2,6%	2,6%	2,6%	2,6%		
Implied GWP growth		1,9%	0,2%	5,0%	4,4%	5,1%	2,0%	2,0%
Retention ratio		94,4%	93,8%	94,1%	94,1%	94,1%	94,1%	94,1%
NEP as % of NWP		97,1%	95,7%	96,4%	96,4%	96,4%	96,4%	96,4%
Combined Ratio Evolution								
Claim ratio		77,2%	74,7%	75,9%	75,9%	75,9%	75,9%	75,9%
Base case				75,9%	75,9%	75,9%		
Upside case	(2,0)%			73,9%	73,9%	73,9%		
Downside case	2,0%			77,9%	77,9%	77,9%		
Expense ratio		15,8%	15,8%	15,8%	15,8%	15,8%	15,8%	15,8%
Combined ratio		92,9%	90,5%	91,7%	91,7%	91,7%	91,7%	91,7%
Other Company Assumptions								
Investment Yield		3,3%	2,4%	2,9%	2,9%	2,9%	2,9%	2,9%
Effective tax rate		25,5%	26,5%	26,0%	26,0%	26,0%	26,0%	26,0%
Reserves/ GWP		169,5%	169,8%	169,7%	169,7%	169,7%	169,7%	169,7%
Solvency requirement as % of NWP		16,0%	16,0%	16,0%	16,0%	16,0%	16,0%	16,0%
Payout ratio		60,0%	60,0%	60,0%	60,0%	60,0%	60,0%	60,0%

Table 9.3 The valuation of General Insurance – Financial statements

Financial Statements

Selected scenario | Base

			Explicit Forecasts			Normalisation Years	
	2011A	2012A	2013E	2014E	2015E	2016E	2017E

Balance Sheet
$Bn

	2011A	2012A	2013E	2014E	2015E	2016E	2017E
Assets							
Investments	454	459	479	503	531	547	564
Intangible assets	10	8	8	8	8	8	8
Fixed assets	19	16	17	17	18	19	20
Other Assets	5	8	9	9	10	10	10
Total Assets	487	491	512	537	566	584	602
Liabilities							
Reserves	342	344	362	378	397	405	413
Debt	33	14	8	9	9	9	9
Other liabilities	22	23	25	26	27	28	28
Total Liabilities	397	381	395	412	432	441	450
Capital & Reserves	90	110	110	117	126	134	143
Retained earnings for the year	-	-	8	8	8	9	9
Shareholders' funds	90	110	117	126	134	143	152
Total Liabilities and Equity	487	491	512	537	566	584	602
Check	-	-	-	-	-	-	-

Income Statement
$Bn

	2011A	2012A	2013E	2014E	2015E	2016E	2017E
Gross written premiums	201,9	202,3	213,1	222,5	233,8	238,5	243,2
Net written premiums	190,7	189,8	200,6	209,5	220,1	224,5	229,0
Net earned premiums	185,2	181,7	193,5	202,0	212,2	216,5	220,8
Claims (net of reinsurance)	(142,9)	(135,8)	(146,9)	(153,4)	(161,2)	(164,4)	(167,7)
Expenses	(31,8)	(31,9)	(33,6)	(35,1)	(36,9)	(37,6)	(38,4)
Underwriting result	10,5	14,0	12,9	13,5	14,2	14,5	14,8
Net investment result	13,1	11,1	13,1	13,7	14,4	15,1	15,6
Other income/ expenses	0,3	0,6	-	-	-	-	-
Profit before tax	23,9	25,7	26,0	27,2	28,5	29,6	30,4
Taxes	(6,1)	(6,8)	(6,8)	(7,1)	(7,4)	(7,7)	(7,9)
Net profit	17,8	18,9	19,3	20,1	21,1	21,9	22,5

Other items
$Bn

	2011A	2012A	2013E	2014E	2015E	2016E	2017E
Solvency requirement	31	30	32	34	35	36	37
Solvency capital	44	54	62	70	79	87	96
Dividends	11	11	12	12	13	13	13
Tangible book value	81	102	110	118	126	135	144

Key Ratios

	2011A	2012A	2013E	2014E	2015E	2016E	2017E
GWP growth	1,3%	0,2%	5,4%	4,4%	5,1%	2,0%	2,0%
Retention ratio	94,4%	93,8%	94,1%	94,1%	94,1%	94,1%	94,1%
NEP as % of NWP	97,1%	95,7%	96,4%	96,4%	96,4%	96,4%	96,4%
Claim ratio	77,2%	74,7%	75,9%	75,9%	75,9%	75,9%	75,9%
Expense ratio	15,8%	15,8%	15,8%	15,8%	15,8%	15,8%	15,8%
Combined ratio	92,9%	90,5%	91,7%	91,7%	91,7%	91,7%	91,7%
Net investment return	3,3%	2,4%	2,9%	2,9%	2,9%	2,9%	2,9%
Effective tax rate	25,5%	26,5%	26,0%	26,0%	26,0%	26,0%	26,0%
Reserves/ GWP	169,5%	169,8%	169,7%	169,7%	169,7%	169,7%	169,7%
Investment growth	13,2%	1,1%	4,3%	5,0%	5,5%	3,1%	3,1%
Solvency ratio	145,5%	179,1%	193,5%	209,3%	223,2%	243,2%	263,0%
RoAE	20,4%	18,9%	16,9%	16,5%	16,3%	15,8%	15,3%
RoTBV	22,9%	20,7%	18,2%	17,6%	17,3%	16,8%	16,1%

Table 9.4   The valuation of General Insurance – Cost of equity

Cost of Equity

Beta calculation

$Bn

	Mkt Cap	Beta	Adjusted Beta
Tryg	187	1,48	1,32
Topdanmark	133	1,93	1,62
RSA	136	2,03	1,69
Intact	33	1,51	1,34
Progressive	64	1,05	1,03
Average		1,60	1,40
Weigthed Average		1,68	1,45

Cost of Equity

Risk-free rate	1,75%
Beta	1,40
Equity risk premium	6,14%
Cost of Equity	10,4%

techniques. Such methodology is extremely sensitive to terminal value calculation. As a result, we present three alternative ways to estimate such value:

- Gordon growth formula: based on assumed cost of capital and long-term growth rate.
- WEM exit multiple: based on assumed cost of capital, long-term growth rate and ROE.
- 1-year forward P/E: based on current trading multiples for selected peers.

The final valuation range has been computed in two steps. As a first step, each methodology has been applied to financial projections in the three scenarios considered, resulting in a probability weighted average valuation. Secondly, we have computed the average point for the list of results deriving from the application of the different valuation techniques. The valuation range was established by allowing for a customary +/– 10% interval around this value.

See Tables 9.2–9.8 for the detailed valuation of General Insurance.

Table 9.5   The valuation of General Insurance – Dividend discount model

Dividend Discount Model

Selected scenario   Base

				Explicit Forecasts			Normalisation Years	
	2010A	2011A	2012A	2013E	2014E	2015E	2016E	2017E
Excess Capital Method								
$Bn								
Dividend Calculation								
Solvency capital BoP				54	58	60	63	65
Net Income				19	20	21	22	22
Loss of investment yield on extra-dividend				-	(0.1)	(0.2)	(0.4)	(0.5)
Solvency Capital EoP - Pre-Dividend				74	78	81	85	87
Solvency requirement				32	34	35	36	37
Solvency Ratio Pre-Dividend				229%	232%	231%	236%	236%
Solvency Ratio Target				180%	180%	180%	180%	180%
Dividend				16	17	18	20	21
Solvency Capital EoP - Post-Dividend		54		58	60	63	65	66
Adjusted RoE Calculation								
Equity BoP				110	113	116	119	120
Adjusted Net Income				19	20	21	22	22
(-) Dividends				(16)	(17)	(18)	(20)	(21)
Equity EoP			110	113	116	119	120	121
Tangible equity EoP			102	106	108	111	112	114
Adj RoE (excl. excess capital)				17,3%	17,5%	17,8%	18,0%	18,2%
Adj RoTBV (excl. excess capital)				18,5%	18,7%	19,0%	19,3%	19,4%
Discounting and Terminal Value								
Time				30-giu-13	30-giu-14	30-giu-15	30-giu-16	30-giu-17
Period				0.50	1.49	2.49	3.50	4.50
Discount Factor		10%		0,95	0,86	0,78	0,71	0,64
Dividends				16	17	18	20	21
Terminal Value								252
Present value				15	15	14	14	175
Value		234						

Sensitivity on Terminal Value
$Bn

Key Inputs	
Cost of Equity	10.4%
Long Term Growth Rate	2.0%
P/BV WM	1.94x
P/E 1yr fwd	11.2x

Terminal Value Calculation	
Perpetual Dividend Growth	162
WarrantedM Book Exit Multiple	151
P/ E1yr fwd Exit Multiple	162

Valuation	
Perpetual Dividend Growth	234
WarrantedM Book Exit Multiple	223
P/ E1yr fwd Exit Multiple	233

Table 9.6 The valuation of General Insurance – Warranted equity method

Warranted Equity Method

Selected scenario | Base |

WEM

$Bn

Equity 2012A	110
Excess capital	16
Equity 2012A net of excess capital	94
CoE	10,4%
Long Term Growth Rate	2,0%
Long Term RoE - Adj.	18,2%
WEM P/ BV	1,94x
Value	198

		Long Term Growth Rate		
		1,5%	2,0%	2,5%
	9%	225	233	242
CoE	10%	193	198	203
	11%	181	185	189

Table 9.7 The valuation of General Insurance – Trading comps and regression based valuation

Trading Comps and Regression Based Valuation

Selected scenario | Base |

	P/EPS Multiple			P/BV Multiples		P/TBV Multiples		RoAE			RoTBV		
	2012A	2013E	2014E	2012A	2013E	2012A	2013E	2012A	2013E	2014E	2012A	2013E	2014E
Selected Peer Statistics													
Tryg	9,4x	9,0x	8,5x	0,96x	1,09x	1,29x	1,16x	11,1%	10,4%	10,3%	13,7%	12,9%	12,4%
Topdanmark	48,7x	12,4x	9,5x	0,60x	0,85x	0,92x	0,86x	1,8%	5,0%	6,2%	1,9%	6,9%	8,3%
RSA	11,6x	9,7x	8,4x	0,71x	0,78x	0,86x	0,80x	4,1%	7,2%	7,8%	7,4%	8,2%	8,7%
Intact	14,0x	12,5x	11,1x	0,94x	2,09x	2,65x	2,12x	7,1%	7,0%	7,9%	18,9%	16,9%	17,6%
Progressive	12,0x	11,2x	10,5x	1,86x	2,20x	2,65x	2,34x	14,2%	16,0%	15,5%	22,0%	21,0%	20,0%
Average		11,0x	9,6x		1,40x		1,46x			9,5%			13,4%
Median		11,2x	9,5x		1,09x		1,16x			7,9%			12,4%

Valuation
$Bn

Selected multiple	11,2x	9,5x		1,09x		1,16x		
Company metric	19	20		117		110		
Value	216	191		128		128		

Regression Based Valuation
$Bn

Company Metric	
TBV 2013E (net of excess capital)	106
Excess capital	16
RoTBV 2014E (excl. excess capital)	18,7%
Regression (RoTBV 2014E vs. P/TBV 2013E)	
Constant	(0)
Slope	14
R2	98%
Implied Multiple	2,18x
Implied Valuation	246

Table 9.8   The valuation of General Insurance – Valuation summary

Valuation Summary

Selected scenario | Base |

Football Field

$Bn

	Min	Valuation Value	Max	Gap
Trading Valuation				
P/E 2013E	194	216	237	43
P/E 2014E	172	191	210	38
P/ BV 2013E	115	128	140	26
Reg. P/ TBV 2013E vs. RoTBV 2014E	222	246	271	49
WEM				
Long term growth 02%	173	193	212	39
Long term growth 02%	178	198	217	40
Long term growth 03%	183	203	224	41
DDM				
Via Gordon	210	234	257	47
Via P/ BV Warranted Exit Multiple	200	223	245	45
Via P/ E 1yr fwd Exit Multilpe	210	233	257	47
Average	186	206	227	41

Base Case

$Bn

	Min	Valuation Value	Max	Gap
Trading Valuation				
P/E 2013E	194	216	237	43
P/E 2014E	172	191	210	38
P/ BV 2013E	115	128	140	26
Reg. P/ TBV 2013E vs. RoTBV 2014E	222	246	271	49
WEM				
Long term growth 02%	173	193	212	39
Long term growth 02%	178	198	217	40
Long term growth 03%	183	203	224	41
DDM				
Via Gordon	210	234	257	47
Via P/ BV Warranted Exit Multiple	200	223	245	45
Via P/ E 1yr fwd Exit Multilpe	210	233	257	47
Average	186	206	227	41

(*continued*)

Table 9.8   *(Continued)*

Upside Case

$Bn

Trading Valuation				
P/E 2013E	224	249	274	50
P/E 2014E	200	222	244	44
P/ BV 2013E	116	129	142	26
Reg. P/ TBV 2013E vs. RoTBV 2014E	265	294	323	59
WEM				
Long term growth 02%	202	224	246	45
Long term growth 02%	208	231	254	46
Long term growth 03%	215	238	262	48
DDM				
Via Gordon	248	276	303	55
Via P/ BV Warranted Exit Multiple	243	270	297	54
Via P/ E 1yr fwd Exit Multilpe	247	275	302	55
Average	217	241	265	48

Downside Case

$Bn

Trading Valuation				
P/E 2013E	165	183	201	37
P/E 2014E	144	160	176	32
P/ BV 2013E	114	126	139	25
Reg. P/ TBV 2013E vs. RoTBV 2014E	182	202	223	40
WEM				
Long term growth 02%	150	166	183	33
Long term growth 02%	153	170	187	34
Long term growth 03%	156	173	191	35
DDM				
Via Gordon	173	192	211	38
Via P/ BV Warranted Exit Multiple	167	186	204	37
Via P/ E 1yr fwd Exit Multilpe	174	194	213	39
Average	158	175	193	35

Weighted Average

$Bn

Trading Valuation				
P/E 2013E	197	219	241	44
P/E 2014E	175	194	213	39
P/ BV 2013E	115	128	141	26
Reg. P/ TBV 2013E vs. RoTBV 2014E	227	252	277	50
WEM				
Long term growth 02%	177	197	216	39
Long term growth 02%	182	202	222	40
Long term growth 03%	187	208	229	42
DDM				
Via Gordon	214	238	262	48
Via P/ BV Warranted Exit Multiple	206	229	252	46
Via P/ E 1yr fwd Exit Multilpe	214	238	262	48
Average	189	210	232	42

Table 9.8   (*Continued*)

Valuation Summary

Weighted Average

$Bn

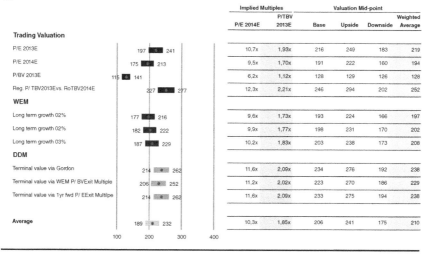

	Implied Multiples		Valuation Mid-point			
	P/E 2014E	P/TBV 2013E	Base	Upside	Downside	Weighted Average
Trading Valuation						
P/E 2013E	10,7x	1,93x	216	249	183	219
P/E 2014E	9,5x	1,70x	191	222	160	194
P/BV 2013E	6,2x	1,12x	128	129	126	128
Reg. P/ TBV2013Evs. RoTBV2014E	12,3x	2,21x	246	294	202	252
WEM						
Long term growth 02%	9,6x	1,73x	193	224	166	197
Long term growth 02%	9,9x	1,77x	198	231	170	202
Long term growth 03%	10,2x	1,83x	203	238	173	208
DDM						
Terminal value via Gordon	11,6x	2,09x	234	276	192	238
Terminal value via WEM P/ BVExit Multiple	11,2x	2,02x	223	270	186	229
Terminal value via 1yr fwd P/ EExit Multilpe	11,6x	2,09x	233	275	194	238
Average	10,3x	1,85x	206	241	175	210

10

The Valuation of Other Financial Companies

Although the intermediation activity carried out by banks and insurers covers the largest chunk of the finance industry, other niche finance companies have emerged over time and do coexist with the traditional players. Such finance companies are either specialized subsidiaries of financial institutions or independent organizations. Mostly, these companies can be valued using the methods we have already presented in Chapter 5 and 9, but some aspects deserve further consideration. Finally, funds nowadays represent the leading force of financial markets at large, and we will touch briefly on some valuation issues related to them.

10.1 THE VALUATION OF FINANCE COMPANIES

Innovation, regulation, and country-specific consumer behavior gave rise to a wide array of companies offering specialized financial services and products. Among them and without this list being exhaustive:

- *Consumer loan companies* mostly provide financing for the customers of retailers or wholesalers either directly or via a credit card system. Personal loans are typically offered to individuals to finance purchases of goods (i.e., automobiles, large household items), or even to buy real estate properties.
- Asset management companies do professionally manage investments in various *securities* (shares, bonds, and other securities) and *assets* (e.g., *real estates*) in order to meet specified investment goals for the benefit of the (institutional or private) investors.
- *Business finance and leasing companies* provide commercial loans to businesses. Business finance companies may also act as factors for accounts receivable: they purchase receivables at a discount and they process and collect the balances of these accounts. The finance company may or may not incur any losses due to bad debt depending on the type of contract (which might be with or without recourse). Finance companies may also provide financing by leasing: they purchase specific machinery or equipment and then they lease it to businesses.

As for the valuation of these companies, the bank and insurance valuation techniques can be used in most circumstances even though the capital regulation tends to be solely national and less strict than for banks and insurance companies.

Consumer and business finance companies have the same intermediating role of financial resources that banks have, and this is reflected in the adoptable valuation techniques.

In particular, consumer loans companies should be valued using the same approaches seen for banks, namely the equity side discounted results models and the equity-side multiples with the P/E and the P/BV generally being the most accurate. Asset/liability based valuation can be used as well with the usual disclaimer about the method capturing only the value of the company as it is, thus excluding the value of potential future growth opportunities.

Leasing companies are somehow closer to insurers than to banks from a valuation standpoint, because a portfolio of leasing contracts is, in a way similar to a portfolio of insurance policies. The appraisal value method can therefore be applied to leasing companies by valuing the present value of the future cash flows the portfolio of existing contracts will generate, and separately the value of the new business the company expects to deliver. The latter estimation can be done either via discounting the future results of expected new contracts or by using a multiple as we have seen for the new business valuation in insurance companies.

Beyond the specific techniques, the valuation of finance companies should include, as far as possible, a thorough analysis of the company business strategy, of the national industry structure and of the forces influencing it, and, finally, of the macroeconomic and financial markets conditions. For example, if a portfolio of lease contracts was originally negotiated in conditions that substantially differ from those prevailing on the market at valuation date and there was no hedge against such change, the analyst should try to assess specifically the impact of the new situation on the assets' value. Importantly, the analysis should not just focus on the finance sector but it should cover the industries toward which factoring or leasing services providers are exposed. In fact, it is not rare for finance companies to specialize in serving just one or few industries. For companies having such a business model, the evolution of the sector(s) they serve might even be more important than the sole analysis of the industry they belong to.

Finance companies are often subsidiaries of (or somehow controlled by) banks or other large financial institutions. For such cases, and depending on the purpose of the valuation (e.g., spin-off, IPO), it is appropriate to analyze if and to what extent the cost and conditions of financing for the company are affected by the affiliation to a larger financial group. In other terms, the valuator should assess the finance company's stand-alone capacity of raising financial resources.

As for the risk profile of factoring companies, a key aspect is the type of contracts they mostly offer. For example, the risk profile of a factoring "without recourse" (or non-recourse factoring) is higher than the one of "with recourse" type because for the former the rights and the obligations (including the risk of the receivables turning out to be a bad debt) are transferred to the factoring company. In practice, without recourse factoring has higher fees to compensate for the higher risks. This element should be adequately reflected in modeling the expected cash flows as well as in the choice of comparables, which should be really analogous in terms of exposure and kind of contracts offered.

Asset management companies vary widely because of their size, type of managed investments, investing style, degree of activeness in the relationship with the investee assets, and other legal features. In general, the income of the managing company is based on a fixed fee (as a percentage of the assets under management) and/or on a fee related to the performance of the invested funds, with the performance typically assessed against a predetermined benchmark or threshold. It is important to stress that in the asset management industry the managing company is, with few exceptions, a separate legal entity from the funds and vehicles it manages (whose valuation will be touched in the next paragraph). So the valuation approaches may be different depending on the fact that, at the same asset manager, it is the managing company rather than the managed funds the object of the valuation.

From the point of view of operations, a managing company is actually not different from a non-financial company. In fact, the financial statement structure is not different from the one of the service companies outside the financial industry (i.e., there is no major role or no role at all for finance-specific items such as loans, deposits, or leasing contracts). As a consequence, a managing company can be valued even using asset-side valuation approaches such as the enterprise DCF or asset-side multiples (e.g., EV/Sales, EV/EBITDA). As for models based on discounting results while the expected stream of fixed percentage fees is usually reasonably simple to forecast, the income component (if any) related to the performance of the fund against, for example, the market is usually difficult to estimate in a reliable way. When working on discounted results models the recommendation is usually to look at the historical average performance and to consider, as far as possible, that the economy and the financial markets usually follow a cyclical pattern. If the managing company fees are positively related to market behavior (which is not the case for specialty funds that do better when the market is depressed), some special care should especially be taken for the terminal value estimation. In particular, "normalized" mid-cycle dividends, cash flows, or excess returns should be considered: in fact, using the cycle's bottom or peak levels for the terminal value may bias the valuation. Finally, multiple-wise there is a specific multiple for asset management companies, namely the P/AUM that we have already encountered in the valuation SOP for the asset management operations of banks and insurers.

10.2   THE VALUATION OF FUNDS

We do not even attempt to list the types of funds – or, to be more precise, of the collective investments schemes – that are currently active in the world. Just a major distinction is worth mentioning because it helps frame the valuation issues we are going to touch upon: open-end versus closed-end funds. The former are "open" to investors, in the sense that they may sell shares to new investors at any time, and they allow existing investors to sell or redeem the shares back at any time as well. Thus, the number of shares of an open-end fund may change and fluctuate constantly. Closed-end funds on the contrary have a fixed, or "closed", capitalization. They issue shares and use the proceeds to make investments in securities or other assets. New investors potentially interested in the fund can buy the shares on a stock exchange (if the fund is listed) or in a private transaction (if the fund is unlisted) but the fund capitalization does not change.

While open-end funds do not usually pose major valuation issues, the closed-end ones do. Actually, listed closed-end funds are characterized by one of the most puzzling and investigated anomalies in valuation, namely the "closed-end discount." In fact, typically the shares of these funds are issued at a premium to the NAV; subsequently, the premium turns into a discount and eventually, upon termination, the discount disappears (Dimson and Minio-Kozerski, 1998).

Figure 10.1 shows the average discount in US closed-end funds from 2001 to 2013. From the figure it is apparent that the discount can be substantial.

The existence and significant magnitude of such discounts violates the market rationality and efficiency assumptions, and several theories have attempted to explain such a phenomenon. Explanations range from tax considerations, to ownership and managerial aspects, to market segmentation issues. Without entering

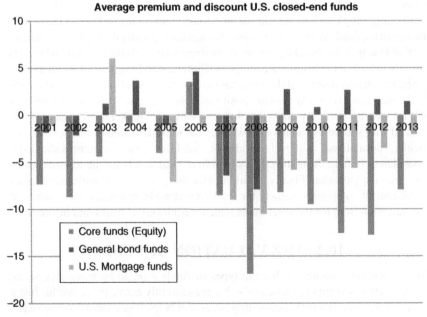

Figure 10.1   Closed-end fund discount in the US
Source: Lipper, A.: Thomson Reuters Company.

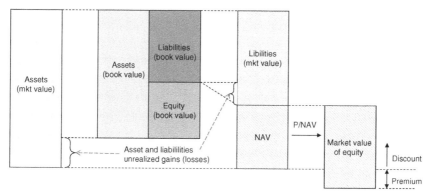

Figure 10.2   NAV and premium (discount) for funds

into the academic debate about the discount determinants, we will point out a few relevant issues for practical valuation purposes.

In practice, the P/NAV multiple is the leading approach to value funds (Figure 10.2), but in order to use such a multiple effectively the elements likely to have an impact on the discount/premium should be considered.

When a listed fund is to be valued it is necessary to assess whether the discount or premium (if any) is consistent with the general and fund-specific features. To do so, the macroeconomic and financial conditions (which are shared by all the funds with the same profile) have to be assessed along the fund-specific issues such as the quality of the management or the uncertainties affecting the valuation of the assets the fund is invested in. Importantly, the life stage of the fund should be taken into account: for example, newly launched funds usually cannot be compared to staged ones. In fact, there is a tendency in private equity funds, to deliver negative returns in early years and investment gains in the subsequent years as the portfolios of companies mature (the so-called "J-Curve effect"). In the early years of funds, a number of factors contribute to negative returns including investment costs, management fees, and under-performing investments that are identified early and written down. Over time the divestment process – through IPOs, trade sale, secondary buyouts, or leveraged recapitalizations – will allow funds to progressively realize the gains from investee assets.

References

Allen, F. and Santomero, A.M. (1998), The theory of financial intermediation, *Journal of Banking & Finance*, 21, 1461–1485.

Avramova, S. and Le Leslé, V. (2012), *Revisiting Risk-Weighted Assets* "Why Do RWAs Differ Across Countries and What Can Be Done About It?", IMF Working Paper.

Ball, M. (1996), Equity tailored to suit the strategy, *Corporate Finance*, October, 18–20.

Beccalli, E. and Frantz, P. (2008), M&A Operations and performance in banking, *Journal of Financial Services Research*, 36 (2), 203–226.

Blume, M. (1975), Betas and their regression tendencies, *The Journal of Finance*, 30 (3), 785–795.

Bruner, R.F. (2004), *Applied Mergers and Acquisitions* (University Edition edn), Hoboken, New Jersey, John Wiley & Sons, Inc.

Campbell, M.P. (2012), A tale of two formulas: Solvency II SCR and RBC, *The Financial Reporter*, 91, 10–13.

Cass, D. (1965), Optimum growth in an aggregative model of capital accumulation, *The Review of Economic Studies*, 32 (3), 233–240.

Damodaran, A. (2012), *Investment Valuation: Tools and Techniques for Determining the Value of Any Asset* (2nd university edn), New York, John Wiley & Sons, Inc.

Díaz, B., Azofra, S.S. and Gutiérrez, C.L. (2009), Are M&A premiums too high? Analysis of a quadratic relationship between premiums and returns, *Quarterly Journal of Finance and Accounting*, 48 (3), 5–21.

Dimson, E. and Minio-Kozerski, C. (1998), Closed-end funds: A survey, *Financial Markets, Institutions & Instruments*, 8 (2), 48 pages.

Frost, S.M. (2005), *The Bank Analyst's Handbook: Money, Risk and Conjuring Tricks*, Chichester, John Wiley & Sons, Ltd.

Grier, W.A. (2010), *Valuing a Bank under IFRS and Basel III*, UK, Euromoney Books Ltd.

Hajek, S. (2011), *Solvency II Strumenti per il risk management delle aziende assicurative* (1st edn). Milano, Egea.

JPMorgan (2008), *Accounting Issues Q&A on Financial Instrument Accounting during the Credit Crunch*. Global Equity Research.

King, M.R. (2009), The cost of equity for global banks: a CAPM perspective from 1990 to 2009, *BIS Quarterly Review* September, 59–73.

Koller, T., Goedhart, M. and Wessels, D. (2010), *Valuation Measuring and Managing the Value of Companies* (5th edn), Hoboken, New Jersey, John Wiley & Sons, Inc.

NAIC (2009), NFI working paper, available online at: www.naic.org/Releases/2009_docs/090305_vaughan_presentation.pdf (accessed September 18, 2013).

Nelson, K.K. (2000), Rate regulation, competition, and loss reserve discounting by property-casualty insurers, *The Accounting Review*, 75, 1155Acc.

Nissim, D. (2010), *Analysis and Valuation of Insurance Companies*, Center for Excellence in Accounting & Security Analysis.

Painter, R.A. and Isaac, D. (2007, May), *A Multi-Stakeholder Approach to Capital Adequacy*, Conning Research & Consulting.

Pettway, R.H., Kanedo, T. and Young, M.T. (1991), International bank capital standards and the costs of issuing capital securities by Japanese banks, *Journal of Banking & Finance*, 15 (3), 559–580.

PricewaterhouseCoopers (2009), *Financial Instruments under IFRS A Guide through the Maze*, PricewaterhouseCoopers' IFRS and Corporate Governance Publications and Tools.

PricewaterhouseCoopers (2008), *IAS 39 – Derecognition of Financial Assets in Practice*.

Ramsey, F.P. (1928), A mathematical theory of saving, *The Economic Journal*, 38 (152), 543–559.

Randall, S. (1999), Insurance regulation in the United States: Regulatory federalism and The National Association of Insurance Commissioners, *Florida State University Law Review*, 26, 635–699.

Resti, A. and Sironi, A. (2007), *Risk Management and Shareholders' Value in Banking*, Chichester, John Wiley & Sons Ltd.

Schuermann, T. and Stiroh, K.J. (2006), *Visible and Hidden Risk Factors for Banks*, Federal Reserve Bank of New York Staff Reports, no. 252.

Stever, R. (2007), *Bank Size, Credit and the Sources of Bank Market Risk*, BIS Working Papers No 238, Basel.

Studenmund, A.H. (2011), *Using Econometrics: A Practical Guide* (6th edn), Pearson Addison Wesley.

Index

Printed and bound by CPI Group (UK) Ltd, Croydon, CR0 4YY

23/04/2025

14660944-0002